Disordered Violence

Series Editors: Victoria M. Basham and Sarah Bulmer

The Critical Military Studies series welcomes original thinking on the ways in which military power works within different societies and geopolitical arenas

Militaries are central to the production and dissemination of force globally but the enduring legacies of military intervention are increasingly apparent at the societal and personal bodily levels as well, demonstrating that violence and war-making function on multiple scales. At the same time, the notion that violence is as an appropriate response to wider social and political problems transcends militaries: from private security, to seemingly 'non-military' settings such as fitness training and schooling, the legitimisation and normalisation of authoritarianism and military power occurs in various sites. This series seeks original, high-quality manuscripts and edited volumes that engage with such questions of how militaries, militarism and militarisation assemble and disassemble worlds touched and shaped by violence in these multiple ways. It will showcase innovative and interdisciplinary work that engages critically with the operation and effects of military power and provokes original questions for researchers and students alike.

Titles in the *Advances in Critical Military Studies* series include:

Published:

Resisting Militarism: Direct Action and the Politics of Subversion
Chris Rossdale

Forthcoming:

The Military-Peace Complex: Gender and Materiality in Afghanistan
Hannah Partis-Jennings

Inhabiting No-Man's-Land: Army Wives, Gender and Militarisation
Alexandra Hyde

Making War on Bodies: Militarisation, Aesthetics and Embodiment in International Politics
Catherine Baker

Disordered Violence

How Gender, Race and Heteronormativity Structure Terrorism

CARON E. GENTRY

EDINBURGH
University Press

I have had the distinct pleasure of being mentored and encouraged throughout my education and my career by truth-tellers, dedicated teachers and talented scholars. Thank you Kavita, Nick, Mel, David, Fred, Tony and Frank.

Edinburgh University Press is one of the leading university presses in the UK. We publish academic books and journals in our selected subject areas across the humanities and social sciences, combining cutting-edge scholarship with high editorial and production values to produce academic works of lasting importance. For more information visit our website: edinburghuniversitypress.com

© Caron Gentry, 2020, 2021

Edinburgh University Press Ltd
The Tun – Holyrood Road, 12(2f) Jackson's Entry, Edinburgh EH8 8PJ

First published in hardback by Edinburgh University Press 2020

Typeset in 10.5/13 ITC Giovanni Std by
IDSUK (DataConnection) Ltd

A CIP record for this book is available from the British Library

ISBN 978 1 4744 2480 6 (hardback)
ISBN 978 1 4744 9189 1 (paperback)
ISBN 978 1 4744 2481 3 (webready PDF)
ISBN 978 1 4744 2482 0 (epub)

The right of Caron Gentry to be identified as the author of this work has been asserted in accordance with the Copyright, Designs and Patents Act 1988, and the Copyright and Related Rights Regulations 2003 (SI No. 2498).

CONTENTS

ACKNOWLEDGEMENTS

Multiple people have been instrumental in bringing this book to publication. First, a very big thank you to Victoria Basham and Sarah Bulmer as series editors and Jenny Daly at Edinburgh for their faith in me and in this idea. It was a needed push to write the book I kept putting off for later. Second, I have benefited from the feminist and Terrorism Studies communities that surround me. This means I was able to workshop chapters out of the book in multiple places, finding both encouragement and challenges that helped me make this project stronger and better. An early version of Chapter 3 was presented at the *International Feminist Journal of Politics* annual conference in San Francisco, 2018. The first few chapters were workshopped at the Handa Centre for the Study of Terrorism and Political Violence. Lydia Cole served as a discussant par exemplar, daring me to throw down a larger gauntlet to the Terrorism Studies community. I raced to finish Chapter 4 for a School of International Relations seminar here at St Andrews and benefited massively from Kieran McConaghy's feedback and positivity. In that seminar, Nick Brook also provided needed commentary. I owe Kristen Harkness for helping me nuance the rationality discussion in Chapter 4. I truly have great colleagues – all mistakes, however, are mine alone.

Additionally, I was able to discuss this project at a Gender and Terrorism workshop Swati Parashar and I organised for the European Workshops in International Studies in Groningen 2018. That workshop was a positive experience of bringing together those of us who have been working on this topic for a long time, including Laura Sjoberg, Katherine Brown and Claudia Brunner, with a newer crowd, including two of my own PhD students, Rabea Khan and Toni Niehuss. Finally, I was invited to give one of the keynotes at the Studies in Critical

Terrorism conference in September 2018 and I based it upon this book. Thank you to Alice Martini and Michael Lister for inviting me.

Throughout my career I have found that my students energise me, push me and help me formulate new ideas. This book is loosely based upon the Gender and Terrorism module I developed when I moved to St Andrews. As different students cycled in and out of that class they brought with them new ideas and new perspectives; I have tried to capture this throughout the pages of this book. Indeed, in my first year, a student, Sophie-Charlotte Schippman, wrote a paper with me on intimate terrorism. Without her and the other students in that module, the chapter on misogynistic terrorism would not exist. I have also benefited from the student research assistant internship programme provided by the School's International Security Studies programme. In 2017, two students were instrumental in providing research for Chapter 3. Both women were stellar research assistants, and I look forward to seeing their career paths unfold: thank you Méabh Flanagan and Maryam Nahhal for your insight and attention to detail!

And then there are those who need to be thanked and recognised in a way that words are simply not enough. First, my husband. I promise: I will never write two books in three years again. Thank you for putting up with my crazy decision to go flat-out on writing, while we also moved house and then renovated said house. You are my favourite person.

Second, my life at St Andrews comprises two phases: my PhD and then my return as a member of staff. In both phases, Nick Rengger was always present. He was my first lecturer at St Andrews when I began the International Security Studies degree. I never knew someone who could talk so much with so much knowledge without notes. Nick was a source of encouragement: without him, I would never have centred my PhD on feminist thought. He introduced me to Cynthia Enloe's and Jean Bethke Elshtain's scholarship and interventions. He taught me it was possible to be both a compassionate and challenging lecturer. When I returned to St Andrews as a staff member, Nick was there to welcome me. When I began to think about rationality and terrorism, he pointed me to Stephen Toulmin. When I decided to write the book, he could think of no better project. His death is a heartbreaking and devastating loss to his family and to the field of International Relations. I do not know how to think of a School of International Relations at St Andrews without him.

Introduction:
Welcome to the Grey

In January 2016, an armed right-wing militia, Citizens for Constitutional Freedom, took over the Malheur National Wildlife Refuge in Harney County, Oregon. During the siege, other militias set up a defensive parameter around the headquarters and the police allowed members to leave and enter the refuge at will. It was not until the fourth week of the siege that law enforcement attempted to intercept some of the leaders, resulting in a shooting, a car chase and arrests. Still the siege went on for another two weeks before the remaining members surrendered to the FBI. None of the men involved were charged with acts of terrorism – even though they tried to supplant the US government's federal authority in this area; used the threat of force to achieve their goals; and shot at the police and resisted arrest.

The founder of the Citizens for Constitutional Freedom, Ammon Bundy, is a white, middle-class Mormon man who had managed a fleet of cars in Arizona but whose father is a rancher in Harney County. Bundy believed he was ordained by God to end the federal government's ownership of the mostly rural land in Harney County. Imagine if Bundy was not white, not middle-class and not a Mormon. What if he was brown, an immigrant, and believed he was ordained by Allah, convinced that the US federal government had perpetrated harms in other parts of the world? Would law enforcement still have stayed away? Would the charges have included terrorism? The label of terrorism was largely avoided by the media and by the government response to the occupation – instead this was largely seen as a protest of (possibly) infringed upon white men. This is a rather telling and blunt example of how race (and gender) is implicated in the narration and labelling of political violence as terrorist.

Even though the violence in Charlottesville, Virginia in the summer of 2017 forced Americans and other Western countries to realise that terrorism and political violence linked to white supremacy and nationalism are indeed rising (this has been demonstrated by the University of Maryland's Global Terrorism Database [START 2017] and somewhat in Terrorism Studies [Rosenfeld 2017; White 2016]), the denial of it continues on some level. The initial response of the Austin police to a series of mail bombings between the 2nd and 20th of March 2018, primarily targeting prominent members of the black community in east Austin, revealed some of the racialised assumptions that drive public responses to terrorism. The first victim of the bomber, Anthony Stephen House, was also one of the first suspects. A black man, he was apparently described as unsmiling and technically astute (Wallace-Wells 2018). Three days after his murder, Austin's associate police chief explained why they were not yet treating it as murder: 'We can't rule out that Mr House didn't construct this himself and accidentally detonate it, in which case it would be an accidental death' (Wallace-Wells 2018). When it was discovered that the bomber was a twenty-three-year old white man from a Christian family who had been homeschooled, the response from the police was tellingly gracious. The interim police chief stated the actions were the

> outcry of a very challenged young man talking about challenges in his life that led him to this point . . . I know everybody is interested in a motive and understanding why. And we're never going to be able to put a (rationale) behind these acts. (Hanna, Karimi, Morris, and Almasy 2018)

This was after the bomber died by setting off his own bomb, in his car, while driving it along I-35, the interstate that runs through the middle of the United States connecting Mexico to Canada, going straight through Austin (Almasy 2018). Somehow, I find it highly unlikely that a similar statement would be made if it had been a man of colour who had perpetrated these bombings and died, effectively, as a suicide bomber. I would also not imagine that the same conversations would have been happening if the bomber were a woman.

It seems that it is still difficult to conceive of women who actively participate in political violence, even after copious amounts of research to demonstrate women's long-standing involvement in terrorist groups (Henshaw 2016; Gentry and Sjoberg 2015; Parashar 2014; Alison 2009; Eager 2008). Surprise and shock were the dominant reactions to Tasheen Malik's wilful participation in the San Bernardino shootings in December 2015. One terrorist expert from Brookings indicated a woman's involvement in terrorism was a complete surprise to him, ostensibly both historically and because she was a mother (Easton 2015; see also Glenza et al. 2015). Similar surprise is found in the current research on women joining ISIS (see Loken and Zelenz 2018 for a discussion of this). Yet, research on women and terrorism is not new – it goes back at least to the 1970s, even if this work was deeply problematic (see Gentry 2018). It continued in the 1980s with limited, yet influential work by Robin Morgan (1989) and Eileen MacDonald (1991). The most significant gains were made in the mid-2000s, when a group of feminist scholars began to work on terrorism (Gentry and Sjoberg 2015; Sjoberg and Gentry 2011, 2007; Parashar 2011, 2009; Brown 2011, 2008; McEvoy 2009).

The differential and subjective treatment of individuals within terrorism and even the violence itself has long been acknowledged (Hoffman 2006; Jackson 2005; Herman and O'Sullivan 1989). Most scholars note that terrorism is a pejorative term, a way of passing judgement and denoting which subjects are credible and legitimate. Yet, somehow, these scholars who note it as a pejorative do not feel the need to discuss why this is. This book aims to explain this silence: this book is about why terrorism is a 'bad word' and how it became a 'bad word'. Terrorism is always seen as evil, bad, reprehensible and as perpetrated by those who are also viewed as equally suspect. Subjectivity and the power differentials that arise from it is an issue that has plagued the field of Terrorism Studies since its inception (see Stampnitzky 2013); it also has to do with how terrorism in policy and in cultural politics has been drawn along race, religious and geopolitical lines. Thus, the violence known as terrorism is 'disordered': it does not fit into the 'scheme of things' – it is violence that does not belong to a state, when a state has the monopoly on legitimate violence; it is a violence that does not belong to the hegemonic ideal, when the hegemonic ideal is often a white, Western male; it is a violence that challenges the status quo, when the status quo is often determined by Western norms and values.

This book aims to explore how we got to this moment in the 'fight against terror' – why terror is drawn along lines of long-standing, pre-existing cultural biases; how this leads to a seemingly stark binary between the good counter-terrorist and the bad terrorist; thus, how terrorism is drawn not as a political struggle but as a moral one. This book argues that Terrorism Studies and the policy-makers within the field need to construct terrorism as the greatest moral challenge of the twenty-first century (as disordered morally), even as it seeks to explain and understand it. Instead of revisiting how terrorism is securitised, this book uncovers how and why it is – not as a way of instrumentalising human response, but how such an instrumentalisation maintains power hierarchies.

Lisa Stampnitzky's (2013) sociological historiography of Terrorism Studies is revealing. While many have argued that Terrorism Studies is dominated by inner circles (see Ranstorp 2009; Silke 2009; Herman and O'Sullivan 1989) and 'subjugated knowledges' (see Jackson 2012), Stampnitzky's book is a thorough investigation of how this inner circle came together (calling themselves the 'terrorism' mafia [Stampnitzky 2013: 39–45]) through the 1970s and how this inner circle constructed what violence is included in the label of terrorism and what actors are described as terrorist. What Stampnitzky's excellent book does not do is discuss how these definitions and descriptions are dependent upon race, particularly 'Arab', and how this is tied to religion and geopolitical location, as long critiqued by Edward Said (1978) in his deconstruction of Orientalism. This happens in spite of the interventions made by Critical Race scholars, and other critical scholars, on how terrorism is conceptualised (Barkawi and Laffey 2006; Tuastad 2003; Herman and O'Sullivan 1989). Yet what has not been noted in its entirety is how gender, sexuality, class and economic imperialism play into this, and how the 'disorder' of terrorism is often linked to these attributes.

The best way to illustrate these intersections and the disorder of terrorism is by situating the book at the crossroads of three interconnected sub-disciplines of International Relations: Critical Military Studies (CMS), Critical Terrorism Studies (CTS) and Feminist Security Studies (FSS). All three of these examine power hierarchies, particularly those that privilege Western and Westphalian state primacy, protecting certain kinds of violence (military and police mainly) in ways that conform to gendered and racialised understandings. CMS aims to be 'sceptically curious' about the 'character, representation, application, and effects' of military power (Basham, Belkin and Gifkins 2015: 1; Enloe 2015). For the founders of CMS this is particularly apt in looking at the way 'in which military apparatuses classify and bureaucratise bodies and minds' (Basham, Belkin and Gifkins 2015: 1). This becomes more pertinent as one looks at how military efforts by Western states, particularly the US, were meant to spread civilising conditions (Mabee 2016; Kienscherf 2015). While there are roots of this in colonial practices and evidence of it in the Cold War, in terms of terrorism, this attitude became more pertinent during the War on Terror. For instance, Kienscherf (2015: 189) argues that 'political instability' and/or insurgency in non-Western states is evidence of 'irresponsible self-governance', what some might call civic or political 'disorder', which requires Western intervention as seen in the War on Terror (Kienscherf 2015: 189). In an early contribution to *Critical Military Studies*, Markus Kienscherf (2015) argues that Western counterinsurgency is premised on the legitimacy of Western forms of governance, policing and military practices – ones that need to be (re)established in (non-Western) states experiencing terrorism. Such intervention is 'strikingly similar to old imperial practice[s]' (Kienscherf 2015: 175). Mabee (2016) makes a similar argument that the military practices of the War on Terror were legitimated by the relationship between liberal democracies and their militaries as contrasted against illiberal states and their 'atavistic and warprone' violence (Mabee 2016: 246). Thus, there are some violences which are seen as 'good', 'acceptable' and 'legitimate' by their relationship with the (Western) state, and some violences that are always disordered by their relationship with illiberal (non-Western) states. Particular bodies and societies are therefore implicated in the binary between legitimate militarism of liberal states against illegitimate militarism of illiberal states and the political violence of non-state actors, for instance as illustrated by the superiority of the elite US Special Forces, which were created to counter 'guerrilla warfare, terrorism, sabotage, subversion, and insurgency' (Warren 2019: 48).

Similar binaries are troubled by Critical Terrorism Studies (CTS), which began by setting its sights on the discursive dominance of the War on Terror. CTS exposed the neo-Orientalist bias of Terrorism Studies as well as Terrorism Studies' acceptance of the primacy of the state and the state's monopoly on the legitimate use of violence (see Wight 2015; Blakeley 2009; Brunner 2007; Jackson 2005). Such assumptions do not just hierarchically order actors from state downward to non-state, but also maintain Westphalian norms on sovereignty (De Carvalho et al. 2011), one that is also linked to international raced structures, like the imperialism mentioned above (Vitalis 2015; Bonilla-Silva 1997). Finally, CTS also tackled the neo-Orientalist bias within mainstream Terrorism Studies (Gentry 2016a; Jarvis 2009; Jackson 2005).

Feminist Security Studies (FSS) aims to bring out how the personal and the individual experience are situated within security concerns (Gentry et al. 2018; Wibben 2011). Christine Sylvester's (2010) criticism that feminism has held itself as above the fray, as above war, is important. Instead, feminism should be able and willing to engage in the examination of the very nature of war by looking at the individual, the personal and the experiential. Therefore, this book uses intersectional analysis to not only avoid abstractions and their harmful elisions of hierarchical power, but to also bring out gendered and racialised hierarchies, demonstrating that they are long-standing in the field of Terrorism Studies and thereby impact how particular societies, communities and individuals are perceived. Without understanding these, we cannot understand why violence continues to erupt and how the label of terrorism is a violence in itself that materialises in physical violence against particular populations.

Thus, it is easy to illustrate how all three of these sub-disciplines work to trouble the (already often troubled) War on Terror; yet, the aim of the book is to suggest that the critique of terrorism and Terrorism Studies should not begin nor end just with post-9/11 events. The Bush administration's construction of the War on Terror is 'low hanging fruit' in some ways. The Bush administration built the War on Terror on racism and the fear of the Other by pitting the neo-liberal democratic (white) West against the illiberal undemocratic despotic (Arab conflated with Muslim) non-West. In this oversimplification and neo-Orientalist perspective of global politics as a West/non-West binary – in the construction of Islam as antithetical to reason and intellect (Jackson 2007; Said 1978); in the collapsing of Muslim identity to violence, irrationality and backwardness (for a critique see Hellmich 2008; Tuastad 2003; for those works that do this see Pipes 2018; Pinker 2011: 435–55); in the expansion of Islam/Muslim to anyone with any tacit connection to the religion, whether it be a geopolitical proximity to so-called 'Muslim states' (Tuastad 2003); in the colour of their skin or in the wearing of a turban (for instance, the targeting of Sikh men in anti-Muslim violence because they wear turbans [Green 2015]) – creates a very specific and very simplistic notion of what terrorism is and how it became the all-consuming security threat. Neo-Orientalism's conflation of Islam with terrorism invaded people's everyday lives with purposeful intent: the dropped bombs and shelling of Iraq, Afghanistan, Pakistan, Yemen, Palestine and Syria; the 2,208 suicide attacks in Iraq between 2003 and 2016 (using the Chicago Project on Security and Terrorism database for suicide attacks in Iraq between those dates); the slow removal of civil liberties and protections in the US and other liberal democracies; the travel bans and the refusal to resettle refugees in the US, particularly after Trump's election. And this all results in and stems from the fear that grips people's hearts, not just in war-torn places but in places of relative peace, and that drives the security agenda. Thus, critical terrorism scholarship paid close attention to how terrorism became 'sticky' with Islam and Muslims.[1]

The oversimplification, or abstraction, of 'Islam' and 'Muslim' is a harm that continues past the supposed end of the War on Terror under the Obama administration with the drone strikes in Yemen and Pakistan and currently with Trump's 'Muslim Ban' executive order, but more insidiously, with the continued, random street attacks on people perceived to be Muslim.[2] Yet neo-Orientalism works in tandem with gender, whether this is in how women who are affiliated with al Qaeda and Islamic State (IS) are discussed (Loken and Zelenz 2018; Sjoberg 2018; Gentry and Sjoberg 2016; Sjoberg and Wood 2015) as feminised to the point of victimhood, with their political violence described in such a way as to absent these women of agency; or in how the men are described as barbaric, hypersexualised and hyperviolent (Aslam 2012; Shepherd 2006; Nayak 2006; White 1990). These observations are all apt, but perhaps they are not as new nor as particular to radical Islamist violence as suggested. The next two examples help to illustrate this point.

First, when 9/11 happened and the investigations into the nineteen hijackers were concluded, much was made of the evidence that suggested that while the hijackers were in flight school in Florida, they spent their evenings at strip clubs or with prostitutes in their hotel rooms (Chesler 2015). When the Bin Laden compound was raided, it was reported that porn was found, and even though this has been discredited it still comes up in news stories (Schmidle 2011). To suggest and then to repeat what amounts to falsehoods serves a specific purpose: to weaken the image of hijackers and later their leader with hypocrisy. If al Qaeda claimed that the main rationale for their violence was a religious one and such a religious objective demanded their own personal religious piety, then to plant any hint of doubt about their religious credibility subsequently discredits the *raison d'être* of their violence.

The second example picks up a similar thread – sexuality – but in an older, and some might conclude unrelated, example. It has been well documented that the Western Marxist-Leninist movements that emerged out of the student movements in the 1960s were plagued by sexual politics (see Aust 2008; Gentry 2004; Ayers 2002; Morgan 1989; Stern 1975). These politics were not just about a continued male dominance in leadership, but also in the male-centric concerns of the protests and later the violence and in how individuals expressed their sexuality. In the US Weather Underground, monogamy in the group was banned; male members and leaders were especially known for sleeping around; Bernardine Dohrn, one of the female leaders, dressed provocatively, in a way that spoke to body politics but also to a way of gaining attention and, therefore, power. Yet, while these sexual dimensions may have existed, they were also used to discredit. Dohrn's choice to wear miniskirts (it was the late 1960s, after all) with tall boots and no bra was often focused upon instead of her politics (see Kolbert 2001).

The sexual dimension of the reporting becomes clearer in a group that seemed to have less sexual politics than the Weather Underground. Two women, Ulrike Meinhof and Gudrun Enslinn, and one man, Andreas Baader, led the West German Red Army Faction's first generation. Baader was known for his unsettled temperament and affinity for violence. This gets translated, somehow, into the anecdote that he 'developed an almost sexual relationship with pistols' and equated 'fucking and shooting' (Hoffman 2006: 246). Let that one sink in, but perhaps not for too long. This anecdote joins with how poorly the first generation RAF's training by Fateh in the Jordanian desert went. Baader, for one, came dressed in too-tight trousers to run the assault course. Even if these stories are false and/or overplayed, they serve a similar narrative to the ones about porn and al Qaeda: to minimise the politics of the people and therefore the groups.

The question then becomes: if sexuality has repeated itself, then what are the other discrediting means that keep circulating? This is more than history repeating itself; instead, this is about how there are easily found narratives within Terrorism Studies that are built upon previous knowledge, establishing coherence and therefore acceptance in its audience: whether that is government officials, members of the public or both. For instance, Jackson (2005: 111) notes that the early War on Terror fear that loosely networked al Qaeda sleeper cells existed in the US was almost verbatim to a theory put forward by Claire Sterling in the 1980s about Soviet sleeper cells in the US. Furthermore, this is even deeper than easily found narratives; this is about identifying the various discursive structures at play in Terrorism Studies and how they shape our conceptions about credibility, legitimacy and morality.

These three sub-fields, CMS, CTS and FSS, work together in critically calling out the racialised and gendered structures that inform and construct hierarchies within the discipline of International Relations, but also in practice. Terrorism Studies, as an interdisciplinary field of study strongly influenced by International Relations and the Westphalian narrative, is not innocent of these hierarchies. Therefore, the argument the first part of the book makes revolves around the idea of 'aphasia'. While 'aphasia' is more commonly known as a medical condition where language skills are reduced due to a brain injury such as a stroke, Critical Race scholars have appropriated the concept of aphasia to refer to the 'calculated forgetting, an obstruction of discourse, language, and speech' within International Relations at the very least (Thompson

2014: 45). In this instance, Critical Race scholars have used 'aphasia' to draw attention to the way that International Relations, amongst other fields, have conveniently forgotten the violent history of colonialism and how this perpetuates a white supremacist system. Rather problematically, however, aphasia simply pathologises these forgettings, which decentres the fact that these structural hierarchies and forgettings are intentional and purposeful.[3] Therefore, while the concept is apt, the term is not and the rest of the book will describe 'aphasias' as forgettings. In addition to racial forgettings, in Chapter 1, I argue that the functioning of International Relations and particularly Terrorism Studies is also owed to forgettings on gender, sexuality and the rationality order dictated by the Western Enlightenment. As such, this means we have a biased sense of what is normal, right and credible. This has a bearing on what violences we see, what victims we recognise and what perpetrators we do (or do not) hold accountable, all of which will be explored throughout the book.

The forgettings and related hierarchies of gender, race, religion and class do not work independently of each other. Instead, they work in tandem and often in ways that make it hard to tease out which one is at play. Therefore, the feminist theory and method of intersectionality is particularly helpful to this project. When it is used by academics and activists, 'intersectionality helps reveal how power works in diffuse and differentiated ways through the creation and deployment of overlapping identity categories' (Cho et al. 2013: 797). Intersectionality came to prominence in the 1980s when Kimberlé Williams Crenshaw (1989) used it to theorise the multiple oppressions black women face under the law. She explains it with this analogy:

> Consider an analogy to traffic in an intersection, coming and going in all four directions. Discrimination, like traffic through an intersection, may flow in one direction, and it may flow in another. If an accident happens in an intersection, it can be caused by cars traveling from any number of directions and, sometimes, from all of them. Similarly, if a Black woman is harmed because she is in an intersection, her injury could result from sex discrimination or race discrimination [. . .] But it is not always easy to reconstruct an accident: Sometimes the skid marks and the injuries simply indicate that they occurred simultaneously, frustrating efforts to determine which driver caused the harm. (Crenshaw 1989: 149)

While Crenshaw remains one of the immediately recognisable scholars on intersectionality, intersectionality was articulated earlier in response to the feminist and civil rights movements in the United States.

Black women felt neither of these prominent movements fully recognised their needs or even cared about their struggle: the feminist
movement was dominated by and seemed exclusively oriented towards
the experiences of white women; the civil rights movement was led by
and concerned with the struggles of black men (see The Combahee
River Collective 1977: 211). This was not the first time that black
women had been secondary concerns: their rights were subordinated
by Civil War-era abolitionists for the suffrage of black men, and their
voting rights were not part of the early twentieth-century suffragette
struggle. Black women found themselves once again being ignored in
the movements of the 1960s and 1970s.

In response, the Combahee River Collective issued 'A Black Feminist
Statement'. The Collective was active in Boston in the 1970s and 1980s
and named themselves after 'the guerrilla action conceptualised and led
by Harriet Tubman on June 2, 1863 . . . in South Carolina. This action
freed more than 750 slaves . . .' (Combahee River Collective 1977: 210).
The very beginning of their statement holds a nascent definition of
intersectionality:

> The most general statement of our politics at the present time would be that
> we are actively committed to struggling against racial, sexual, heterosexual,
> and class oppression and see as our particular task the development of inte-
> grated analysis and practice based upon the fact that the major systems of
> oppression are interlocking (Combahee River Collective 1977: 210).

The Collective articulates how the American white patriarchy plays out
on their lives, their bodies, their sexuality and their agency. The *Statement* (1977: 213) further enumerates that 'We also often find it difficult
to separate race from class from sex oppression because in our lives they
are most often experienced simultaneously . . .'. From this awareness of
oppression comes the necessity of activism:

> The inclusiveness of our politics makes us concerned with any situation that
> impinges upon the lives of women, Third World, and working people. We
> are of course particularly committed to working on those struggles in which
> race, sex and class are simultaneous factors on oppressions. (Combahee
> River Collective 1977: 217)

It may seem odd to discuss the Combahee River Collective's statement
in the context of International Relations and Terrorism Studies: what
does a thirty-year-old statement on black feminism have to do with this?

Most easily, when thought about in the context of Terrorism Studies, the *Statement* helps me immediately acknowledge some of the grey areas of Terrorism Studies. While a media driven by soundbites promotes black-and-white answers, Terrorism Studies scholars, along with Critical Terrorism Studies scholars, admit that the subject is riddled with grey areas. The questions that many would like to be clear-cut, such as 'What is terrorism?' and 'Who is a terrorist?', are not clear-cut at all. Furthermore, what differentiates Critical Terrorism Studies from 'orthodox' Terrorism Studies – like an emphasis on emancipation and the subjectivity of the discourse – also demands nuance and attenuation to the 'grey'. One of the first things I say to students in my Terrorism Studies courses is 'Welcome to the grey', and I'm told I'm not alone in this practice.

One such nuance is actually highlighted in the Collective's statement. It is perhaps coincidental that the Collective named itself after 'guerrilla' action by Tubman to free slaves. Throughout the history of Terrorism Studies, two relevant tensions have existed. The first tension lies in the semantic differentiation of terrorist from guerrilla. For some, there is a significant difference between the two, arguing that guerrillas are more professional in training and in the wearing of uniforms and because guerrillas, not terrorists, accept the rules of war (Stampnitzky 2013: 53; Richardson 2006: 22; Ganor 2002). This amounts to a moralistic and politicised need to establish discursively hierarchical divisions, as will be addressed in the first two chapters, between various actors, in a similar move to the one that makes terrorists immoral criminals and guerrillas more credible political actors. Actions like Tubman's could reside in this grey area: certainly one of the black heroines of the Civil War who was an armed spy and scout for the US Army is not easily recognised as a terrorist or as a guerrilla – even if this is the word the Collective uses to describe her. This begins to illustrate not just how subjective terrorist/guerrilla are, but also how such subjectivity shifts in different contexts: the Collective was comfortable with this word in the era of post-colonial Marxist-Leninist violence, but in the early decades of the twenty-first century, it is a decidedly uncomfortable description of Tubman.

Second, towards the end of the *Statement*, the Collective begins to realise the necessity of recognising how race/class/gender affect those in the then-Third World. Barkawi and Laffey (2006: 330) make it clear that 'terrorism' is assigned to the post-colonial struggles that defy and seek to harm Western power and hegemony. Even though Critical Terrorism Studies has problematised Terrorism Studies' relationships with governments that do the oppressing and explicitly introduced an emancipatory agenda to Terrorism Studies (à la the Frankfurt School [McDonald 2009]), Stampnitzky (2013: 63–5) demonstrates that the story is not as clear-cut. Instead, Terrorism Studies has for decades wrestled with how to acknowledge (or not) these issues, particularly in post-colonial struggles, while also trying to not appear as if it is justifying terrorism. Terrorism Studies has been concerned with how marginalisation, economic and political grievances, and oppression 'push' people towards terrorism and political violence (see Stampnitzky 2013: 63; McCauley and Moskalenko 2011; Taylor and Horgan 2006). Yet, this has been hampered by the primacy of the state within IR and Terrorism Studies.

In their highly regarded textbook, V. Spike Peterson and Ann Sisson Runyan (2009) begin with an important discussion of intersectionality and how it is related to the state-centrism of IR. Firstly, intersectional analysis is an important tool for de-abstracting the state as the dominant actor. Secondly, it helps us see where dominance (or hegemony) and oppression (or subaltern) lie. For instance, they argue that it is no small coincidence that the majority of our global leaders are Western, white men who are highly educated and from wealthy backgrounds (Peterson and Runyan 2009: 7). Power begets power: IR has created a system of dominance that looks like those who wrote the history, made the policy, started the wars and engaged in imperialism (see for instance Vitalis 2015; De Carvalho et al. 2011). And so has Terrorism Studies. Therefore, as Nira Yuval-Davis (2006: 201) asserts, intersectionality helps one see these systems' dominance thereby 'challeng[ing] hegemonic approaches to the study of stratification [and] reified forms of identity politics'. Yet, intersectionality cannot remain focused on these abstractions.

As Marsha Henry (2017) reminds us, feminist IR enquiry into multiple oppressions and power hierarchies came out of consciousness-raising struggles such as the Combahee River Collective. To lose sight of the multiple, felt oppressions of the Collective – and other minorities in similar positions – does their struggle and contribution a disservice. Therefore, I use the Combahee River Collective as a starting point to discuss the ways in which terrorist actors are oppressed by the dominant hierarchies of IR and Terrorism Studies. They are oppressed along race, gender, class and religious lines – amongst others. To look at their oppressions is not to validate or justify the use of violence; instead, it is to look at how their violence is written as different and therefore worse than similar state violence, and then how their personhood and agency are written as immoral and illegitimate in comparison to those who act on the behalf of states. Additionally, it helps to demonstrate that identifying oppressors are part and parcel of a system of oppression.

Clearly, intersectionality begins to complicate things, making what seemed to be clear murky – and this is a good thing. Because intersectionality has been discussed, debated and expanded upon since 1977, some conceptual diffusion has taken place:

> Controversies have emerged about whether intersectionality should be conceptualised as a crossroad, as 'axes' of difference or as a dynamic process. It is not at all clear whether intersectionality should be limited to understanding individual experiences, to theorising identity, or whether it should be taken as a property of social structures and cultural discourses. (Davis 2008: 68)

Yet, in spite of these 'problems', Davis (2008) lands on the belief that these all combine to create a richness and depth for an analytical tool that acknowledges experience, analyses such experience for hegemony and oppression and then uses it to make things better. The point of the Combahee River Collective was to name the problem and to make women's lives better (for a similar argument, see Collins and Bilge 2016). This book aims to do the same, noting that by

> examin[ing] how the categories of race, ethnicity, sexuality, culture, nation, and gender not only intersect but are mutually constituted, formed, and transformed within transnational power-laden processes such as European imperialism and colonialism, neoliberal globalisation, and so on (Patil 2013: 847–8)

Therefore, it can examine the underlying forgettings that shape our understanding of terrorism. How does the racism, misogyny, heteronormativity, religious bias, geopolitical structuring and state-centrism of IR *harm* the way that we see, locate, construct and therefore combat terrorism? How do such biases lead to problematic counter-terrorism policies? How do they reify where power is held?

Furthermore, while intersectionality *is* a theory for understanding oppressions, *it is also* a method for analysing them (see Cho et al. 2013: 785).[4] It is a *method* as opposed to a *methodology* because an intersectional method is not designed nor does it prioritise a scientific, replicable result. Instead, as a method, it recognises, in the words of Ann Tickner (1997: 619), that

With a preference for hermeneutic, historically based, humanistic, and philosophical traditions of knowledge accumulation, rather than those based
on the natural sciences, feminist theorists are often sceptical of empiricist
methodologies that claim neutrality of facts. While many feminists do see
structural regularities, such as gender and patriarchy, they define them as
socially constructed and variable across time, place, and cultures, rather than
as universal and natural.

Because of feminism's post-positivist leanings, feminist research is concerned with empirical, not 'empiricist', frameworks; it identifies more
with method than methodology for gathering and analysing evidence
(Tickner 2005: 3). Feminism pays attention to individuals, oppression
and marginalisation as a means of challenging IR's focus on the state and
state-level activity: 'Feminist inquiry is a dialectical process – listening
to women and understanding how the subjective meaning they attach
to their lived experiences are so often at variance with meanings inter-
nalised from society' (Tickner 2005: 4). Furthermore,

[w]hat makes feminist research unique . . . is a distinctive methodological
perspective that fundamentally challenges the often unseen androcentric
or masculine biases in the way that knowledge has traditionally been constructed in all the disciplines. (Tickner 2005: 3)

This resistance to social scientific methodologies and how much they
dominate IR, particularly North American IR, works well with intersectionality as a method.

Intersectionality is not going to value replicable data as much as
it is going to value individual experiences (see Parashar, Tickner and
True 2018; Al-Ali and Pratt 2016; Wibben 2011). Catherine MacKinnon
(2013: 1020) argues that intersectionality

does not simply add variables. It adopts a distinctive stance, emanates from
a specific angle of vision, and, most crucially, embodies a particular dynamic
approach to the underlying laws of motion of the reality it traces and traps
while remaining grounded in the experiences of classes of people within
hierarchical relations.

Importantly, intersectionality is '[i]mbued with . . . potent observations
of reality, contending' with very real 'complexit[ies]' (MacKinnon 2013:
1020). Therefore, Cho, Crenshaw and McCall (2013: 795) find 'that
intersectionality is best framed as an analytic sensibility' that 'adopt[s]'

an intersectional way of thinking about the problem of sameness and difference and its relation to power. This framing – conceiving of categories
not as distinct but as always permeated by other categories, fluid and
changing, always in the process of creating and being created by dynamics of power – emphasises what intersectionality does rather than what
intersectionality is.

Thus, intersectionality is key to uncovering these various means of what
power *does* and *how* it works to discredit those associated with terrorist violence because this violence is embedded in the patriarchal white
supremacist politics of International Relations (see Anievas et al. 2014;
Krishna 2001; Bonilla-Silva 1997).

This book then adopts an intersectional analytical sensibility by
'asking the other question' (Matsuda 1991). When those from divergent
backgrounds work together:

> we compare our own struggles and challenge one another's assumptions. We
> learn of the gaps and absences in our knowledge. We learn a few tentative,
> starting truths, the building blocks of a theory of subordination. (Matsuda
> 1991: 1188)

Because the questioning of these knowledge gaps leads to the recognition of the interconnectedness of all oppressions, Matsuda (1991: 1189)
proposes a 'a method' of 'ask[ing] the other question':

> When I see something that looks racist, I ask, 'Where is the patriarchy in
> this?' When I see something that looks sexist, I ask 'Where is the heterosex-
> ism in this?' When I see something that looks homophobic, I ask, 'Where are
> the class interests in this?'

'Asking the other question' keeps the intersectional dynamic at the
forefront of the researcher's/student's mind(s). Therefore, even if the
subject of Terrorism Studies may rarely be the black woman that intersectionality began with,[5] the subject of Terrorism Studies is often an
individual where 'asking the other question' reveals a site of multiple
oppressions.

However, *how* this 'question' is asked is also another question. What
does it mean to actively pursue an intersectional analytic sensibility that
asks the other question? A post-structural/Foucauldian discourse analysis is the one most readily apparent. In order to establish the forgettings
hidden within Terrorism Studies, it becomes necessary to analyse the
very texts that make up this sub-discipline and how these help produce

material hierarchies (as explored in Chapter 1). Critical Terrorism Studies scholarship is most often dependent upon discourse analysis, and perhaps frustratingly so (see Stump and Dixit 2013). Yet, at the heart of it, the core challenges that have been levelled at Terrorism Studies are often Foucauldian: that there is a core group of Terrorism Studies scholars who existed before 9/11 and who reify power structures so they may be funded by or in close relationship with a Western state (most often the US and UK governments) (see Stampnitzky 2013, chapter 3; Silke 2009; Ranstorp 2009); therefore, these scholars subjugate certain knowledges about terrorism, terrorist actors and terrorist violence in order to maintain state power.

IR and Terrorism Studies are interested in teaching, telling and producing scholarship that adheres to certain information, norms and ways of knowing. Thus, it creates an epistemic narrative, one that this chapter refers to as the 'Westphalian' narrative, meaning the foundational idea in International Relations' scholarship of the primacy and legitimacy of sovereign states, their militaries and, subsequently, their violences will be explored in Chapter 2. Information that coheres to this narrative maintains narrative fidelity and is privileged above any information that challenges it (Fisher 1989: 47; see also Wibben 2011: 2). From this stems a power-wielding epistemic bias against non-state actors. In order to maintain the 'truth' of this narrative, anything that challenges the primacy of states, such as non-state violence, must be discounted. 'Terrorist organisations', 'terrorism' and 'terrorists' are labels that purposefully discount and discredit certain actors based upon a variety of identities – gender, race, religion, geographic location and, arguably, lack of statehood. These differentiations, which are important to intersectionality, are also discursive constructions of power that produce material realities and productive hierarchies.

Chapters 1 and 2 discuss 'terrorist' and 'terrorism' as thick signifiers and essentially contested concepts. They are deeply contentious terms that even most Terrorism Studies scholars acknowledge as pejorative as they automatically conjure up illegitimacy and immorality. Chapter 1 critically examines the quest for a definition of terrorism within the scholarly literature. Instead of trying to parse out an acceptable definition of terrorism, Chapter 1 looks for the motivation behind the 'quest', or the need to find and establish a definition of terrorism that goes uncontested. Finding a purely objective definition that multiple constituencies, such as academics from different approaches, governments with different agendas, and the varied media sources, can agree on is an impossibility. It is a deflection away from the various contingent and contested structures – the forgettings – that shape International Relations and Terrorism Studies, particularly gendered, raced, heteronormative and classed structures.

Chapter 2 explores how these forgettings have led to a particular way of assigning credibility and legitimacy within the international system as particularly related to the Westphalian narrative. Chapter 2's purpose is to look at what is meant to be reflected in the designation of terrorism, particularly how rationality and morality are used against those associated with terrorist violence. It relies upon Carole Pateman's (1980) article, 'The Disorder of Women', which parses out how women were constructed as the non-rational, non-credible subject who would only bring civilisation to ruin. Terrorists are constructed in a suspiciously similar manner. Terrorism and terrorists are constructed out of a Western epistemic bias built upon gendered and raced legacies, making it near impossible to see this style of violence as anything but moral, credible and rational. It ends by asking: what responsibility do Terrorism Studies scholars have to bear for these constructions and how they impact various lives?

Thus, Chapter 3 begins by asking if the Westphalian narrative of state morality and legitimacy, as built by colonial legacies and dependent upon gender hierarchies, bleeds downwards, impacting how we see different individuals. It moves away from larger generalisations and abstractions and turns to how these forgettings inform how particular terrorist actors have been narrated within Terrorism Studies. It begins with an overview of the intersectional work within Terrorism Studies and concludes with eight intersectional profiles of these terrorist actors. These actors were chosen because they have largely captured the public imagination, but also because they represent different ideologies and geopolitical locations over time and across genders. By taking the intersectional approach outlined in Chapter 1, the emphasis is on 'asking the other question' (Matsuda 1991), which acknowledges the obvious factors in a profile but it also demands that one looks for what is deflected or unacknowledged. As such, certain similarities between the profiles emerge, creating strange 'bedfellows' between and across different, seemingly unrelated eras of terrorism, as shown above with the connections of sexualisation between al Qaeda and the Marxist-Leninist groups of the 1960s. This is evidence of how terrorism is related to manufactured narratives that draw upon similar descriptions and notions over and over again, forming a sense of intelligibility about terrorist actors, their motivations and their credibility.

Chapter 4 homes in on rationality and how Terrorism Studies tries to, belatedly, 'grant' terrorists legitimacy via a rationality claim. The chapter probes exactly why this is problematic: rationality is a legacy of the Enlightenment, which also justified Western imperialism. As the West expanded into 'far-flung' lands, it systematically categorised those places and the things within them, including people. This information was used to build research and scientific knowledge whilst simultaneously reifying Western modernity and progress, whereas the subjected colonial spaces were fabricated in stark contrast as pre-modern, anti-progressive and hence irrational. Thus, rationality became tied to both gender and race. Terrorism Studies picks up this thread of rationality, and not without some substantial problems. These problems come to a head in the literature on radicalisation, which is in opposition to rationality. This tension between rationality and radicalisation only reifies the counter-terrorist as a white Western person (male) and the terrorists as a black/brown non-Western person (also male). This has stark consequences for how Terrorism Studies and policy-makers perceive the terrorist threat.

Moreover, how these produce subjugated knowledges of *particular types of violence* demands exploration. Even within the obsession of defining *what* exactly constitutes terrorism, there are violences other than state terrorism that are minimised. It is often argued that 9/11 was exceptionalised – it became the exemplar terrorist attack, as a non-state actor originating from the Global South conducted a terrorist attack unprecedented for the number dead. Yet, the majority of victims of terrorism live outside of the Global North. Terrorism is attached to Kashmir, the Palestinian conflict, the Kurdish struggle, but these are often also forgotten in common parlance because the violence in those places does not threaten the international system. Instead, it is unspectacular/unnoticed because it *upholds* the system as the Global South is where violence is 'meant' to be located. Accordingly, political violence, such as war or terrorism, is not 'meant' to happen in the Global North, and masculine Global North actors are often conceived of as *the* counter-terrorists. Therefore, there are violences that are missed or discounted, particularly when they are perpetrated by those conflated with counter-terrorists: white men in the Global North. Chapter 5 will argue why what has been known as patriarchal terrorism must be articulated and explored *within* mainstream Terrorism Studies. It breaks away from the previous literature, however, by renaming this style of violence 'misogynistic terrorism', connecting the previous idea of patriarchal terrorism with rising alt-right misogynist violence that works alongside white supremacy in the United States.

In a study ostensibly about power, the conclusion returns to power and the centrality of epistemic power to Terrorism Studies. In it, I recognise my own epistemic power, as someone educated by one of the key orthodox Terrorism Studies scholars, but never fitting well into that stream of scholarship. At the same time, I have never had an easy relationship with Critical Terrorism Studies scholarship either – perhaps because I was not 'raised' in the University as a post-structuralist, even if I am a post-structural feminist now. Nevertheless, an academic in a field that has had direct impact on conflict and people affected by conflict means that we can never escape multiple, criss-crossing layers of power. How then does one proceed?

Notes

1. Sara Ahmed (2004) persuasively argues that emotions – such as fear and anxiety – become stuck to particular objects. In this instance, fear, anxiety, terror and threat have become stuck to Muslims just because they are associated with Islam, and Islam has been declared the biggest threat to the West (see also Gentry 2015; Daase and Kessler 2007; Massumi 2005).
2. For instance, the one in Portland, Oregon that began with the harassment of two women in hijab and ended with the death of two men who came to their defense (Guardian Staff 2017).
3. Recognition of this problem goes to Claudia Brunner, who pointed this out at a EWIS workshop.
4. McCall (2005), however, sees the development of intersectionality as a method as potentially limiting.
5. Although this should not be dismissed. As one of the founders of the Black Lives Matter movement, Patrisse Khan-Cullors (2018) has written strikingly about being labelled a terrorist for her political position and activity.

References

Al-Ali, Nadje, and Nicola Pratt (2016), 'Positionalities, Intersectionalities, and Transnational Feminism in Researching Women in post-Invasion Iraq', in Annick Wibben (ed.), *Researching War: Feminist Methods, Ethics, and Politics* (Abingdon: Routledge), pp. 76–92.

Alison, Miranda (2009), *Women and Political Violence: Female Combatants in Ethno-National Conflict* (Abingdon: Routledge).

Almasy, Steve (2018), 'Video Shows Austin Bomber Blow Himself Up as Officers Closed In', CNN, 31 August, <https://edition.cnn.com/2018/08/31/us/austin-serial-bomber-video/index.html> (last accessed 21 November 2018).

Anievas, Alexander, Nivi Manchanda and Robbie Shilliam (eds) (2014), *Race and Racism in International Relations: Confronting the Global Colour Line* (Abingdon: Routledge).

Aslam, Maleeha (2012), *Gender-Based Explosions: The Nexus between Muslim Masculinities, Jihadist Islamism and Terrorism* (Tokyo: United Nations University Press).

Aust, Stefan (2008), *The Baader-Meinhof Complex* (London: Bodley Head).

Ayers, Bill (2002), *Fugitive Days: Memoirs of an Antiwar Activist* (Boston: Beacon Press).

Barkawi, Tarak, and Mark Laffey (2006), 'The Post-colonial Moment in Security Studies', *Review of International Studies*, 32(2): 329–52.

Basham, Victoria, Aaron Belkin and Jess Gifkins (2015), 'What is Critical Military Studies?', *Critical Military Studies*, 1(1): 1–2.

Blakeley, Ruth (2009), *State Terrorism and Neoliberalism: The North in the South* (Abingdon: Routledge).

Bonilla-Silva, Eduardo (1997), 'Rethinking Racism: Toward a Structural Interpretation', *American Sociological Review*, 62(3): 465–80.

Brown, Katherine (2008), 'The Promise and Perils of Women's Participation in UK Mosques: The Impact of Securitisation Agendas on Identity, Gender and Community', *British Journal of Politics and IR*, 10(3): 472–91.

Brown, Katherine (2011), 'Blinded by the Explosion? Security and Resistance in Muslim Women's Suicide Terrorism', in Laura Sjoberg and Caron E. Gentry (eds), *Women, Gender, and Terrorism* (Athens: University of Georgia Press), pp. 194–226.

Chesler, Phylis (2015), 'Why Are Jihadis so Obsessed with Porn?', *New York Post*, 17 February, <https://nypost.com/2015/02/17/why-are-jihadis-so-obsessed-with-porn/≥ (last accessed 21 November 2018).

Cho, Sumi, Kimberlé Williams Crenshaw and Leslie McCall (2013), 'Toward a Field of Intersectionality Studies: Theory, Applications, and Praxis', *Signs: Journal of Women in Culture and Society*, 38(4): 785–810.

Collins, Patricia Hill, and Sirma Bilge (2016), *Intersectionality* (Hoboken, NJ: John Wiley & Sons).

The Combahee River Collective (1977), 'The Combahee River Collective Statement', <https://americanstudies.yale.edu/sites/default/files/files/Keyword%20Coalition_Readings.pdf> (last accessed 21 November 2018).

Crenshaw, Kimberlé Williams (1989), 'Demarginalising the Intersection of Race and Sex: A Black Feminist Critique of Antidiscrimination Doctrine, Feminist Theory, and Antiracist Politics', *University of Chicago Legal Forum* 1: 139–67.

Daase, Christopher, and Oliver Kessler (2007), 'Knowns and Unknowns in the "War on Terror": Uncertainty and the Political Construction of Danger', *Security Dialogue*, 38(4), 411–34.

Davis, Kathy (2008), 'Intersectionality as Buzzword: A Sociology of Science Perspective on What Makes a Feminist Theory Successful', *Feminist Theory*, 9(1): 67–85.

De Carvalho, Benjamin, Halvard Leira and John M. Hobson (2011), 'The Big Bangs of IR: The Myths that Your Teachers Still Tell You About 1648 and 1919', *Millennium*, 39(3): 735–58.

Dugard, John (1974), 'International terrorism: Problems of definition', *International Affairs*, 50(1): 67–81.

Eager, Paige Whaley (2016), *From Freedom Fighters to Terrorists: Women and Political Violence* (Abingdon: Routledge).

Easton, Nina (2015), 'How ISIS is Recruiting Women – And Turning Them into Brutal Enforcers', *Fortune*, 5 May, <http://fortune.com/2015/05/05/isis-women-recruiting> (last accessed 21 November 2018).

Enloe, Cynthia (2015), 'The Recruiter and the Sceptic: A Critical Feminist Approach to Military Studies', *Critical Military Studies*, 1(1): 3–10.

Fisher, Walter R. (1989), 'Human Communication as Narration: Toward a Philosophy of Reason, Value, and Action', *Philosophy and Rhetoric*, 22(1): 71–4.

Ganor, Boaz (2002), 'Defining Terrorism: Is One Man's Terrorist Another Man's Freedom Fighter?', *Police Practice and Research*, 3(4): 287–304.

Gentry, Caron E. (2004), 'The Relationship between New Social Movement Theory and Terrorism Studies: The Role of Leadership, Membership, Ideology and Gender', *Terrorism and Political Violence*, 16(2): 274–93.

Gentry, Caron E. (2015), 'Anxiety and the Creation of the Scapegoated Other', *Critical Studies on Security*, 3(2): 133–46.

Gentry, Caron E. (2016), 'The Mysterious Case of Aafia Siddiqui: Gothic Intertextual Analysis of neo-Orientalist Narratives', *Millennium*, 45(1): 3–24.

Gentry, Caron E. (2018), 'Gender and Terrorism', in Caron E. Gentry, Laura Shepherd and Laura Sjoberg (eds), *The Routledge Handbook on Gender and Security* (Abingdon: Routledge), pp. 140–50.

Gentry, Caron E., and Laura Sjoberg (2015), *Beyond Mothers, Monsters, Whores: Rethinking Women's Violence in Global Politics* (London: Zed Books).

Gentry, Caron E., and Laura Sjoberg (2016), 'Female Terrorism and Militancy', in Richard D. Jackson (ed.), *Routledge Handbook of Critical Terrorism Studies* (Abingdon: Routledge), pp. 145–56.

Gentry, Caron E., Laura Shepherd and Laura Sjoberg (eds) (2018), *The Routledge Handbook on Gender and Security* (Abingdon: Routledge).

Glenza, Jessica, Tom Dart, Andrew Gumbel and Jon Boone (2015), 'Tasheen Malik: Who was the "Shy Housewife" Turned San Bernardino Killer?', *The Guardian*, 6 December, <http://www.theguardian.com/us-news/2015/dec/06/tashfeen-malik-who-was-the-shy-housewife-turned-san-bernardino-killer> (last accessed 21 November 2018).

Green, Emma (2015), 'The Trouble with Wearing Turbans in America', *The Atlantic*, 27 January, <https://www.theatlantic.com/politics/archive/2015/01/the-trouble-with-wearing-turbans-in-america/384832/≥> (last accessed 21 November 2018).

Guardian Staff (2017), 'Portland Man Accused of Fatal Train Stabbing Has Outburst in Court', *The Guardian*, 31 May, <https://www.theguardian.com/

us-news/2017/may/30/portland-stabbing-anti-muslim-jeremy-joseph-christian-court≥ (last accessed 21 November 2018).

Hanna, Jason, Faith Karimi, Jason Morris and Steve Almasy (2018), 'Police: Austin Bomber Left 25-Minute Confession Video on Phone', *CNN*, 31 August, <https://edition.cnn.com/2018/03/21/us/austin-explosions/index.html≥ (last accessed 21 November 2018).

Hellmich, Christina (2008), 'Creating the Ideology of al Qaeda: From Hypocrites to Salafi-Jihadists', *Studies in Conflict and Terrorism*, 31(2): 111–24.

Henry, Marsha (2017), 'Problematising Military Masculinity, Intersectionality, and Male Vulnerability in Feminist Critical Military Studies', *Critical Military Studies*, 3(2): 182–99.

Henshaw, Alexis (2016), *Why Women Rebel: Understanding Women's Participation in Armed Rebel Groups* (Abingdon: Routledge).

Herman, Edward S., and Gerry O'Sullivan (1989), *The Terrorism Industry: The Experts and Institutions That Shape Our View of Terror* (New York: Pantheon).

Hoffman, Bruce (2006), *Inside Terrorism* (New York: Columbia University Press).

Jackson, Richard D. (2005), *Writing the War on Terrorism: Language, Politics, and Counterterrorism* (Manchester: Manchester University Press).

Jackson, Richard D. (2007), 'Constructing Enemies: "Islamic Terrorism" in Political and Academic Discourse', *Government and Opposition*, 42(3): 394–426.

Jackson, Richard D. (2012), 'Unknown Knowns: The Subjugated Knowledge of Terrorism Studies', *Critical Studies on Terrorism*, 5(1): 11–29.

Jackson, Richard D., Marie Breen Smyth and Jerone Gunning (eds) (2009), *Critical Terrorism Studies: A New Research Agenda* (Abingdon: Routledge).

Jarvis, Lee (2009), *Times of Terror: Discourse, Temporality, and the War on Terror* (Basingstoke: Palgrave MacMillan).

Khan-Cullors, Patrisse (2018), *When They Call You a Terrorist: A Black Lives Matter Memoir* (Edinburgh: Canongate).

Kienscherf, Markus (2016), 'Producing "Responsible" Self-Governance: Counterinsurgency and the Violence of Neoliberal Rules', *Critical Military Studies*, 2(3): 173–92.

Krishna, Sankaran (2001), 'Race, Amnesia, and the Education of International Relations', *Alternatives*, 26(4): 401–24.

Loken, Meredith, and Anna Zelenz (2018), 'Explaining Extremism: Western Women in Daesh', *European Journal of International Security*, 3(1): 45–68.

Mabee, Bryan (2016), 'From "Liberal War" to "Liberal Militarism": United States Security Policy as the Promotion of Military Modernity', *Critical Military Studies*, 2(3): 242–61.

McCall, Leslie (2005), 'The Complexity of Intersectionality', *Signs: Journal of Women in Culture and Society*, 30(31): 1771–802.

McCauley, Clark R., and Sophia Moskalenko (2011), *Friction: How Conflict Radicalises Them and Us* (Oxford: Oxford University Press).

MacDonald, Eileen (1991), *Shoot the Women First* (Washington, DC: Fourth Estate).

McDonald, Matt (2009), 'Emancipation and Critical Terrorism Studies', in Richard D. Jackson, Marie Breen Smyth and Jerone Gunning (eds), *Critical Terrorism Studies: A New Research Agenda* (Abingdon: Routledge), pp. 109–23.

McEvoy, Sandra (2009), 'Loyalist Women Paramilitaries in Northern Ireland: Beginning a Feminist Conversation about Conflict Resolution', *Security Studies*, 18(2): 262–86.

MacKinnon, Catherine A. (2013), 'Intersectionality as Method: A Note', *Signs: Journal of Women in Culture and Society*, 38(4): 1019–30.

Massumi, Brian (2005), 'Fear (The Spectrum Said)', *positions: east asia cultures critique*, 13(1): 31–48.

Matsuda, Mari J. (1990), 'Beside My Sister, Facing the Enemy: Legal Theory Out of Coalition', *Stanford Law Review*, 43(6): 1183–992.

Morgan, Robin (1989), *The Demon Lover: The Roots of Terrorism* (New York: Washington Square Press).

Nayak, Meghana (2006), 'Orientalism and "Saving" US State Identity after 9/11', *International Feminist Journal of Politics*, 8(1): 42–61.

Parashar, Swati (2009), 'Feminist International Relations and Women Militants: Case Studies From Sri Lanka And Kashmir', *Cambridge Review of International Affairs*, 22(2): 235–56.

Parashar, Swati (2011), 'Gender, Jihad, and Jingoism: Women as Perpetrators, Planners, and Patrons of Militancy in Kashmir', *Studies in Conflict and Terrorism*, 34(4): 295–317.

Parashar, Swati (2014), *Women and Militant Wars: The Politics of Injury*, Abingdon: Routledge.

Parashar, Swati, Jacqui True and J. Ann Tickner (eds) (2018), *Revisiting Gendered States: Feminist Imaginings of the State in International Relations* (New York: Oxford University Press).

Pateman, Carole (1980), '"The Disorder of Women:" Women, Love, and the Sense of Justice', *Ethics*, 91(1): 20–34.

Patil, Vrushali (2013), 'From Patriarchy to Intersectionality: A Transnational Feminist Assessment of How Far We've Really Come', *Signs: Journal of Women in Culture and Society*, 38(4): 847–67.

Peterson, V. Spike, and Anne Sisson Runyan (2009), *Global Gender Issues in the New Millennium* (Boulder, CO: Westview Press).

Pinker, Stephen (2011), *The Better Angels of Our Nature: A History of Violence and Humanity* (New York: Penguin).

Pipes, Daniel (2018), <https://www.danielpipes.org/> (last accessed 21 November 2018).

Ranstorp, Magnus (2009), 'Mapping Terrorism Studies After 9/11: An Academic Field of Old Problems and New Prospects', in Richard D. Jackson, Marie Breen Smyth and Jerone Gunning (eds), *Critical Terrorism Studies: A New Research Agenda* (Abingdon: Routledge), pp. 13–33.

Richardson, Louise (2006), *What Terrorists Want: Understanding the Terrorist Threat* (London: John Murray).

Rosenfeld, Jean E. (2017), 'Fascism as Action Through Time (Or How It Can Happen Here)', *Terrorism and Political Violence*, 29 (3): 394–410.

Said, Edward (1978), *Orientalism* (London: Vintage).

Schmidle, Nicholas (2011), 'Getting Bin Laden', *The New Yorker*, 8 August, <https://www.newyorker.com/magazine/2011/08/08/getting-bin-laden≥ (last accessed 21 November 2018).

Silke, Andrew (2009), 'Contemporary Terrorism Studies: Issues in Research', in Richard D. Jackson, Marie Breen Smyth and Jerone Gunning (eds) (2009), *Critical Terrorism Studies: A New Research Agenda* (Abingdon: Routledge), pp. 34–48.

Shepherd, Laura J. (2006), 'Veiled References: Constructions of Gender in the Bush Administration Discourse on the Attacks on Afghanistan Post-9/11', *International Journal of Feminist Politics*, 8(1): 19–41.

Sjoberg, Laura (2018), 'Jihadi Brides And Female Volunteers: Reading The Islamic State's War To See Gender And Agency In Conflict Dynamics', *Conflict Management and Peace Science*, 35(3): 296–311.

Sjoberg, Laura, and Caron E. Gentry (2007), *Mothers, Monsters, Whores: Women's Violence in Global Politics* (London: Zed Books).

Sjoberg, Laura, and Caron E. Gentry (eds) (2011), *Women, Gender, and Terrorism* (Athens: University of Georgia Press).

Sjoberg, Laura, and Reid Wood (2015), 'People, Not Pawns: Women's Participation in Violent Extremism across MENA', *USAID Research Brief*, 15 September 2015, <https://www.usaid.gov/sites/default/files/documents/1866/CVE_RESEARCH-BRIEF_PEOPLENOTPAWNS.pdf> (last accessed 25 November 2018).

Stampnitzky, Lisa (2013), *Disciplining Terrorism: How 'Experts' Invented Terrorism* (Cambridge: Cambridge University Press).

START (2018) 'PIRIUS: Frequently Asked Questions', <https://www.start.umd.edu/pirus-frequently-asked-questions#q7> (last accessed 22 November 2018).

Stern, Susan (1975), *With the Weathermen: The Personal Journal of a Revolutionary Woman* (Garden City, NJ: Doubleday).

Stump, Jacob L., and Priya Dixit (2013), *Critical Terrorism Studies: An Introduction to Research Methods* (Abingdon: Routledge).

Sylvester, Christine (2010a), 'Tensions in Feminist Security Studies', *Security Dialogue*, 41(6): 607–14.

Taylor, Max, and John Horgan (2006), 'A Conceptual Framework For Addressing Psychological Process in the Development of the Terrorist', *Terrorism and Political Violence*, 18(4): 585–601.

Thompson, Debra (2014), 'Through, Against, and Beyond the Racial State: The Transnational Stratum of Race', in Alexander Anievas, Nivi Manchanda and Robbie Shilliam (eds), *Race and Racism in International Relations: Confronting the Global Colour Line* (Abingdon: Routledge), pp. 44–61.

Tickner, J. Ann (2005), 'What Is Your Research Program? Some Feminist Answers to International Relations Methodological Questions', *International Studies Quarterly*, 49(1): 1–21.

Tuastad, Dag (2003), 'Neo-Orientalism and the New Barbarism Thesis: Aspects of Symbolic Violence in the Middle East Conflict(s)', *Third World Quarterly*, 24(4): 591–9.

Vitalis, Robert (2015), *White World Order, Black Power Politics: The Birth of American International Relations* (Ithaca, NY: Cornell University Press).

Wallace-Wells, Benjamin (2018), 'The Inscrutable Terror of the Austin Bombings', *The New Yorker*, 28 March, <https://www.newyorker.com/news/dispatch/the-inscrutable-terror-of-the-austin-bombings≥ (last accessed 21 November 2018).

Warren, Stephen (2019), 'US Special Forces: An Other within the Self', *Critical Military Studies*, 5(1): 40–62.

White, Jonathan R. (2016), *Terrorism and Homeland Security* (Boston: Cengage Learning).

White, Louise (1990), 'Separating the Men from the Boys: Constructions of Gender, Sexuality, and Terrorism in Central Kenya, 1939–1959', *The International Journal of African Historical Studies*, 23(1): 1–25.

Wibben, Annick (2011), *Feminist Security Studies* (Abingdon: Routledge).

Wight, Colin (2015), *Rethinking Terrorism: Terrorism, Violence and the State* (London: Palgrave MacMillan).

Yuval-Davis, Nira (2006), 'Intersectionality and Feminist Politics', *European Journal of Women's Studies*, 13(3): 193–209.

CHAPTER 1

The Structural Signification of Terrorism

This chapter digs deeper into one of the key contentions within Terrorism Studies: how to define terrorism. There are multiple stakeholders in this debate: scholars, who wish to study terrorism via various disciplinary approaches (Jackson et al. 2009; Herman and O'Sullivan 1989); governments, who need to show that they are combating terrorism effectively (Wight 2015: 7; Stampnitzky 2013; Lum et al. 2006); and media sources, who, depending upon their ideological leanings, present terrorism in ways that sell (Nacos 2000; Wilkinson 1997). Quite often these stakeholders cannot agree on a definition. Therefore, articles or books like this one often dedicate precious word limits to a discussion of the definition debate. What is it about the lack of agreement on the terrorism definition that is so troubling to particular scholars and practitioners? To answer this question, it is first important to explore what the tensions are in the 'definition' debate before looking at it as a contested concept that structures social relations.

There are multiple fissures that perpetuate the debate. First, it is often noted that terrorism is a pejorative, discrediting label (Hoffman 2006: 21–3; Jenkins 1980: 10). An additional concern stems from the idea that a lack of a concrete definition results in less than social scientific objectivity (Richards 2015: 8). While many academics have settled on basing the definition as a form or method of political violence, what exactly this method *is* or *does* is not always clear (see for instance Jongman's [2017] discussion of this: 7, 13–25). Furthermore, negative connotations remain, primarily because the label of terrorism is not uniformly applied to all actors who use this method. As such, the chapter begins to also establish how terrorism is constructed as 'disordered' – outside of the hegemonic order of Westphalia and Western dominance, but also as violence belonging to an Other who is also a threat to the hegemonic order. Therefore, the purpose of this chapter is not to fulfil the quest for the Golden Fleece and provide a definition, but instead to establish that a definition cannot be agreed upon because the definition quest actually, intentionally or otherwise, represents gender, racial and imperial, and heteronormative aphasias, or preferably, 'calculated forgetting[s]' (Thompson 2014: 45).

Scholarship on these forgettings is clear that the global and political order is dependent upon the divisions of the world and power between European whites and people of colour (Anievas et al. 2014). Thus, this chapter begins to set out the argument, which is carried through to the rest of the book, that racial forgettings are also present in Terrorism Studies. Furthermore, if we ask the other question, racial forgettings are not the only 'calculated' discursive obstruction present: there are also signs of gendered and heteronormative forgettings within IR that also apply to Terrorism Studies. This comes through in investigating the reasons why Terrorism Studies persists in finding an 'objective' or hard and fast definition of terrorism that all can agree on. And this, in my opinion, is an impossible quest.

It is an impossible quest because terrorism is a 'thick signifier', or a discursive way of organising social relations into ones that revolve around the (extra)normative ideation of terrorist violence. Terrorism as a signifier is indicative of social structures and hierarchies of race, gender and heteronormativity, if not others. It results in what Richard Jackson (2012: 13) calls 'subjugated knowledges', or the diminishment of certain forms of knowledge as 'non-knowledge' because of ontological, epistemological or methodological biases.[1] The very reason why we cannot settle on a definition is owed to these hierarchies and knowledge diffusions. The field persists in its quest to have an objective definition because arriving at a definition means that one does not have to deal with the power dynamics of applying the label. And this is what this chapter attempts to tease out: *why* the term is subjective and discrediting, how this is linked to different ways of being, knowing and seeing as related to race, gender and sexuality. Furthermore, this chapter will end on how race, gender and sexuality are all linked to organising concepts in IR and Terrorism Studies, such as rationality, legitimacy and morality.

The Definition Quest

The lack of an agreed-upon terrorism definition is often seen as one of the largest faults within the field:

> If the international community is ultimately to respond effectively to terrorism in the longer term, and if states are to avoid charges of hypocrisy

and double standards, then there is a need to conceptualise *and apply* the term more objectively. By refraining from defining terrorism according to perceived state or national interests, or 'in the service of power', there might then be potential for a more comprehensive, neutral, honest, and analytical approach to the concept of terrorism. (Richards 2015: 25)

For Richards (2015: 6), one part of his aim is to make the term of terrorism less prone to 'manipulation' for political purposes, to be used against 'those one "does not like"' (2015: 15). Yet, he does not address the permissibility on which this manipulation rests and believes finding an objective definition will end this struggle. Additionally, to have a fixed definition would mean that Terrorism Studies needs to be better than other fields. It assumes that other fields and disciplines have fixed, stable definitions with an underlying assumption that such definitions lends credibility and legitimacy to it (see also Crenshaw 2014: 557). Yet, other fields do not have fixed, stable and non-contested definitions: there are multiple definitions and ideas of what 'feminism' is (from 'radical', 'liberal', 'standpoint', to 'post-structural'); there are multiple ways of approaching 'sovereignty' (see for instance Weber 1998); and expanding the definition of 'security' has been one of the key conversations in security studies for the past twenty years (see for instance Huysmans 2014; Fierke 2015; Buzan et al. 1998). It belies a particular social scientific epistemology that values a neo- or positivist methodology that results in objective 'truths'. It also fails to engage in depending upon other ways of knowing that do not assume a social scientific approach.

It is largely held within Terrorism Studies that terrorism is a method – a method that all actors can employ (Schmid and Jongman 1988: 13). For Richards (2015: 69–75), this does not mean enumerating what type of attacks constitute terrorism (from hijackings or bombings to assassinations), but instead realising that the point of this 'act of violence . . . is to generate a psychological impact beyond the immediate victims' (2015: 73). The insistence on method has a relationship with Hannah Arendt's (1970: 51) idea of violence:

[v]iolence is by nature instrumental; like all means, it always stands in need of guidance and justification through the end it pursues. And what needs justification by something else cannot be the essence of anything.

According to Arendt, violence is a method which only derives its meaning by those who wield it. This aligns with this idea of terrorism as a method, an instrumental use of force. Arendt (1970: 52), however, is able to acknowledge that violence is always illegitimate, whereas Terrorism Studies is really only able to see terrorism (even if it is a method all actors can use) as belonging to non-state actors and therefore illegitimate.

In spite of the emphasis on terrorism as a method of violence, there are still identifying elements that are often included in notions and definitions of terrorism. One of the most cited resources that highlight the intricacies of the definition debate is Alex Schmid and Albert Jongman's various editions of *Political Terrorism* (1988 and 2005; Jongman 2017). In the 2005 edition, Schmid and Jongman surveyed academics and practitioners for each individual's definition of terrorism. Of the 109 different definitions that they received, they coded them for the top twenty-two frequencies as listed in Table 1.1 (Schmid and Jongman 2005: 5–6). The expected is there: that violence, political and terror are the top three most frequent concepts is a given. However, it is a bit surprising that violence, political and terror do not show up in 100 per cent of the definitions. Instead, violence is only identified in 83.5 per cent and political in 65 per cent, whereas fear or *terror* is only in 51 per cent. Beyond these fairly substantial differences, there are further elements that reveal, perhaps, the subjective nature of the term. For instance, Schmid and Jongman (2005: 5, 25–8) work through some of the leading Terrorism Studies scholarship, discussing what is meant by 'extranormative', including the targeting of innocent 'civilians, noncombatants, neutrals', and that non-state 'groups, movements, organisations perpetrate it'.

The extranormative angle is potentially one of the most deeply held elements of the definitions that do exist. The immorality of terrorism is quite often linked with the targeting of civilians and non-combatants, particularly when they are seen as 'innocent'. In her introductory text to the subject, Louise Richardson's (2006: 20) primary definition of terrorism reads: 'Terrorism, simply put, means deliberately and violently targeting civilians for political purposes.' She builds upon this primary definition through seven elaborated points, the last of which focuses on the targeting of civilians. She argues the

> deliberate targeting of civilians . . . is what sets terrorism apart from other forms of political violence, even the most proximate form, guerrilla warfare. Terrorists have elevated practices that are normally seen as the excesses of warfare to routine practice, striking at non-combatants . . . as deliberate strategy. (Richardson 2006: 22)

The targeting of civilians is linked with other troubling behaviours.

Table 1.1 Schmid and Jongman's top twenty-two frequencies for a terrorism definition.

	Element	Frequency
1	Violence, force	83.5%
2	Political	65%
3	Fear, terror emphasised	51%
4	Threat	47%
5	(Psychological) effects and (anticipated) reactions	41.5%
6	Victim–target differentiation	37.5%
7	Purposive, planned, systematic, organised behaviour	32%
8	Method of combat, strategy, tactic	30.5%
9	Extranormality, in breach of accepted rules without humanitarian constraints	30%
10	Coercion, extortion, induction of compliance	28%
11	Publicity aspect	21.5%
12	Arbitrariness; impersonal, random character; indiscrimination	21
13	Civilians, non combatants, neutrals, outsiders as victims	17.5%
14	Intimidation	17%
15	Innocence of victims emphasised	15.5%
16	Group, movement, organisations as perpetrator	14%
17	Symoblic aspect, demonstration to others	13.5%
18	Incalculability, unpredictability, unexpectedness of occurrence of violence	9%
19	Clandestine, covert nature	9%
20	Repetitiveness; serial or campaign character of violence	7%
21	Criminal	6%
22	Demands made on third parties	4%

Terrorists are differentiated from other politically violent actors because they are untrained, non-uniformed, and therefore not beholden to the rules of war. It this lack of training and uniformity, indicating a betrayal of the rules of war, that leads to the intentional murder of civilians and non-combatants (Ganor 2002: 288). Killing of civilians violates one of the prime principles in the Just War tradition's *jus in bello* norm of proportionality. According to Just War scholar Alex Bellamy (2008: 30), terrorism is illegitimate and immoral 'in every circumstance' because it intentionally targets non-combatants for political purposes. While Bellamy (2008: 29) recognises that the label of terrorism is subjective, it is nevertheless a 'moral definition'. This conceptualisation of terrorism as immoral is important and linked with Westphalian norms that support the primacy of the state. While the connection with immorality will be explored in the next chapter, for now the focus remains on how Westphalian norms protect the state from the terrorism label.

This protection is dependent upon the Westphalian norm that states possess the monopoly on the legitimate use of violence. Louise Richardson (2006: 21) pointedly declares that 'terrorism is the act of sub-state groups, not states'. Although they may be sponsors of terrorism and states may take 'action that is the moral equivalent of terrorism', for 'analytical clarity' 'we must understand [terrorist actors] as sub-state actors' (Richardson 2006: 21–2). This sentiment is echoed in Colin Wight's *Rethinking Terrorism*, where terrorist groups are *always* sub-state and *always* protest groups against the state (2015: 12), although they are not always illegitimate (2015: 18). He concurs with Richardson (2006) that 'state terrorism . . . provides no additional purchase on a critique of unacceptable state practices beyond that already covered by international law' (Wight 2015: 15).

A more nuanced approach is found in Bruce Hoffman's oft-cited *Inside Terrorism* (2006). In his discussion of the definition quest, he works through various US government definitions, including the US Department of State (DoS), the FBI, the Department of Homeland Security (DHS) and the Department of Defense (DoD) (Hoffman 2006: 31). As Hoffman (2006: 31) notes, 'each of the . . . definitions reflect the priorities and particular interests of the specific agency involved' as well as, it should be added, the US government. All of the definitions emphasise that terrorism is a 'subnational' activity (DoS), to 'intimidate' or 'coerce' (FBI, DHS and DoD) a 'government' or 'civilian population' or both (FBI, DHS, DoD). These intimate that terrorist actors are *only* groups, movements and/or organisations, and *not* states. While Hoffman (2006: 14) discusses the state terrorism of 'totalitarian states and dictatorial leaders', state terrorism is seemingly consigned to history and the focus of the book is on sub-state groups or, in the conclusion, the state sponsors of terrorism as identified by the US government (Hoffman 2006: 256–67). Another scholar, in one of the field's introductory readers, includes state terrorism in his definition but also recognises the controversy in doing so (Gibbs 2012: 66–7).

Therefore, coming back to the declaration of many Terrorism Studies scholars that terrorism is a pejorative is deeply relevant. In one of the clearest explanations of this subjectivity, Richardson (2006: 19) compares the idea of terrorism with a statement that Justice Potter Stewart made in the decision on obscenity in US Supreme Court case *Jacobellis v Ohio*. Describing what did or did not qualify as obscene hardcore pornography, Justice Stewart wrote, 'I know it when I see it.' She extemporises, 'We know terrorism when we see it, or do we? We know we don't like it. . . . Terrorism is something the *bad guys* do' (Richardson 2006: 19, emphasis added). The use of terrorism and terrorist are not neutral. They do not reflect an objective and unbiased reality – and to argue that Terrorism Studies can be objective fails to recognise the power dynamics and social hierarchies that this field is built upon. Why would it make many Americans uneasy, if not queasy, to go with the Combahee River Collective's identification of Harriet Tubman as a 'guerrilla' as discussed in the introduction? How do we think about the American revolutionaries that dumped tea in the Boston Harbour and instigated a war against King George III of Britain? Or, how do we remember Nelson Mandela? As the first black president of South Africa and a figure of peace or as a guerrilla, the crime which sent him to Robben Island for eighteen years? Why is it that 9/11 was so quickly recognised as terrorism and has become a touchstone for the conceptualisation of terrorism, but the majority of the world remains ignorant of the death toll in Kashmir (approaching 50,000, not including disappearances, since it began in 1947 [see CNN Library 2018])?

Choosing not to examine *why* terrorism is a pejorative is deeper than one person's or one group's claim to legitimacy. Choosing not to dig more deeply is a 'moment of antagonism', one in which political contestations are ignored in order to shore up the status-quo power dynamic. A moment of antagonism, Jenny Edkins (1999: 5) illuminates, is a way of understanding how these calculated forgettings work. For instance, '[s]ocial order is characterised by antagonisms that bring to light . . . the contingency of the institutionalised frameworks of society within which everyday social practices tak[e] place' (Edkins 1999: 5). In these contingencies a social dynamic is at play: we can either make the contingent known, reveal subjectivity and expose the operational dynamics of politics; or we can fold to the norm: subsuming ourselves and others to the everyday politics upon which, I argue, calculated forgettings are dependent. A judgement call is made when something is pronounced (or not) 'terrorism' and the calculated forgettings of race, gender, class and heternonormativity remain forgotten. The pejorative element does not matter because erasures support the way the world is meant to be ordered.

Fearful Words: The Discursive Power of Terrorism

Discourse is key to understanding how Terrorism Studies has governed itself – determining the debates, conversations, what subjects matter and where the knowledge of these subjects comes from. Richard Jackson (2012) argues that Terrorism Studies rests on 'subjugated knowledge'. Taken from Foucault, the idea of subjugated knowledge refers to forms of knowledge that 'have been disqualified as nonconceptual knowledges [and] as insufficiently elaborated' because they are seen as 'naïve' and 'hierarchically inferior' (Foucault 1997: 7 as cited in Jackson 2012: 13). While the violence and destruction are real, 'terrorism is a social fact rather than a brute fact', meaning that the significance of the act is derived from 'symbolic labelling, social agreement, and a range of inter-subjective practices' (Jackson 2008: 28). Terrorism is seen as a 'pejorative rather than analytical term' (Jackson 2008: 29) because those in power, in that moment of antagonism, often use it as a label to delegitimise and remove moral authority from the terrorist actor (and to reify their own legitimacy and moral authority; see Gentry 2014). While Critical Terrorism Studies (CTS) has already highlighted the tensions and the power differentials, this scholarship has not gone far enough.

Within post-structuralism, 'language is "the primary social institution"' (Searle 1995: 59–60 as quoted within Epstein 2013: 502). Language

> generat[es] structures that are always charged with relations of domination, and temporarily fixed within historically contingent sets of meanings (discourses), the settling of which is the outcome of a political struggle. *Discourse is the primary site for the exercise, not of consensual reasoning, but of power.* (Epstein 2013: 502, emphasis added)

The structures that language establishes also temper 'the condition of possibility for acting in' (Epstein 2013: 506). Thus, the language we use to describe terrorism, terrorists and counter-terrorism/terrorist determines the conditions for action, legitimacy and credibility.

When, in the moment of antagonism, an act of violence is called terrorism, it is being interpellated – it is being constituted and, in this case, as an 'utterance' (Butler 1997: 2). Butler specifically explores 'injurious speech' and how 'utterances' work to harm (and possibly empower, as to be called a name is to be in some way recognised). Utterances may be quotidian and mundane, but they are also

> ritual or ceremonial. As utterances, they work to the extent that they are given in the form of a ritual, that is repeated in time, and, hence, maintain a sphere of operation that is not restricted to the moment of the utterance itself. The

> illocutionary speech act performs its deed *at the moment* of the utterance, and yet to the extent that the moment is ritualised, it is never merely a single moment. The 'moment' in ritual is a condensed historicity: it exceeds itself in past and future directions, an effect of prior and future invocations that constitute and escape the instance of utterance. (Butler 1997: 3)

In such a way, we come close to understanding how words form structures. Through the performativity of ritual and ceremony, the way that the moment reaches backwards and forwards temporally, the utterances play into the ways that society and cultural relations have been structured.

For instance, in the 1990s after the fall of the Soviet Union, Chechens began an armed struggle for an independent state apart from Russia. They won the first war and the US government was verbally supportive of the Chechen struggle for self-determination. Yet, Russia insisted that the Chechens were terrorists, emphasising Chechen tactics including suicide attacks, attacks on the International Committee for the Red Cross and hospitals. What the Russians deflected or denied was their own use of ethnic cleansing and genocidal violence. Yet, after 9/11, when the US ramped up the War on Terror, the US named multiple Chechen groups as terrorist, thus interpolating that conflict as between legitimate state violence and illegitimate terrorist violence (see Gentry and Whitworth 2011; Bhattacharji 2010).

In this book, a book that specifically targets how Terrorism Studies and, to a lesser extent, CTS structure the field, it is imperative to understand who gets to speak and be heard. It is imperative to understand the performative nature of power and who gets to perform it: not just who gets to engage in the moment of antagonism, but who gets heard at the conclusion of that moment. In *Excitable Speech*, Butler (1997: 6) works through a parable written by Toni Morrison, an African American former Nobel Laureate in Literature:

> In the parable, young children play a cruel joke and ask a blind woman to guess whether the bird that is in their hands is living or dead. The blind woman responds by refusing and displacing the question: 'I don't know . . . but what I do know is that it is in your hands. It is in your hands.'

Reversing Morrison, who 'analogi[ses]' the blind woman as a 'practiced writer' (Butler 1997: 8), I argue that academics in this context are the children who taunt the woman and are possibly harming the bird. How the bird is treated – how those who are *our subject* are treated – is in *our hands*. In Terrorism Studies, the power to determine credibility and legitimacy and then how we respond to terrorism is in our hands. Do we always exercise this power with recognition of common humanity, or do we use this power to foster further separations between the self and Other? This is examined in the next chapter by looking at the emergence of the new terrorism thesis.

Language, after all, is agency, 'an extended doing, a performance with effects' (Butler 1997: 7). While Butler offers us a way out of the reification of power structures in this work, within Terrorism Studies the charges that CTS has brought need to be further interrogated. While CTS brought a necessary critique to the War on Terror, the racial, gendered and heteronormative power structures that inform Terrorism Studies go further back than 2001 or the 1990s. They are rooted in the same structures as IR – a once and always colonial subject designed to support hierarchical racial and gendered imperialism (see Vitalis 2015 and further exploration of this in Chapter 4). Therefore, we have to ask how the authority has been granted to Terrorism Studies – as a subject with a strong relationship to governments – and how we have come to accept such authority. For example, Boaz Ganor, an Israeli academic and counter-terrorism advisor, uses deeply troubling language to discuss counter-terrorism. While I have been told that to use Boaz Ganor is picking the low-hanging fruit, the fruit Boaz produces has no less power. For a social scientist, his citation record is impressive and his h-index score is high: he has power. Therefore, why is it that Ganor can use language like the 'eradication of terrorism' through 'destroy[ing] the organisation's motivations', and 'completely eliminat[ing] the enemy' (Ganor 2005: 26)? And how are we meant to make sense of Ganor's (2005: 28) mentioning of these previously articulated Israeli counter-terrorism positions: 'terrorism can be wiped out using offensive means, but the international climate does not allow Israel to do so', or 'our hope was to exterminate terrorism. We learned and understood that it is really impossible to exterminate terrorism . . .'? Especially when these are offered to the readers of his counter-terrorism textbook without any kind of explanation of what 'wiped out' or exterminate' mean, and without any kind of critique?

To 'speak' terrorism, as borrowed from the Copenhagen School's notion of speaking security (as explored further on), is injurious and it works to solidify particular identities. As Butler continues, 'hate' or injurious

> speech reinvokes the position of dominance and reconsolidates it at the moment of utterance. As the linguistic rearticulation of social domination, hate speech becomes . . . the site for the mechanical and predictable reproduction of power. (Matsuda 1993 as cited in Butler 1997: 19)

By uttering terrorism in that moment of antagonism, a judgement is passed. Who becomes rational, legitimate or moral within political violence tends to track along a state/non-state binary and how these are linked with, at the very least, race and gender. While the utterance of terrorism immediately reflects an existential security crisis, the utterance deflects away from these discursive structures.

Therefore, it is my belief that the quest to establish a *definitive* definition of terrorism fails to grapple with the reasons why there will *never be* a universal definition of terrorism. Terrorism is what William Connolly (1993) calls an 'essentially contested concept', because certain concepts 'essentially involve endless disputes about their proper uses on the part of their users' (Connolly 1993: 10). Terrorism is an essentially contested concept because there are deeper legacies of racism, colonialism and gendered practices that go into qualifying this style of violence and those who perpetrate it. Karin Fierke (2015: 34) expands on this: essentially contested concepts 'generat[e] debates that cannot be resolved by reference to empirical evidence because the concept contains a clear ideological or moral element and defies precise, generally accepted definition' (Fierke 2015: 34). There are three criteria which allows this contestation to happen:

1. 'the concept is appraisive or describes a valued achievement';
2. it is an 'internally complex [practice] and involves reference to several dimensions';
3. 'if the agreed and contested rules of application are fairly open, making it possible for users to interpret the shared rules in different ways as new and unforeseen events arise' (Fierke 2015: 35)

First, as will be demonstrated throughout the pages of this book, to label an activity as terrorism allows the one doing the labelling to gain an upper hand, to become the one appraising the activity and determining its (illegitimate and immoral) value. In her discussion of terrorism and ethics, Virginia Held (2008: 4) argues that 'international law is itself evolving and has serious limitations. As currently formulated, it is highly biased in favour of existing states and against non-state groups . . .'. This is reflected in Andrew Valls' (2000: 66) discussion of just war theory and terrorism:

> In the public and scholarly reactions to political violence, a double standard is often at work. When violence is committed by states, our assessment tends to be quite permissive, giving states a great benefit of the doubt about the

propriety of their violent acts. However, when the violence is committed by nonstate actors, we often react with horror, and the condemnations cannot come fast enough.

This division of state versus non-state is a logocentric binary, where one term is superior, here states (and typically democratic ones [see Gentry 2014]), and one is inferior, non-state actors, particularly ones that use violence. This is why Critical Terrorism Studies' early agenda centred on state terrorism, refuting the protection afforded states by Westphalian norms (see Blakeley 2009). How this logocentrism also implicates automatic connotations of morality/immorality will be further explored in Chapter 2.

The state centrism of Terrorism Studies and the articulation of terrorism as illegitimate is one way of subjugating specific knowledges about post-colonial or irredentist anti-state violence (see for instance Barkawi and Laffey 2006). It follows the Westphalian norms of state sovereignty and the state as having the monopoly on the legitimate use of force, but it must now be acknowledged that state lines defend colour lines. In International Relations specifically and in the West (far) more generally, such legitimacy is tied to Westphalia and to notions of legitimate authority and the legitimate use of violence, which is tied closely to *white, Western* liberal democracies (see Gentry 2014; de Carvalho et al. 2011; Kochi 2009). Therefore, terrorism in many definitions becomes something that *non-Western, non-white* non-state actors use, but somehow not something states do. In fact, Terrorism Studies goes to great lengths to set apart state violence. Isn't this why an Israeli counterterrorist can use the words 'eradication' and 'elimination', because terrorism is tied to particular brown bodies? How is it that scholars accept the US's designation of what states sponsor terrorism without discussing in turn the US's relationship with the *mujahideen* in Afghanistan, or the complicity and support offered via Operation Condor in South America? Terrorism then is a discursive phenomenon that orders the international hierarchy, distinguishing between state and non-state, credible and non-credible, legitimate and illegitimate. The very existence of the idea of terrorism and the continued use of the label is owed to social power and practice.

All terrorism is an egregious harm, but to differentiate between the actors who utilise this 'method' of violence is also harmful. Such declarations and labels perpetuate further harm, keeping some away from power while allowing others to continue to hold and wield power. Thus, subjugated knowledge is closely related to the other Foucauldian principle of the power/knowledge praxis, which holds that knowledge produces power and power relies upon knowledge to shape intent. Stabilising a definition of terrorism determines which forms and types of knowledge and information count – in this case, a stable definition of terrorism becomes the apex of the power/knowledge intersection. The gendered and racialised tensions of these hierarchies are the very reasons why a fixed definition will never emerge.

This is clear if we mind our history: there is a reason why the UN resisted adopting a definition of terrorism until after 9/11. '[T]he definition conundrum has entangled the UN for four decades' because some states 'condemn as terrorism all acts that endanger or take innocent lives' while '[o]thers have emphasised the need to include state-sponsored acts within the definition' (Cortright et al. 2007: 44). Specifically, in the first thirty years of the UN, within the looming backdrop of the Cold War, the developing world (mainly) was casting off their colonial masters. Part of this casting-off process was post-colonial violence, violence that was often written as terrorist (Barkawi and Laffey 2006: 330). During the Cold War, not only was there tension on the Security Council between the US and the USSR, but the UNGA, as controlled by the G-77 and the Non-Aligned Movement, would not adopt a definition that implied post-colonial violence was 'terrorist' and therefore illegitimate (Dugard 1974: 73). Indeed, a UNGA group made up of 'Afro-Arab and East European states' rejected the suggestion of a Western-controlled UNGA group to 'prevent and punish terrorism'. They 'refused to support any measures which might interfere with the activities of liberation movements or which failed to condemn organised state terror on the part of "colonial, racist and alien regimes"' (Dugard 1974: 74). This overlaps with the state of Terrorism Studies at the time. It was emerging as an academic field led by a close-knit group of scholars and policy-makers who met over and over again from the 1960s onwards (Stampnitzky 2013: 39–45; Ranstorp 2009: 20). These scholars came primarily from the Global North, few were women, and many had government and military ties (Stampnitzky 2013: 31–9) – all of which speak to specific perspectives and objectives in how they studied terrorism and for what purpose, which closely align with the tensions found at the UN.

Second, determining what is terrorism is an activity that relies upon several other dimensions of knowledge and practice. Why are mass shootings in the US not seen as an act of terrorism if they are perpetrated by white men, but are when they are perpetrated by brown men? More specifically, why was Major Nidal Hasan, the Fort Hood shooter, often described as a terrorist and not a mentally ill lone gunman? (This will be explored in Chapter 3.) Why would the takeover in Oregon, as mentioned in the Introduction, not be seen as terrorism? Terrorism happens in a context – typically political – that differentiates itself from another event. This too is loaded: given all of the mass shootings that happen in the US on a daily/monthly basis, where women are often the target or the majority of the victims, why is this not seen in light of patriarchy as a political system and ideology? (This will be explored later in Chapter 5). This 'knowledge' of terrorism is intimately tied to 'knowledges' of race, gender and religious bias – if not of sexuality and class as well.

Third, the instability of terrorism – as not having a fixed definition and for its notorious subjectivity – enables the manipulation of the concept as new events arise, as Richards (2015: 15) acknowledges. Looking back from 2019, this is most obvious in the events that followed 9/11 and the construction of the Bush administration's War on Terror. Several key texts within Critical Terrorism Studies focus on the discursive machinations of the Bush administration. Richard Jackson (2005) looks at the discourses used to justify and win support for the War on Terror, particularly in the creation of the Muslim Other. Lee Jarvis (2009) looks at the construction of time as particularly linked to progressive Western civilisation against an 'atavistic' Islamic one as well as the framing of the War on Terror within Biblical concepts. Yet, the discourse used here, of fanaticism, fundamentalism, 'radical', shares commonalities with discourse used against non-Islamic and non-religious terrorism in the 1960s and 1970s, as the next few chapters will illustrate.

Terrorism has historically been utilised to serve political purposes. For instance, an identity crisis emerged within Terrorism Studies when its attempt to understand the phenomenon collided with the US government's need to ramp up the Cold War in the 1980s by invoking terrorism (Stampnitzky 2013, chapter 3). Many respected Terrorism Studies scholars, including ones who had previously worked with or for the US government, were challenged for arguing against the construction of terrorism as irrational and fanatical, trying to offer instead an understanding of why people turned to terrorism. These scholars were seen as sympathetic to terrorism and as anti-government (Stampnitzky 2013: 70–5). The discourse of fanaticism effectively shut out those who might criticise the US government (as its policies perhaps contributed to the conditions that led people to terrorism), and amplified the voices that argued for heavy-handed counter-terrorism, justifying an increase in spending and military operations.[2] It was not surprising, then, when I heard at an inter-governmental training on counter-terrorism that successful counter-terrorism scenarios included the 2009 Sri Lanka military campaign against the LTTE, which some have called a genocide, and the Russian campaign against the Chechens, which included elements of ethnic cleansing, gender-based violence and genocide.

Such a result – increasing the power and capability of a government to militarily respond to terrorism – begins to hint at the stratifications that Terrorism Studies and the definition problem rest upon. It is not just that terrorism is an essentially contested concept but it is also a 'thick signifier', or the understanding that a term does not just point to an object but also 'organises social relations' (Huysmans 1998: 232). In a classic text in Critical Security Studies, Huysmans (1998: 228) argues that

> 'Security' refers . . . to a wider framework of meaning (call it symbolic order, or culture or, as I will call it, discursive formation) within which we organise particular forms of life. The question about the meaning of security should thus be pursued a bit further. It should lead to the exploration of the wider cultural framework(s) within which security receives its meaning, and which are often implied in the daily use of the label 'security'. To do this we should move away from approaching 'security' as a definition or as a concept and instead interpret it as a thick signifier.

While he also argues that security, like terrorism, has multiple definitions that impact/reify multiple ways of seeing security, Huysmans (1998) ultimately argues that the most productive way of grappling with security is to do so through de Saussure's post-structural semiotics.

De Saussure splits a sign into a signifier, the word or sound, and the signified, the image or the concept the sign represents. Signifiers receive meaning through what they are *not*. This means, in this instance, the signifier 'security' is not neutral; instead security 'has a history and implies a meaning, a particular signification of social relations' (Huysmans 1998: 228). In a foundationalist approach, security 'assumes an external reality', but in a post-structural approach,

> 'security' becomes self-referential. It does not refer to an external, objective reality but establishes a security situation by itself. . . . Thus, the signifier has a performative rather than descriptive force. Rather than describing . . . , it organises social relations into security relations. (Huysmans 1998: 232)

This has significant bearing on terrorism and the quest for a definition. When terrorism is spoken, those who hear it *know* what it means and what the response should be. It is so loaded that it invokes an immediate claim on our time, attention and emotions. It demands a particular action. But this knowledge is tied to particular ways of being and exclusions from power structures.

The case that IR is deeply structured and hierarchical has been made quite well for a long time (Vitalis 2015; Sjoberg 2013; Peterson and Runyan 2009; Barkawi 2010; Barkawi and Laffey 2006; Tickner 1992); yet, to see Terrorism Studies as additionally embedded in these structures and therefore potentially resistant to change has only been more recent (see Stump and Dixit 2013; Jackson et al. 2009; Jackson 2005). That 'terrorism' is a discursive, problematic concept is well known and, indeed, it has often been seen as the driving force behind the emergence of Critical Terrorism Studies in 2006. While these scholars have looked at the reification of the Westphalian state-system within the West, others have noted, separately, the issues of racialised religious bias (Jarvis 2009; Jackson 2005; Tuastad 2003) and gender (Gentry 2018a and 2016b; Sjoberg 2009), very few have brought these together (see Stump and Dixit [2013, chapter 5] for an exploration of this critique and Parashar [2011] for how it can be done). Indeed, many have failed to dig more deeply into *why* the definition is derogatory and this failure can be related to forgettings.

Calculated Forgettings: The Intersecting Structures of Terrorism Studies

This section attempts to draw out the *systematic* and *system of* gendered, racial and heteronormative exclusions that the field of IR makes. Terrorism Studies is deeply tied to IR and is filled with these same exclusions. The chapter, however, does not necessarily argue that the scholars themselves are sexist or racist, as they are simply navigating a series of exclusions and hierarchies themselves. Thus, the next section does not make the claim that the scholars cited are *individually* problematic, but that their *scholarship* could only be welcomed into an exclusionary system if it does not challenge it. Thus, all scholarship, all knowledge and all practices are navigations of power and systemic exclusions. That is why the 'definition debate' becomes a perfect exemplar for demonstrating the power hierarchies within the field: the need to arrive at a definition is in an effort to create an objective, rational and credible social scientific field of Terrorism Studies. Yet, this drive is based upon certain erasures and exclusions and fails to recognise that credibility does not lie within a settled

debate – instead it lies within a field of study willing to have difficult conversations about how best to continue to navigate the power/
knowledge nexus.

Racial Forgetting

This section will build upon the notion of aphasia within Critical Race
theory, arguing that multiple forgettings are at play, not just the wilful
'ignorance' of the white supremacist system of IR, which encompasses
Terrorism Studies. 'Forgetting' in this regard is a discursive manoeuvre
to deny how much IR depends upon race dominance in IR, or what multiple Critical Race scholars call 'white supremacy' (Vitalis 2000; Mills
1997). While some may be resistant to the use of 'white supremacy' in
this regard, thinking it is better served describing the overt racism of the
Ku Klux Klan, Critical Race scholars maintain that the world 'has been
foundationally shaped for the past five hundred years by the realities
of European domination' (Mills 1997: 20, italic emphasis removed).
Indeed, the trick of racism is to see it as a 'remnant' of the past, instead
of part of the ordering of the present (Bonilla-Silva 1997: 468). Thus,
it is important to see that the international system is a 'racialised social
syste[m]' so dependent upon the racial categorisations of actors that
it leads to 'economic, political, social, and ideological' hierarchies
(Bonilla-Silva 1997: 469).

The continuance of the white supremacist system is predicated on
'forgetting' (Mills 1997). Mills (1997: 19) argues that

> white misunderstanding, misrepresentation, evasion, and self-deception on
> matters related to race are among the most pervasive mental phenomena
> of the past few hundred years, a cognitive and moral economy physically
> assigned for conquest, colonisation, and enslavement. And these phenomena
> are in no way *accidental*, but *prescribed* by the terms of the Racial Contract,[3]
> which requires a certain schedule of structural blindness and opacity in order
> to establish and maintain the white polity.

The reason why IR relies so heavily upon abstractions (or the over-gen-
eralisations which feminists also critique [see Sylvester 1999]) is that the
subject is 'premised on a desire to escape history, to efface the violence,
genocide, and theft that marked the encounter between the rest and the
West in the post-Columbian era' (Krishna 2011: 401). Krishna continues that IR is '[f]ounded . . . on discourse that justified, abstracted, and
rationalised the genocide of populations of the so-called new world, the

enslavement of Africans, and the colonisation of Asians.' The silence and the abstraction are a

> substitute truth that renders existence at least partly bearable. *It is . . . then a quintessentially white discipline.* It is not that race disappears from IR; it is rather that race serves as the crucial epistemic silence around which the discipline is written and coheres. *That which is made to appear in IR discourse is that which conceals the silent presence of race.* (Krishna 2001: 407, emphasis added)

When the question is posed, 'Is this IR?' or when epistemologies and methodologies that fall outside of a social scientific approach are dismissed, discouraged or denigrated, these discursive acts then designate what is to appear as 'IR discourse'. These mask different ways of knowing and of being because they uphold a very strict way of thinking about IR, war, security and political violence (see also Krishna 2006). Such questions are aimed to make IR scholars forget (or never know) the origins of our field.

Following from this, then, is how '[f]orgetting empire is often a focus of Eurocentrism, of the unreflective assumption of centrality of Europe and latterly the West in human affairs' (Barkawi 2010: 4). Such 'forgetting' is illustrated by looking at the dubious origins of the field's most illustrious journal, *Foreign Affairs*. It began as the *Journal of Race Development*, a publication that aided the efficiency and efficacy of colonial policy and governance (Vitalis 2015; see also Barkawi 2010: 10). Therefore,

> [w]e have to acknowledge, nonetheless, that the collectivity that identifies itself as the 'the field of [IR]' in the US is tightly, organically bound to a particular place, history, and social formation. This inescapable fact, which applies equally across 'schools' of thought and methodological 'approaches' goes far to explain why IR today has little to say about racism as an international institution or white supremacy . . . that the field's founders embraced and elaborated. (Vitalis 2000: 355)

Barkawi, however, argues that this responsibility is not solely located within IR in the US, it can be traced to IR in Europe as well. The legacy and purpose of *The Journal of Race Development* forged the 'imperial origins of the discipline' as a whole (Barkawi 2010: 10), which shaped its ontological, epistemological and formational perspectives.

More specifically, IR's origins are linked to the formation of security studies and, more particularly, to how terrorism is understood as a security threat. For instance, '[u]nderstanding security relations, past and present, requires acknowledging the mutual constitution of Europe and a non-European world and their joint role in making history' (Barkawi and Laffey 2006: 330). Violent conflict between these two constituencies 'is very old' and, within security studies, the conflicts are often viewed as 'small wars or asymmetric conflict and conceived as peripheral to, and derived from the main action among great powers . . .' (Barkawi and Laffey 2006: 330). Post-colonial conflicts, or 'resistance movements', which are 'armed resistance to Northern domination', are 'subsumed largely' as 'terrorism' (Barkawi and Laffey 2006: 330). This is a self-affirming cycle: legitimate state violence begets illegitimate non-state violence, which often originates from the Global South. Western inter-ventions are often conducted in non-Western states (see for instance Brown 2002) and often result in unintentional ripple effects, such as the emergence of anti-Western or anti-Northern violence. Determining this violence as terrorism 'legitimates state power and delegitimates the use of force by non-state actors. It assumes in advance that "terrorist" acts are always illegitimate and unjustified' (Barkawi and Laffey 2006: 332). Barkawi and Laffey (2006) illustrate this with al Qaeda's origins in *mujahideen*, which were armed by the US in the 1980s in order to resist the Soviet invasion of Afghanistan.

The construction of Western versus non-Western identity inter-sects with feminist critiques of masculinity and femininity. As Kimberlé Crenshaw (1995: 142) writes, 'rationality, neutrality, and objectivity' were associated with 'white men who live in Europe and North America'; they are, in other words, 'simply elements' that are naturalised into the 'domi-nant worldview of white elites' and are reluctantly granted to people of colour (see also Crenshaw 1995: 130). During the colonial period, the 'negotiation' of colonising/colonised subjects became structured along the lines of the increasingly entrenched 'rational' and 'objective' Enlightened identity of Europeans, leaving people of colour on the opposite end of the binary: irrational and subjective (Quijano 2007).

'Rationality, progress, and development' are key concepts to con-structing what is 'Western' (and as will be explored below, what is 'masculine'), as are 'agency', 'power' and 'morality' (Barkawi and Laffey 2006: 346). Indeed, because non-Western subjects (and often women) were found to be 'lacking' in these areas, Europeans and later those within the wider West could 'locat[e] civilisation and law' there and not 'over there' (Barkawi and Laffey 2006: 347). Rationality, as will be explored in Chapters 2 and 4, is central to how terrorism is understood and it cannot be separated from the location of terrorism as often within non-Western/non-European places, nor from the positing irrationality within the same population/locale.

Gendered Forgetting

Rationality, agency and morality are also deeply gendered (and tied to heteronormativity), and related to the construction of the state system. Gender – the socially constructed division of bodies into masculine and feminine – 'fosters dichotomisation, stratification, and depoliticalisation in thought and action, sustaining global power structures' (Peterson and Runyan 2010: 2). Masculinity assumes a certain association with violence due to the assumed natural capacity of a man to be violent. In turn, this creates a particular link between men, masculinity and warfare (see Hutchings 2008; see also the *Critical Military Studies* 2017 special issue on militarised masculinity), a link the Westphalian system is dependent upon.

When a subject or an object is gendered, this means that certain expectations are automatically imparted. These expectations are related to the socially constructed gender binary between what is masculine and feminine. As a construction, masculinity conveys logic, rationality, dispassion and autonomy. In co-constitutive tension with masculinity, femininity conveys the reverse: illogical, irrational, emotional and dependent (Peterson and Runyan 2010: 2; Tickner 1992: 7). Since the Enlightenment, Western political thought has been dependent upon masculine idealisations of the political actor (traditionally constructed as Western, white, rational men) as fully autonomous – able to make (rational) decisions with no constraint placed upon it (him) (see Peterson and Runyan 2010: 7).

This perspective is also supported by the work on hegemonic masculinity, which is

> the ideal form of masculinity performed by men with the most power attributes, who not incidentally populate most global power positions – typically white, Western, upper-class, straight men who have conferred on them the complete range of gender, race, class, national, and sexuality privileges. (Peterson and Runyan 2010: 7)

This idealised masculinity is transposed to the state – qualifying the state, a sovereign, autonomous, rational actor, as a masculinised actor and non-state actors as feminised ones (Tickner 1992: 42). The masculinised state has the sole access to credibility and the legitimacy to use violence via the monopoly on power, rendering other actors, such as politically violent ones, as non-credible and illegitimate (see Gentry 2016b; Kochi 2009; Sjoberg 2009). While the monopoly on violence works domestically through the criminal justice system, it works externally through the threat of and the credible ability to wage war. War is 'man's work', a sentiment explored in great depth by Cynthia Enloe (2014 and 2000), and a state defends its sovereignty via the military and its ability to wage war effectively. In addition to the relationship between masculinity and war (see also Hutchings 2008), being a good and capable citizen has been dependent upon a person's ability to be a good soldier (Elshtain 1987) – something historically limited to men (see MacKenzie 2015). The supremacy and primacy placed upon such masculine ideals and their conflation with particular roles and positions as citizens and as states place those on the outside of it – like women or feminised (or 'devalorised' [Peterson 2010: 17]) subjects (i.e., not masculine subjects like states) in subordinate positions. Laura Sjoberg (2013) has taken this one step further, arguing that the international state system is not driven by anarchy, but by a gendered hierarchy, where conforming to gendered idealised types determines the esteem an actor may have. States as a transposition of idealised masculinity dominate; non-state actors, like terrorist groups, cannot gain access to or be recognised idealised masculine traits (see Sjoberg 2009; Gentry 2018a and 2014).

Indeed, in neo-Realism, a state's rationality is tied to its military capability, embedding the Thucydian notion of 'might makes right' (see Walzer 1977: 4). Terms associated with the rationality-based study of IR and latterly terrorism are inherently loaded. For instance, asymmetric warfare is a restatement of the 'weapon of the weak' cliché, which, when put into realist language, is a less capable actor making a (costly) decision to fight a more capable actor (Stepanova 2008). This is also known as 'irrational' in the realist paradigm. Or reference to terrorism, even within rationality discourse, as an 'illegitimate method' or an 'unjustified use of force' removes the supposed neutrality of rationality and inscribes the activity with (im)moral weight (see Kochi 2009; Held 2008).

Yet, hegemonic masculinity also determines how the 'idealised actor' is determined, often as white, masculine, wealthy, assertive/dominant, powerful and rational (see also Connell and Messerschmidt 2005). In terms of the military this is related to 'militarised masculinity', which requires physical strength, assertiveness, resoluteness or stoicism, diminishing the feminine (see Eichler 2014). This contrasts substantially with the construction of the individual terrorist, which will be explored further in Chapter 3. Robert Pape (2003: 343) makes the distinction between the rationality of a group's decision to use suicide terrorism and the irrationality of those who carry out the suicide mission. Similarly, Boaz Ganor (2005: 30) claims that politically violent actors are motivated by emotions weighed against a 'rational calculation'; more precisely, he argues the emotions belonging to 'leaders, terrorists, supporters, and activists' are 'irrational' (Ganor 2005: 36) (as will be discussed further in Chapter 4). In such ways, terrorism falls outside of idealised types, becoming subordinate within a hegemonic masculine system. More recent literature has tied this gendered hierarchy of the international system with the emergence of neo-Orientalism, thereby bringing the racialised religious bias against Islam together with gender in a complex manner (Narozhna and Knight 2016, chapter 3).

Hannah Partis-Jennings (2017) explores this interplay when she looks at the 2011 murder of a Taliban 'insurgent' (a term often linked with terrorism) by a UK soldier on patrol. The case of Marine A was well known, in part because he was convicted of murder in the context of war but in part because, after he shot the Afghan man, he recited a line from Shakespeare's *Hamlet*, 'shuffle off this mortal coil . . .', with the addition of 'you cunt'. While Partis-Jennings undertakes a creative intertextual investigation, the focus here is on how she develops Marine A's identity within a militarised masculinity, one that is able to dehumanise the Afghan man he murdered. For instance, she argues.

> if you look at the logic of the killing, especially when elucidated through a gender-sensitive ethical framework, it is hardly differentiated from the founding parameters of war-fighting writ large. As Sandra Whitworth points out, military training is 'in short . . . about preparing people to destroy other human beings by force'. (Partis-Jennings 2017: 7, citing Whitworth 2004: 151)

Where the soliloquy in which Hamlet contemplates death is a reflection on humanity, in the instance of Marine A those same words are used to show the negated relationship between Marine A and the insurgent. In reflecting on the audio recording of the patrol's encounter with the Afghan man,

> one of the most interesting moments takes place just after the shooting. Marine A speaks to the other soldiers, declaring, 'it's nothing he wouldn't do to us'. One of them agrees, 'I know, exactly.' This sentiment points to an instant in which relationality is banished and reiterated simultaneously;

> Marine A is actively justifying his actions in terms of the relationship between them (British soldiers) and the Taliban and simultaneously delineating it as one of mutual unrecognisability. He shuts down the possibility of seeing a person lying dead on the ground, of understanding that this person is human like him, by defining him in terms of his capacity to do them harm (Partis-Jennings 2017: 8).

The relationship between these two humans is broken by Marine A's commitment to his masculine, soldiering identity, particularly in projecting and realising it as superior to the Taliban (Partis-Jennings 2017: 10).

There is a particular gendered dimension to this, one that speaks to the gendered forgetting within terrorism quite specifically. Partis-Jennings (2017: 11) asserts:

> A gendered 'shame-to-power conversion' by the soldiers is visible in the feminising and killing of the injured Afghan insurgent; Marine A manifests the desire to control his identity in an uncontrollable context, to regain agency by denying agency to the Other, shaming him, dehumanising him, committing violence against him, and in doing so striving to regain some semblance of the promised military masculine power.

This need to project a superior, masculine identity by those who counter terrorism is a rarely noted dynamic within Terrorism Studies. That Partis-Jennings points out the soldier's actions as happening in a situation out of control is important to considering a 'gendered forgetting' within Terrorism Studies. By searching for an objective, social scientific definition, Terrorism Studies can remain grounded in a foundationalist ontology, where rationality exists in a concrete, uncontestable, fully controlled context. Again, this quest depends on reflecting back a particular way of being and doing, one that does not capture the messy complexity of war, and countering what is often deemed to be a grey area: terrorism.

Heteronormative Forgetting

Potentially, heteronormative forgetting is one of the hardest forgettings to see, given the widespread acceptance of heteronormativity – unless, perhaps, one is directly affected by this system that rigidly enforces heterosexual norms. Just as racial and gender essentialisation make assumptions that racial and gender differences are biological and therefore immutable, heteronormativity makes assumptions about sexuality and therefore the organisation of social, legal and political arrangements around these assumptions. Heteronormativity assumes that people fall into one of two ways of being – male or female – and that these lead to complementary sexual, biological and social functions. Bluntly, men can procreate with multiple partners, but by not carrying and then caring for (via the dependency of nursing) they can inhabit the public domain, whereas women are curtailed to the private (see Elshtain 1981; Pateman 1980).

In this light, V. Spike Peterson (2014: 605) points out that 'the *continuity* of state formations' is 'enable[ed]' through 'the normalisation of heteropatriarchal principles' which 'secur[e] appropriate social reproduction[,] reliable transmission of property, and citizenship claims'. Moreover, 'the making of states *is* the making of sex' (Peterson 2014: 605). Unique among political organisations, state making is 'distinguished by their *formal* (legal) codification of marriage (. . . heterosexual matrix and "nuclear" family) and patriarchal inheritance of property and citizenship' (Peterson 2014: 605). In other words, heteropatriarchy (or heteronormativity's relationship with male-dominated societies) is able to locate those who belong to the particular *polis* and those who do not via their lineage as traced through the essentialisation of reproductivity to nuclear family relations. This, therefore, has within it assumptions about legality (marital status, inheritance, taxes, benefits), legitimacy (of heirs and citizenship rights) and morality.

The binary logic (logocentrism) of heteronormativity is then replicated and projected internationally. State versus non-state is one such projection, as highlighted above. Order (resting on the masculine association of rationality and order) versus anarchy (discursively linked with the feminine qualities of irrationality, chaos, hysteria [see for instance Elshtain 1987; see also Enloe's [1983: 117] discussion of Greek patriarchal-order and what lurked or loomed beyond]) is another logocentric binary, one that queer theory in IR 'explicitly engage[s]' reading 'order vs anarchy as normal vs perverse' and, more specifically, as 'hetero/homo-normative vs queer' (Weber 2014: 597). Queer theory, then, begins to interrogate the (overly) simplistic rendering of heteronormatively infused-IR.

In a proto-queer theory article, Cynthia Weber (1998: 93) advances that the state is sexed and gendered in a particular way for a particular purpose:

The state is said to be female and feminine domestically and male and masculine internationally. It is the presumed heterosexual projection of masculine authority into the internal (female/feminine) affairs of other states or

territories, or into the masculine realm of international politics (an anarchi-
cal war of every man against every man) that is the stuff of IR theory and
practice. An application of Butler's performative reading of sex, gender, and
sexuality would not accept these universal[isms] . . . Instead, it would investigate how various, particular, historically-bounded sex and gender codings
participate in affecting the state and sovereignty.

In this passage, Weber begins to queer how the state is signified within
IR. To queer something is to recognise that people, objects, actors do
not always (or ever) 'signify monolithically' (Weber 2014: 597), and
this act of recognition begins to erode some of the power presumed
within heterosexual norms. Therefore to queer is to be 'open' to the

mesh of possibilities, gaps, overlaps, dissonances and resonances, lapses and
excesses of meaning when the constituent elements of anyone's gender, and
anyone's sexuality aren't made (or *can't* be made) to signify monolithically
(Sedgwick 1993: 8 as cited in Weber 2014: 596)

One significant contribution queer theory makes is 'the understanding that codes and practices of "normalcy" simultaneously constitute
"deviancy," exclusions, and "otherings" as sites of social violence' (Lind
2014: 601; see also Peterson 2014: 604). For this study, several queer
theorists have already begun to unpack how the 'terrorist' is portrayed as
'deviant' (see Weber 2016; Puar 2017; Puar and Rai 2002).

In relationship to this sense of interrogating deviancy, queer theory
also 'investigate[s] how queer subjectivities and queer practices . . . are
disciplined, normalised, or capitalised upon by and for states' (Weber
2014: 597). Weber posits 'queer logic' as the 'and/or' that recognises
that 'truths are never stable and their representation is never guaranteed'
(Weber 2014: 598). Therefore, queer scholarship

[t]rack[s] when queer figurations emerge and how they are normalised
and/or perverted as to that they might challenge but also support heterosexual, heteronormative, cis-gendered, homonormative, homophobic, and
trans*phobic assumptions, order, and institutions. (Weber 2014: 598)

What then are heteronormative forgettings when it comes to IR and,
therefore, to Terrorism Studies? One article intersects post-colonial-
ism with queer theory, by 'align[ing] "queer" and "Third World" –
grouping them in their common inheritance of subjugation and
disparagement . . . and a politics aimed at disrupting domination
and status quo' (Kapoor 2015: 1611). Echoing the narrativising of

anti-colonial violence as 'terrorism' (see Barkawi and Laffey 2006), Kapoor's (2015: 1612) article looks at how the 'Third World comes off looking remarkably queer: under Western eyes it has often been constructed as perverse, abnormal, and passive . . . as . . . backward, effete' and as 'never living up to the [Western] mark'. Thus, as hetero-normativity sets up a dominant political system, both domestic and international, forgettings of how this system of operation demarcates abnormality via heteronormativity are established, accepted and constantly reproduced.

While Jasbir Puar (2017) and Cynthia Weber (2016) have spent a significant amount of time parsing out the queer logic of the terror-ist, counter-terrorist and good patriotic citizen, Weber and Melanie Richter-Montpetit (2017: 4–5) identified the need for further research on the topic:

> How do non-normative understandings of gender and sexuality intersect with understandings of racial difference and colonial forms of power to construct internationally dangerous figures – like 'the terrorist' and/or 'the insurgent'?

Weber argues in *Queer International Relations* (2016) that there are four 'undesirable' figures in IR that upset Westphalia-as-Sovereign Male:

Unwanted im/migrant
The terrorist
The Underdeveloped
The Undevelopable

As the following chapters will demonstrate, all four of these at times can be seen in different ways of narrating who the terrorist is and how the terrorist operates. By doing so, it reifies the 'correct' order of things: a state-based system that prioritises both the political and economic operations of the West. While there is some tension with this,[4] queer theory's aim to disrupt, agitate and challenge the hegemonic formations of IR that are inherently dependent upon binary formations enables a way past the binary thinking inherent within IR but, more particularly, Terrorism Studies.

Conclusion

It is therefore apparent that racialised, masculinised and heteronorma-tive idealisations structure IR, and this has an enormous impact on how we proceed as an academic field: in our teaching, in our publishing, in how we advise on policy, all because of what we see as important (see Phull et al. 2018). The language of IR *is* masculinist with its emphasis on the rational, sovereign and powerful. As Critical Military Studies homes in on: it is men who are traditionally associated with war and the wielding of power (Elshtain 1987; Hutchings 2008). From the masculinist identity of soldiering, Western culture has created the idea of a good and able citizen: again, rational, powerful, dominant and intelligent (Elshtain 1987 and 1981; Pateman 1980). From such traits (or idealised discursive descriptions), notions of what is a good government were derived (Elshtain 1987 and 1981; Pateman 1980). Yet, these are not just gendered terms. They are racial terms. They are heteronormative terms. Thus, descriptions of idealised citizens maintain particular boundaries of who belongs, who is credible, who is legitimate and who is moral.

In a recent piece for *Critical Military Studies*, Marysia Zalewski (2017: 203) writes that the relationships between gender, states and militaries is a manipulation:

> Militaries most surely have violence at their heart; . . . this violence persistently masquerades as something 'other' through its sanctioning by the state. Buried in this authoritative frame is a quagmire of hidden violence – state violence itself, gender/sex violence, the violence of colonialism and racial brutality. Paradoxically, the presence of these contradictions makes militaries a significant maker of gender (and other) boundaries, but also extremely vulnerable to their exposure given the colossal amount of work needed to maintain the web of illusions . . .

Feminism and other critical thought uncovers these illusions, showing them as fragile and weak, but oh so necessary to maintaining the structural order of patriarchy, white supremacy and heteronormativity. The violence of the military is not just war: it is indicative of how the state and hegemonic structures maintain power.

Thus, when the state and its sanctioned violence codify legitimacy in particular ways, all other ways of being, knowing and doing become illegitimate. Zalewski (2017 and 2013) also notes that the 'competing imaginaries of masculinity consistently emerge . . . in popular representations of "terrorists" and "western (civilised) leaders"'. The terrorist figure is manufactured, consumed and replicated as everything outside of the idealised images; therefore the terrorist is constructed not by what it is not, but by what else is non-credible, illegitimate, immoral: feminised, radicalised and queer others.

Notes

1. This, of course, relates to the methods section in the introductory chapter and the work that Ann Tickner (2005 and 1997) has done to represent the validity of feminist methods that are not (neo-)positivist.
2. An excellent study correlates politicians' need to stay in their positions by looking 'tough on terrorism' with rapidly changing counter-terrorism measures, which leads to inefficiencies and ineffectiveness (Lum et al. 2006).
3. Mills' Racial Contract is similar to Rousseau's Social Contract, in which the premise of government is a contract between the governed, who give up some rights and grant allegiance to government, which in turn protects the remaining rights of the governed. In the Racial Contract, race is seen as an outcome of the fallibility of humanity – resulting in seeing people of colour as imperfect humans. The Social Contract rests on the subjugation of people of colour in order to protect the primacy of European (and later Global North) states and white supremacy.
4. For instance, conversations at the annual conference of the *International Feminist Journal of Politics* in 2018 seemed to indicate that Queer theory could not be used for its analytical value alone. It also had to reckon with how the use of Queer theory impacted queer individuals and not putting already disenfranchised people at further risk.

References

Anievas, Alexander, Nivi Manchanda and Robbie Shilliam (eds) (2014), *Race and Racism in International Relations: Confronting the Global Colour Line* (Abingdon: Routledge).

Barkawi, Tarak (2010), 'Empire and Order in International Relations and Security Studies', in Bob Denemark (ed.), *The International Studies Encyclopaedia* (Hoboken, NJ: Blackwell), pp. 1360–79.

Barkawi, Tarak, and Mark Laffey (2006), 'The Post-colonial Moment in Security Studies', *Review of International Studies*, 32(2): 329–52.

Bellamy, Alex (2008), *Fighting Terror: Ethical Dilemmas* (London: Zed Books).

Blakeley, Ruth (2009), *State Terrorism and Neoliberalism: The North in the South* (Abingdon: Routledge).

Bonilla-Silva, Eduardo (1997), 'Rethinking Racism: Toward a Structural Interpretation', *American Sociological Review*, 62(3): 465–80.

Brown, Chris (2002), *Sovereignty, Rights and Justice: International Political Theory Today* (Cambridge: Polity Press).

Butler, Judith (1997), *Excitable Speech: A Politics of the Performative* (Abingdon: Routledge).

Buzan, Barry, Ole Wæver and Jaap de Wilde (1998), *Security: A New Framework for Analysis* (Boulder, CO: Lynne Rienner Publishers).

CNN Library (2018), 'Kashmir Fast Facts', *CNN*, 25 March, <https://edition.cnn.com/2013/11/08/world/kashmir-fast-facts/index.html> (last accessed 22 November 2018).

Connell, Robert W., and James W. Messerschmidt (2005), 'Hegemonic Masculinity: Rethinking the Concept', *Gender and Society*, 19(6): 829–59.

Connolly, William E. (1993), *The Terms of Political Discourse* (Princeton, NJ: Princeton University Press).

Cortright, David, George A. Lopez, Alistair Millar and Linda Gerber-Stellingwerf (2007), 'Global Cooperation against Terrorism: Evaluating the United Nations Counterterrorism Committee', in David Cortright and George A. Lopez (eds), *Uniting Against Terrorism: Cooperative Non-military Responses to the Global Terrorist Threat* (Cambridge, MA: MIT Press), pp. 23–50.

Crenshaw, Martha (ed.) (1995), *Terrorism in Context* (University Park: Penn State Press).

Crenshaw, Martha (2014), 'Terrorism Research: The Record', *International Interactions*, 40(4): 556–67.

Critical Military Studies (2017), 3(2), Special Issue on Militarised Masculinities.

De Carvalho, Benjamin, Halvard Leira and John M. Hobson (2011), 'The Big Bangs of IR: The Myths That Your Teachers Still Tell You About 1648 and 1919', *Millennium*, 39(3): 735–58.

Dugard, John (1974), 'International Terrorism: Problems of Definition', *International Affairs*, 50(1): 67–81.

Edkins, Jenny (1999), *Post-structuralism and International Relations: Bringing the Political Back In* (Boulder, CO: Lynne Rienner Publishers).

Eichler, Maya (2014), 'Militarised Masculinities in International Relations', *Brown Journal of World Affairs*, 21(1): 81–95.

Elshtain, Jean Bethke (1987), *Women and War* (Chicago: University of Chicago Press).

Elshtain, Jean Bethke (1981), *Public Man, Private Woman: Women in Social and Political Thought* (Princeton, NJ: Princeton University Press).

Enloe, Cynthia (1983), *Does Khaki Become You? The Militarisation of Women's Lives* (Boston: South End Press).

Enloe, Cynthia (2000), *Manoeuvres: The International Politics of Militarising Women's Lives* (Berkeley: University of California Press).

Enloe, Cynthia (2014), *Bananas, Beaches, and Bases: Making Feminist Sense of International Politics* (Berkeley: University of California Press).

Epstein, Charlotte (2013), 'Constructivism or the Eternal Return of Universals in International Relations. Why Returning to Language Is Vital to Prolonging the Owl's Flight', *European Journal of International Relations*, 19(3): 499–519.

Fierke, Karin M. (2015), *Critical Approaches to International Security* (Hoboken, NJ: John Wiley & Sons).

Foucault, Michel (1997), *Society Must Be Defended: Lectures at the College de France, 1975–76*, ed. Alessandro Fontana and Mauro Bertani (London: Allen Lane).

Ganor, Boaz (2002), 'Defining Terrorism: Is One Man's Terrorist Another Man's Freedom Fighter?', *Police Practice and Research*, 3(4): 287–304.

Ganor, Boaz (2005), *The Counter-Terrorism Puzzle: A Guide for Decision Makers* (London: Transaction).

Gentry, Caron E. (2014), 'Epistemic Bias: Legitimate Authority and Politically Violent Nonstate Actors', in Caron E. Gentry and Amy E. Eckert (eds), *The Future of Just War: New Critical Essays* (Athens: University of Georgia Press), pp. 17–29.

Gentry, Caron E. (2016b), 'Gender and Terrorism', in Simona Sharoni, Julia Welland, Linda Steiner and Jennifer Pederson (eds), *Handbook on Gender and War* (Cheltenham: Edward Elgar Publishing), pp. 146–68.

Gentry, Caron E. (2018a), 'Gender and Terrorism', in Caron E. Gentry, Laura Shepherd and Laura Sjoberg (eds), *The Routledge Handbook on Gender and Security* (Abingdon: Routledge), pp. 140–50.

Gibbs, Jack P. (2012), 'Conceptualisation of Terrorism', in John Horgan and Kurt Braddock (eds), *Terrorism Studies: A Reader* (Abingdon: Routledge), pp. 63–75.

Held, Virginia (2008), *How Terrorism Is Wrong: Morality and Political Violence* (Oxford: Oxford University Press).

Herman, Edward S., and Gerry O'Sullivan (1989), *The Terrorism Industry: The Experts and Institutions that Shape Our View of Terror* (New York: Pantheon).

Hoffman, Bruce (2006), *Inside Terrorism* (New York: Columbia University Press).

Hutchings, Kimberly (2008), 'Making Sense of Masculinity and War', *Men and Masculinities*, 10(4): 389–404.

Huysmans, Jef (1998), 'Security! What Do You Mean? From Concept to Thick Signifier', *European Journal of International Relations*, 4(2): 26–255.

Huysmans, Jef (2014), *Security Unbound: Enacting Democratic Limits* (Abingdon: Routledge).

Jackson, Richard D. (2008), 'An Argument for Terrorism', *Perspectives on Terrorism*, 2(2): 25–32.

Jackson, Richard D. (2012), 'Unknown Knowns: The Subjugated Knowledge of Terrorism Studies', *Critical Studies on Terrorism*, 5(1): 11–29.

Jackson, Richard, Marie Breen Smyth and Jerone Gunning (eds) (2009), *Critical Terrorism Studies: A New Research Agenda* (Abingdon: Routledge).

Jarvis, Lee (2009), *Times of Terror: Discourse, Temporality, and the War on Terror* (Basingstoke: Palgrave MacMillan).

Jenkins, Brian Michael (1980), *The Study of Terrorism: Definitional Problems* (Santa Monica, CA: RAND).

Jongman, Albert J. (2017), *Political Terrorism: A New Guide to Actors, Authors, Concepts, Data Bases, Theories, and Literature* (Abingdon: Routledge).

Kapoor, Ilan (2015), 'The Queer Third World', *Third World Quarterly*, 36(9): 1611–28.

Kochi, Tarik (2009), *The Other's War: Recognition and the Violence of Ethics* (London: Birkbeck Law Press).

Krishna, Sankaran (2001), 'Race, Amnesia, and the Education of International Relations', *Alternatives*, 26(4): 401–24.

Lind, Amy (2014), '"Out" in International Relations: Why Queer Visibility Matters', *International Studies Review*, 16(4): 601–4.

Lum, Cynthia, Leslie W. Kennedy and Alison Sherley (2006), 'Are Counterterrorism Strategies Effective? The Results of the Campbell Systematic Review on

Counter-Terrorism Evaluation Research', *Journal of Experimental Criminology*, 2(4): 489–516.

MacKenzie, Megan (2015), *Beyond the Band of Brothers: The US Military and the Myth that Women Can't Fight* (Cambridge: Cambridge University Press).

Matsuda, Mari J. (1993), 'Public Response to Racist Speech: Considering the Victim's Story', in Mari J. Matsuda, Charles R. Lawrence, Richard Delgado and Kimberlé Williams Crenshaw (eds), *Words That Wound* (Boulder, CO: Westview), pp. 17–52.

Mills, Charles W. (1997), *The Racial Contract* (Ithaca, NY: Cornell University Press).

Nacos, Brigitte L. (2000), 'Accomplice or Witness? The Media's Role in Terrorism', *Current History*, 99(636): 174–8.

Narozhna, Tanya, and W. Andy Knight (2016), *Female Suicide Bombings: A Critical Gender Approach* (Toronto: University of Toronto Press).

Pape, Robert A. (2003), 'The Strategic Logic of Suicide Terrorism', *American Political Science Review*, 97(3): 343–61.

Parashar, Swati (2011), 'Gender, Jihad, and Jingoism: Women as Perpetrators, Planners, and Patrons of Militancy in Kashmir', *Studies in Conflict and Terrorism*, 34(4): 295–317.

Partis-Jennings, Hannah (2017), 'Military Masculinity and the Act of Killing in *Hamlet* and Afghanistan', *Men and Masculinities*, doi: 1097184X17718585.

Pateman, Carole (1980), '"The Disorder of Women:" Women, Love, and the Sense of Justice', *Ethics*, 91(1): 20–34.

Peterson, V. Spike (2010), 'Gendered Identities, Ideologies, and Practices in the Context of War and Militarism', in Laura Sjoberg and Sandra Via (eds), *Gender, War, and Militarism: Feminist Perspectives* (Denver, CO: Praeger), pp.17–29.

Peterson, V. Spike (2014), 'Family Matters: How Queering the Intimate Queers the International', *International Studies Review*, 16(4): 604–8.

Peterson, V. Spike, and Anne Sisson Runyan (2009), *Global Gender Issues in the New Millennium* (Boulder, CO: Westview Press).

Phull, Kiran, Gokhan Ciflikli and Gustav Meibauer (2018), 'Gender and Bias in the International Relations Curriculum: Insights from Reading Lists', *European Journal of International Relations*, doi: 1354066118791690.

Puar, Jasbir K. (2017), *Terrorist Assemblages: Homonationalism in Queer Times* (Durham, NC: Duke University Press).

Puar, Jasbir K., and Amit Rai (2002), 'Monster, Terrorist, Fag: The War on Terrorism and the Production of Docile Patriots', *Social Text*, 20(3): 117–48.

Quijano, Aníbal (2007), 'Coloniality and Modernity/Rationality', *Cultural Studies*, 21(2–3): 168–78.

Richards, Anthony (2015), *Conceptualising Terrorism* (Oxford: Oxford University Press).

Richardson, Louise (2006), *What Terrorists Want: Understanding the Enemy, Containing the Threat* (New York: Random House).

Richter-Montpetit, Melanie, and Cynthia Weber (2017), 'Queer International Relations', *Oxford Research Encyclopaedias*, <http://politics.oxfordre.com/view/10.1093/acrefore/9780190228637.001.0001/acrefore-9780190228637-e-265> (last accessed 25 November 2018).

Schmid, Alex P., and Albert J. Jongman (1988), *Political Terrorism* (London: Transaction).

Schmid, Alex P., and Albert J. Jongman (2005), *Political Terrorism* (London: Transaction).

Searle, John R. (1995), *The Construction of Social Reality* (New York: Penguin Books).

Sedgwick, Eve K. (1993), *Tendencies* (Durham, NC: Duke University Press).

Sjoberg, Laura (2009), 'Feminist Interrogations of Terrorism/Terrorism Studies', *International Relations*, 23(1): 69–74.

Sjoberg, Laura (2013), *Gendering Global Conflict: Toward a Feminist Theory of War* (New York: Columbia University Press).

Stampnitzky, Lisa (2013), *Disciplining Terrorism: How 'Experts' Invented Terrorism* (Cambridge: Cambridge University Press).

Stepanova, Ekaterina A. (2008), *Terrorism in Asymmetrical Conflict: Ideological and Structural Aspects* (Oxford: Oxford University Press).

Thompson, Debra (2014), 'Through, Against, and Beyond the Racial State: The Transnational Stratum of Race', in Alexander Anievas, Nivi Manchanda, and Robbie Shilliam (eds), *Race and Racism in International Relations: Confronting the Global Colour Line* (Abingdon: Routledge), pp. 44–61.

Tickner, J. Ann (1992), *Gender in International Relations: Feminist Perspectives on Achieving Global Security* (New York: Columbia University Press).

Tickner, J. Ann (1997), 'You Just Don't Understand: Troubled Engagements Between Feminists and IR Theorists', *International Studies Quarterly*, 41(4): 611–32.

Tickner, J. Ann (2005), 'What Is Your Research Program? Some Feminist Answers to International Relations Methodological Questions', *International Studies Quarterly*, 49(1): 1–21.

Toulmin, Stephen (1992), *Cosmopolis: The Hidden Agenda of Modernity* (Chicago: University of Chicago Press).

Tuastad, Dag (2003), 'Neo-Orientalism and the New Barbarism Thesis: Aspects of Symbolic Violence in the Middle East Conflict(s)', *Third World Quarterly*, 24(4): 591–9.

Valls, Andrew (2000), 'Can Terrorism Be Justified?', in Andrew Valls (ed.), *Ethics in International Affairs: Theories and Cases* (Lanham, MD: Roman and Littlefield), pp. 65–79.

Vitalis, Robert (2000), 'The Graceful and Generous Liberal Gesture: Making Racism Invisible in American International Relations', *Millennium*, 29(2): 331–56.

Vitalis, Robert (2015), *White World Order, Black Power Politics: The Birth of American International Relations* (Ithaca, NY: Cornell University Press).

Walzer, Michael (1977), *Just and Unjust Wars: A Moral Argument with Historical Illustrations* (New York: Basic Books).

Weber, Cynthia (1998), 'Performative States', *Millennium*, 27(1): 77–95.

Weber, Cynthia (2014), 'From Queer to Queer IR', *International Studies Review*, 16(4): 596–601.

Weber, Cynthia (2016), *Queer International Relations: Sovereignty, Sexuality, and the Will to Knowledge* (New York: Oxford University Press).

Whitworth, Sandra (2004), *Men, Militarism, and UN Peacekeeping: A Gendered Analysis* (Boulder, CO: Lynne Rienner Publishers).

Wight, Colin (2015), *Rethinking Terrorism: Terrorism, Violence, and the State* (Basingstoke: Palgrave MacMillan).

Wilkinson, Paul (1997), 'The Media and Terrorism: A Reassessment', *Terrorism and Political Violence*, 9(2): 51–64.

Zalewski, Marysia. (2017), 'What's the Problem with the Concept of Military Masculinities?', *Critical Military Studies*, 3(2): 200–5.

CHAPTER 2

Intersecting Terrorism Studies

In a rather eloquent presentation for the Handa Centre for the Study of Terrorism and Political Violence, Tim Wilson (2012) spoke about terrorism's 'ability to stop the clocks' and to claim the attention of those who would not normally pay attention to political events. Indeed, the power of terrorism is its ability to grab the world's interest because it is often seen as a spectacular event, a spectacular deviation from the status quo and from the moral norms of protecting innocent life that is held dear. Yet, I would add, that clock only stops for some acts of terrorism, not all.

For instance, in a discussion of 'patriarchal' or 'everyday' terrorism (as will be discussed in Chapter 5), some of my students were resistant to calling this form of domestic abuse terrorism precisely because it was so minimal. To them, terrorism is a deed like 9/11 or the 2017 Manchester Arena suicide-bombing at the end of an Ariana Grande concert. It is spectacular and unswerving in its desire to harm innocents. However, not all terrorism is spectacular, nor does it aim to harm those that are unequivocally innocent. Those who are labelled terrorists target military installations, like the West German Red Army Faction or the Irish Republican Army. When we think of the violence in Kashmir or in Israel-Palestine, this is not always a spectacular violence because it is accompanied by endemic, everyday violence that grinds people and society down. Not all terrorism is perpetrated by those that we easily accept as terrorists, like political violence conducted by our own governments, such as the torture at Bagram, Abu Ghraib and Guantanamo Bay (see Melanie Richter-Montpetit's [2014 and 2007] excellent work on how these are linked with race structures and how this enables a 'blind eye' to them in US society) or in the destabilising of other places, like Operation Condor in the Southern Cone.

While we would recognise that all or most violence treads a fine knife edge when it comes to illegitimacy and immorality, and all of the violence mentioned in the paragraph above has fallen off that knife-edge completely, there are times where charges of immorality are rarely levelled at the violence states perpetrate, where it is almost always levelled at terrorist violence. Therefore, the purpose of this chapter is to interrogate how terrorism and the terrorist actor can only be understood by reflecting on and recognising the charges directed against them: of irrationality, immorality and illegitimacy. This can be initially approached via a gendered lens, but given the intersectional method of asking the other question, the chapter will also show how these gendered assumptions work with and alongside race and imperialism, at the very least.

One way that I illustrate the issue of terrorism's illegitimacy is through the assignment of Carole Pateman's (1980) classic article, 'The Disorder of Women: Women, Love, and the Sense of Justice', to my Gender and Terrorism course. I assign it midway through the semester, when the class begins to shift from feminist theory and methods to interrogating terrorism as a gendered subject. I begin by breaking down the main points in Pateman's article, where some of the sentiments are either familiar or at least coherent with the other feminist work they have been studying. Pateman's (1980: 21) article revolves around two ways of conceiving 'disorder:' first, civil disorder or 'a rowdy demonstration, a tumultuous assembly, riot, breakdown of law and order, arguably infraction of international norms, break with monopoly on violence', or, second, disorder may also 'refer to an internal malfunction of an individual, such as . . . a disordered imagination or a disorder of stomach or intestines'. Pateman then continues to make the connection between a personal disorder and the perception of how this impacts on public life.

Within the gendered confines of femininity, women have long been seen as (biologically) inferior and therefore disordered. As such, they pose a threat to civil order:

> Women, it is held, are a source of disorder because their being, or their natures, is such that it necessarily leads them to exert a disruptive influence in social and political life (Pateman 1980: 22).

To demonstrate how such thinking has been accepted and promoted within Western political theorists, Pateman looks at the work of Jean-Jacques Rousseau, Sigmund Freud and John Rawls and how they conceptualise women, politics and citizenship. In liberal political thought, when political institutions are based on the Social Contract, consent can only be reached via rational, free and equal individuals: men (Pateman 1980: 21). Leaving aside the racial forgettings the Social Contract is dependent upon, as highlighted in the previous chapter (see Mills 1997), it is necessary to understand why women were excluded.

For the Social Contract to work, these rational individuals must achieve justice, which works in opposition to feminine love and emotional bonds (Pateman 1980: 24). Bluntly, women 'lack, and cannot develop, a sense of justice' (Pateman 1980: 20). The private and particular interests of women present a problem, as emotional interests would interfere with the finer virtue of justice, leading to an interruption or interference with the rules of order. Women, according to these thinkers, are unable to handle and bear the weight of civic and political responsibilities, or to learn or grasp full ideas of justice; and they are temperamentally weak and overly emotional. Therefore, only men, as ordered, rational, justice-seeking individuals, can be justice-establishing citizens (Pateman 1980). This ordering of individuals should be familiar to the reader, because it is the same ordering that has been used to explain the primacy of the state in International Relations.

Therefore, to bring this back to terrorism: what happens when I take the quote from above and replace 'women' with 'terrorists'?

> Terrorists, it is held, are a source of disorder because their being, or their natures, is such that it necessarily leads them to exert a disruptive influence in social and political life.

Does this not maintain a logical coherency but with an admittedly altered argument? If I replaced 'women' with 'men' or even 'states', would this maintain the coherency? The coherency found with the substitution 'terrorists' demonstrates how terrorism is feminised (or, again, to be devalorised [Peterson 2010]). Terrorist violence is diminished, not just within the Westphalian system, but through the way terrorism, terrorist violence and terrorists are explained and understood in International Relations, Terrorism Studies and the larger public discourse. In this way, Pateman's article becomes the mechanism through which we can understand the epistemic bias against terrorism, terrorist acts and terrorist actors (see also Gentry 2016b). Therefore, the 'disordering' happens in two related ways, through the labels of irrationality and immorality.

Epistemic Bias and Rationality and Morality in the Study of Terrorism

Richard Jackson (2015) notes that in the binary of terrorist/counter-terrorist, states, politicians and academics automatically align themselves with counter-terrorism and the side of legitimacy (see also Toros 2008). This alignment leads to a 'sentiment' of superiority based upon rationality and morality that defines the field of Terrorism Studies, imbuing our debates with a certain flavour. Thus, this chapter will argue that irrationality serves as one way of discrediting politically violent actors and their violence. This serves as a silencer – or a means for not dealing with the reasons why people actually choose, for political and emotional reasons, to engage in terrorism (see Sjoberg and Gentry 2008a). And while such a silencing/subjugating attempt is well noted in Terrorism Studies (see Jackson 2012), the much deeper structures that lie behind irrationality have been less explored.

Forgettings operate because of the accepted dominance of 'the way things should be'. They work because the dominant worldview determines the way that certain people, populations and actors are perceived as inadequate or lesser than others. To determine that some who commit a particular style or method of violence are irrational, immoral and/ or illegitimate is a further harm, however, and is a mode of oppression. Thus when Critical Race scholars, feminists and queer theorists all note that the Other-of-colour, the gendered Other, the gay/perverse/queer-Other are all seen as deviant from the rational, legal, credible Self, this Self–Other differentiation reflects an epistemic injustice.

An epistemic injustice is a particular way of denying people epistemic authority based on their identity (Fricker 2007: 5). Committing or engaging in this form of injustice is a key way of subjugating knowledge: it is a way of determining that those who fall outside of the dominant position in a hierarchy are not credited with intelligence or with rational and moral agency. Epistemic injustice occurs because of differences within social power – the 'idea that power is a socially situated capacity to control others' action' (Fricker 2007: 4) – something that states have within IR as the primary actor. Furthermore, social power works with 'identity power', power that is derived from the prejudices and biases that society tells about certain people based upon their identities (Fricker 2007: 4). The pejorative label of terrorism works because of social and identity power that is granted to states by those who are socialised through Westphalian norms. When the discursive label of terrorism is successfully applied to sub-state politically violent groups, leading to a belief in those groups' illegitimacy, this is the operation of an 'identity-prejudicial credibility deficit', where simply by belonging to a particular group an actor's epistemic credibility is doubted or denied (Fricker 2007: 4). It is also the notion that all groups labelled as terrorists are automatically denied credibility in International Relations, without denying credibility and legitimacy to states that use terrorist-style violence.

In Terrorism Studies, Claudia Brunner (2015 and 2007) looks at how the conception of the non-Western Other is a form of epistemic bias, as part of the ongoing process of colonisation and imperialism. Even though Chapter 4 has a deeper discussion of rationality and how it forms a logocentric binary with radicalisation, the larger and more historic logocentricism is the Western rationality poised against non-Western irrationality. This feeds into sentiments about legitimacy as well. Relying upon both Gayatri Spivak and Enrique Galván-Álvarez, Brunner (2015) makes the argument that Othering as a colonial practice is an epistemic violence in which the denial of knowledge to and/or for Others is 'one of the key elements in any process of domination' (Galván-Álvarez 2010: 11, as quoted in Brunner 2015: 6). Additionally, Brunner (2015: 7) situates Terrorism Studies 'within the highly asymmetric setting of International Relations in which both political violence . . . and epistemic violence takes place simultaneously and interdependently'. As will be further discussed in Chapter 4, colonialism hierarchically ordered the world into hegemon and subaltern through physical violence, but concurrently hierarchically ordered those within as well. Part of this was in the practice of denying that colonised people were able to be rational. Thus, rationality – and any assessment of it – is a missed moment of antagonism whereby the traditional system of order, the Western imperial system, is maintained. Implicated in this maintenance, of course, is the building of academic knowledge.

Terrorism Studies and Rationality Claims

A distilled definition of rationality reflects the utility of the term: to be rational is to make decisions based upon a cost–benefit analysis (Nussbaum 2003: 22; Rasmussen 2003: 99; Foley 1991: 369). A deeper understanding of the term reveals: 1) that the agent is fully aware of the decision being made and of all known consequences, and is choosing between the proposed ends to the best benefit of the self; and 2) the goals are intellectual as opposed to non-intellectual (Rasmussen 2003: 99; Foley 1991: 371). It is a highly individualistic and autonomous decision-making method: 'the interests of others' are considered 'only to the extent that they affect the rational actor's own interests' (Rasmussen 2003: 99). Further, the decision should be reached without the complication of emotions (Rasmussen 2003: 99) because decisions are meant to be completely 'objective' (Foley 1991: 370).[1] Rationality is seen within a logocentric binary with irrationality, or (excessive) emotion, where emotion is problematic and leads people astray. Therefore, freedom from emotional toil produces only good (Foley 1991: 370), whereas irrationality results in bad consequences or outright failure. Irrationality also brings in (bad) emotions of 'bewilderment' and 'perplex[ity]' (Foley 1991: 368) with implications that the actor has 'act[ed] wrongly' (Foley 1991: 387) and should feel some sense of diminishment. This, of course, has a relationship with a perception of morality and immorality.

Even though this chapter is predicated on the idea that rationality is not extended to those labelled as terrorist, Terrorism Studies has, in fact, spent a significant amount of time explaining just how rational terrorists are. For example, if political violence is rational:

It must make perceptible gains. (Pape 2005: 22, 61; McCormick 2003: 481; Crenshaw 2001 and 1990; Fromkin 1975)

Actors and organisations must be making ordered, strategic and logical decisions – as if operating from a game tree. (Sprinzak 2009; Pape 2003; McCormick 2003: 482)

Organisations are 'collectively rational', meaning that individual rationality is subsumed to a greater group identity. (McCormick 2003: 483; Crenshaw 1990: 1987, 1981)

Interests are posited within gains and strategic advantages, such as media attention or government provocation, not as ones defined by emotional ties. (Abrahms 2008; McCormick 2003: 483–4; Hoffman 2001; Fromkin 1975)

Yet, the language is not as unbiased as it seems. What is hidden in Terrorism Studies is the long-standing discursive divide on the rationality of terrorism.

Terrorism Studies was established in the 1960s, and by the 1970s it was embroiled in a discursive battle that would define the field for years to come. Where many early scholars emphasised the rationality of political violence as prompted by 'specific grievances and motivations' (Stampnitzky 2013: 63), by the late 1970s, the question of attributing rationality to terrorists would become quite contentious . . . [and] the very question of whether terrorists had rational, objective motives would become highly politically charged. (Stampnitzky 2013: 65)

Where the academics pursued (as) objective (as possible) research that led to more slowly conceived and less reactive conclusions, Western, particularly US, politicians were driven by a need to quickly, publicly address violence that was seen to threaten liberal democracies in the Cold War (see Stampnitzky, chapter 3; for more on the problem of rushed counter-terrorism policies, see Lum et al. 2006). Stampnitzky (2013: 50) argues that this led to a new discursive lens through which terrorism was constructed, one in which morality, politicality and rationality of political violence would come to be strongly intertwined with the production and evaluation of experts and expertise.

Stampnitzky (2013: 51) finds that the discourse led to a significant epistemic problematic whereby

the formation of terrorism as a problem with a moral evaluation built into it, attempts to develop a morally neutral terrorism expertise, and sometimes even attempts to understand terrorism at all, became subjects to discrediting attacks as – somewhat paradoxically – politicised knowledge, and this has led to persistent difficulties for those seeking to create rational knowledge about political violence.

While Stampnitzky (2013) focuses her chapter 3 on these tensions between academics and politicians, this chapter will focus on the discursive dynamic of 'rationality' and the gendered and raced dynamics such a word as 'rational' hints at.

There is a reason why Terrorism Studies continues to exhibit tension over the rationality of terrorist violence. Early and now discredited Terrorism Studies literature that suggested terrorists were mentally unstable disturbingly removed political motivation, agency and thus credibility (see Third 2010; Post 1990: 25; Merari 1990: 202). Take for instance this 'conversation' between Martha Crenshaw and Jerrold Post in Walter Reich's 1990 edited volume, *The Origins of Terrorism*. In the volume's first chapter, Crenshaw, barely mincing her words, seeks to counter Post's argument that terrorists are psychologically troubled, by working through the rational utility of terrorism. Terrorism is 'logical' and a 'wilful choice made by an organisation for political and strategic reasons, rather than as the unintended outcome of psychological or social factors' (Crenshaw 1990: 8). According to Crenshaw (1990: 8),

> terrorism is assumed to display a collective rationality. A radical political organisation is seen as the central actor in the terrorist drama. The group possesses collective preferences or values and selects terrorism as a course of action from a range of perceived alternatives. Efficacy is the primary standard by which terrorism is compared with other methods of achieving political goals.

To illustrate her argument, Crenshaw (1990) looks at groups from across the globe and with different ideological stances, including the Weather Underground, the Popular Front for the Liberation of Palestine (PFLP), the Red Army Faction and *Euskadi Ta Askatasuna* (ETA) in Spain. She ends by stating 'that even the most extreme and unusual forms of political behaviour can follow an internal, strategic logic' (Crenshaw 1990: 24). I often taught this chapter alongside David Fromkin's 1975 *Foreign Affairs* article on strategy, using Crenshaw's proposition to formulate Fromkin's historical examples within the Prisoner's Dilemma and game trees.

Post's (1990) chapter, and the rest of the contributions to Reich's volume, makes an opposing argument by claiming that terrorists are psychologically compelled to commit acts of violence – that terrorists possess a 'psycho-logic'. He looks at the now-disputed West German psychological study of those convicted or arrested for terrorism (Post 1990: 29), amongst other studies, and concludes that terrorists' personalities often cannot contend with contrary information, therefore they 'split' or externalise their psychological anguish (Post 1990: 27). Such externalisation leads them to commit violent acts. In these chapters, we have a distillation of another debate which has shaped Terrorism Studies: what are the psychological forces at play in the mind of a terrorist? While there are several ways of attempting to address this question – via a mobilisation argument, a radicalisation argument, or a process theory argument[2] – for a confluence of reasons, Terrorism Studies post-9/11 became rather centred upon the idea of rationality.

Critical Terrorism Studies argues that following 9/11 and the entrance of North American political scientists into the field (even if for only one publication [Silke 2009: 35]), a significant amount of contemporary Terrorism Studies scholarship is now focused on rationality-based models, such as Rational Actor Model (RAM) or Rational Choice (see also Muro-Ruiz 2002). At first glance, the insistence upon the rationality of the terrorist actor is a good thing – rationality's association with both a masculinist and racial ideal seemingly inscribes the terrorist actor with political agency and credibility. Yet, beyond this dependency upon hegemonic structures, there is a tricky discursive manoeuvre in this literature: as one reads deeper, rationality is associated with collective activity and less so with the individual. This will be shown by delving into 'postmodern' or 'new terrorism', whereas Chapter 4 will look more closely at this issue in contrast to radicalisation as the antithesis of rationality.

New Terrorism

The New Terrorism thesis emerged at the end of the 1990s, predominantly argued by Walter Laqueur with a strong contribution by Bruce Hoffman (2002 and 1999). Laqueur (1996) first termed 'new terrorism' as 'postmodern' terrorism: that not *too* much about terrorism has changed over the past fifty years with the exception of an increased 'destructive potential' that requires groups who have little compunction in leveraging such destruction (Laqueur 1996: 28). In his later book, Laqueur (1999) predicts that new terrorism will replace the wars of the nineteenth and twentieth centuries. He holds that 'there has been a radical transformation, if not a revolution, in the character of terrorism' (Laqueur 1999: 4). The perpetrators will act transnationally, in loosely organised networks, take advantage of technology, and will not be sponsored by a state. They will, in some way, be inspired by religion and thus are seen as religious fanatics uninterested in negotiation. They will seek and will use weapons of mass destruction and target indiscriminately. They will commit spectacular attacks:

> Chances are that of 100 attempts at terrorist superviolence, 99 would fail. But the single successful one could claim many more victims, do more material damage, and unleash far greater panic than anything the world has yet experienced (Laqueur 1999: 36).

It is no wonder, given this prescient description, that when 9/11 happened, the postmodern/new terrorism thesis gelled with many even though it contrasted heavily with the reliance upon any rationality and rational actor approach. The new terrorism thesis led to fears of al Qaeda's decentralised global network reaching into multiple ongoing conflicts, such as Chechnya's struggle against Russia; bin Laden's technological acumen; and sleeper cells in the US that could be activated quickly (see Hoffman 2002).

By tying new terrorism to religious 'fanaticism', Laqueur opened the door, presumably unwittingly, to a neo-Orientalist bias, particularly as Laqueur's (1999 and 1996) more global approach, looking at Christian millennialism in the US, Japan's Aum Shinrikyo and other cult and religious violence, disappeared. It seems that after 9/11 the world suddenly accepted Samuel Huntington's (1993: 35) once scorned words that 'Islam has bloody borders' (absent of any critical examination that those same borders were also Western). Terrorism and political violence became tied to 'a new barbarism', described as 'fanatical and truly irrational', and 'naïve, emotional, impulsive . . . and fundamentally uninformed' (Stampnitzky 2013: 65; see also Tuastad 2003). For many of us in either orthodox or Critical Terrorism Studies, this language problematically dominated Western responses to al Qaeda post 9/11 (see Gentry 2015a; Jarvis 2009; Jackson 2005). Therefore, the notion of rationality and strategy are belied and undermined by a neo-Orientalist-infused new terrorism thesis, which converges over religious fundamentalism and intractability.

Neo-Orientalism works on a fulcrum of gendered and raced rationality: one that leverages the supposed rational superiority of the West against the irrational atavistic leanings of the 'Arab' east (see also Brunner 2015). Whereas Edward Said (1978) set out a critique against the historical, cultural and political Orientalist discourse of the West against those associated with Arabia, neo-Orientalism expands this to all people associated with Islam as dictated by their skin colour, dress, country of origin, etc. (Akram 2000: 8; Yeğenoğlu 1998; Nader 1989: 351). Both Orientalism and neo-Orientalism assume that all people associated with Islam are less intelligent and incapable of learning, hyperviolent, hypersexualised and religiously fundamentalist. This works as a gendered neo-Orientalism,[3] as this racialisation of a bastardised form of Islam (that is to say, this is no more representative of Islam than David Koresh's Branch Davidians are representative of Christianity) is also deeply gendered. It is the men who are presumed to be hyperviolent and hypersexual: this is represented in the 9/11 hijackers as watching porn and going to strip clubs before the attacks. And the men use this hyperviolence and hypersexualisation against women, who are submissive, dominated, controlled and abused (Nayak 2006: 51; Shepherd 2006: 25). Hence, why the Bush administration used the circumstances of women to justify the invasion in 2001 (Shepherd 2006: 20). Yet, neo-Orientalism is not the only time that the irrationality charge continues to come up; this is also witnessed in the work on suicide terrorism.

The assignment of emotion/irrationality becomes a way of holding power over those who challenge the dominant narrative of Westphalian state sovereignty. As a gendered construct, rationality discourse inhibits a full understanding of political violence (see Atran 2003). Rationality's connection with the sovereignty system creates a dichotomised state structure. As such, credibility and legitimacy are granted to states but denied to non-state actors, especially to politically violent ones (Heinze and Steele 2009; Sjoberg 2009; Gentry 2016b). This means states, especially powerful ones, can act almost without impunity – breaking international norms and laws at will – and as possessors of the monopoly on violence, they can act violently without necessarily being seen as illegitimate (see Brown 2002: 127). Inevitably, any sub-state actor that chooses political violence is denied a full hearing; Tarik Kochi (2009: 74) describes this as denying the legitimacy of the Other's war and upholding a Western, Westphalian order. As noted above, when an individual deviates from what is seen as rational, the actions and the individual become imbued with immorality.

Morality and the Myth of Westphalia

Most terrorism scholars' definitional discussion indicates that the immorality of terrorism stems from the targeting of innocent non-combatants. However, digging further into the overlapping literature between Terrorism Studies and Just War, there is more behind the immorality designation than this. The sub-state nature of terrorism is key. One of the clichés in the study of terrorism is that terrorism is the 'weapon of the weak'. As a non-state actor, it is not armed with the economic and military *capability* of the state. I emphasise capability because, when I was first a student of International Relations over twenty years ago, the first few chapters of my first textbook linked both 'capability' and 'rationality'. Rationality was a direct reflection of capability, which was defined by a state's strength to wage war. If a state was weaker than its opponent, it would be 'irrational' for that state to start a war: a case in point was often Iraq in the early 1990s, where its army was listed as only the fifth strongest army at the time. While it was superior to Saudi Arabia's capability, it was inferior to Saudi Arabia's ally, the United States. These measurements of capability and assessment of rationality are then taken to the sub-state. After the interventions in Afghanistan (2001) and the reinvasion of Iraq (2003), asymmetric warfare of state militaries against insurgents (rebel groups, terrorists), became the favoured term. This semantic profiling of terrorism as the 'weapon' of this 'weak' irrational actor continues to contribute to the state/non-state binary.

Although Terrorism Studies scholars are not exclusively from an International Relations background, there is a tacit agreement about the international system and where terrorist violence fits within it. This system is largely narrated as the Westphalian system, where states are the dominant actor and they are attributed with sovereignty, rationality and the monopoly on legitimate violence (see Vitalis 2015; Gentry 2014; de Carvalho et al. 2011). It is here – in the relationship between states, authority, power, violence and legitimacy – where conceptual clarity is often lost. The Westphalian system is an ontological arrangement that presumes clarity on the arrangement between these things: state, authority, power, legitimacy and violence. Within this ontological arrangement, states are the primary actor and states practice the Westphalian norms of sovereign equality, non-aggression and non-interference. Thus, states become the ones with authority, which, as defined by Arendt (1970: 45), is the 'unquestioning recognition by those who are asked to obey'. There is often an assumption of Arendtian power that goes alongside this authority – that the state in the Westphalian actor also has the support of its people (as power in a state/government is granted by the population [Arendt 1970: 44]). An assumption of power is also an assumption of legitimacy, as legitimacy in IR is often tied to liberal democratic practices.

Yet, just as the quote from Marysia Zalewski (2017) at the end of the last chapter suggested, hidden within this complex relationship are multiple types of violence. An Arendtian approach to violence in this puzzle is that of literal, physical violence that derives meaning from those who use it (Arendt 1970: 46, 55). Physical violence is problematic: against (the) power (of the people), violence would win, but maintaining power with violence invites only illegitimacy:

> Power and violence are opposites; where the one rules absolutely, the other is absent. Violence appears where power is in jeopardy, but left to its own course it ends in power's disappearance. . . . Violence can destroy power; it is utterly incapable of creating it. (Arendt 1970: 52–3, 56)

Arendt (1970) captures conceptual clarity along with a powerful ethic, one where legitimacy and power are derived from a post-Enlightenment Western liberal ideal. Yet there is potentially a more complex relationship between power, legitimacy and violence, which clouds some of this clarity.

If Westphalia is an ontological arrangement, parsing out the relationship between power, legitimacy and violence is fine, but it does not necessarily capture the discursive, and therefore non-literal, nature of these relationships. Instead, there is far more manipulation of legitimacy, power and therefore violence than Arendt's (1970) definitions would suggest. For instance, Chris Brown (2002: 127), borrowing from Krasner, explores the 'organised hypocrisy' of the sovereignty system; a hypocrisy that privileges the actions not just of sovereign states over non-state actors, but of powerful states over weaker ones (Brown 2002: 79). If weaker states break Westphalian norms, they are often labelled as 'pariah' or 'rogue' states, as the slightly weaker Iraq was. Yet stronger states can break the norms with impunity. This ties power and legitimacy more to the idea of 'the state' rather than to the origins of the state's power – the people – leading to hegemonic relationships amongst states. Furthermore, not only has Westphalia created a stratification among states, but also between states and non-states. While weaker states are punished for contravening international law and norms, when non-state actors, particularly terrorist organisations, break these rules they are seen as even more illegitimate (see Gentry 2014; Kochi 2009: 45; Held 2008: 11).

Additionally, the Westphalian privilege is a violence in itself as a colonial remnant, which reifies Western imagery and identity over others (Vitalis 2015; de Carvalho et al. 2011). Tarik Kochi's (2009) aforementioned criticism is a larger criticism of Just War, Westphalia and the Western sovereignty system. The West, he argues, does not often grant sub-state actors any legitimacy for their use of violence (Kochi 2009: 74–5). If Westphalia previously established that states are the only ones that may be justified in their use of violence, then non-state actors that use violence in an attempt to change their state and possibly influence geopolitics will always be scripted as illegitimate. He argues that this is an evident epistemic bias, one which fails to see the ethics in why non-state and Global South actors chose violent means (Kochi 2009: 249). It is again a bias about identity – of statehood and of Western identity. Thus the narrative of state credibility and legitimacy is strongly linked to Western identity. This speaks to an ongoing pattern where Western regions have more access to legitimacy and credibility than the non-West, yet hold others to norms the West is free to break.

The privileging of states and their monopoly on power in turn delegitimises other claims on power and violence. There is a certain epistemic image of the world and global politics presented in IR that must be adhered to in order to maintain narrative fidelity. As noted by Tickner (1992: 42), states are abstractions of masculine idealisations of privilege: 'in terms of self-help, autonomy, and power seeking'. States in the construction and reification of Western prioritising Westphalia are legitimised as masculine actors, which leads to argument that international politics and conflict are not determined by anarchy but instead by gender hierarchy (Sjoberg 2013). War happens, Sjoberg (2013) argues, because states and other actors engage in a competitive performance of masculinity. By extension this feminises politically violent sub-state actors, who are denied the right to use violence or to be rational actors. Revealing gender's intersection with other identifiers, race, religion, geography and, yes, statehood, challenges the Westphalian narrative, which in turn uncovers the operation of power.

The more immediate issue to the study of political violence is the moral legitimacy that has been invested in states. That the state is the location of various activities, from identity and economics to protection, is not a problem. Yet, there is a conflation of the legal status of a state via procedural authority and the moral credibility of a state (legitimacy), particularly in the evolution of authority and legitimacy within the Just War tradition (Kochi 2009: 45). In *Just and Unjust Wars*, Michael Walzer (1977: 53–4) argues, like Arendt (1970), that states are invested with procedural authority because a (democratic) state is 'the highest representation of the will of the people'. The 'moral standing' of a state stems from 'the reality of the common life it protects' – particularly if this is a democratic state protective of civil rights and liberties.

In discussions of Just War and terrorism, Western democracies are often posed as the essential and necessary protectors of liberal values, which are always differentiated from problematic radical Islamist terrorism in ways that uphold the racialised and Western order (Gentry 2014: 20). In the Just War, legitimate authority is normatively conceived, stemming from Ancient Greek thought in which authority was legitimate if it represented the good of a *polis*. In earlier Christianity, 'the sovereign was the highest authority precisely because God placed him there' (Gentry 2014: 20). Luther, in his challenge to Catholicism, argued that authority belonged to secular powers. With the institutionalisation of Westphalia, states became

> [t]acitly bound by norms . . . overriding the tension, states almost had a free reign in going to war. Thus, the strengthening of the state and its previously held moral credentials led to a binary: state's actions are inevitably viewed as legitimate and substate actors' actions as illegitimate (or less important, valued, credible). (Gentry 2014: 21)

The valorisation of states as not just legitimate authorities but moral ones as well is a way of instantiating the epistemic bias against some actors. Those with privilege and power protect themselves and are based within a particular epistemology that exists because those who create and maintain policy in the international system grant 'truth' to the primacy of the state and thus to the 'logic' and 'reality' of Westphalia. (Gentry 2014: 23)

The conflation of states' legal authority with moral authority 'complicates the discussion' (Brown 2002: 7–9) and may 'contribut[e] to the problem of violence' (Steele and Amoreaux 2009: 179). This echoes a sentiment previously mentioned: that the anti-terror campaigns in Chechnya and Sri Lanka, both of which have involved genocidal and ethnic cleansing acts, were described as 'successful', thereby legitimising these methods by Russia and Sri Lanka. Even though the Chechens won their first war for national self-determination against Russia, with both sides using terroristic violence, Russia is seen as (slightly) more competent and far more legitimate (at least) as a state. The bias in favour of states is an identity prejudice, reflective of an epistemic injustice, rooted in a system that relies upon epistemic violence.

This is why it is important to use the language of 'calculated forgettings' rather than aphasia, as aphasias pathologise the violence, making it a by-product of a broken system, IR and Terrorism Studies scholarship. Instead, these forgettings are not accidental nor passive oppressions, they are purposeful. They are the way the system is meant to work, given its masculinist and imperialist starting points. This leads us to a further discussion: what responsibility do scholars have for how their work replicates these oppressions? This could happen in at least one of two ways: that scholars simply reify and replicate a system of oppression because that is what they have been trained to do; or the theories, hypotheses and suggestions that the scholars make are used by policy-makers in order to perpetuate systemic oppression.

The concern of this chapter and indeed of this book is to not just point out how IR and Terrorism Studies are built upon a series of oppressional hierarchies, but to look at how these oppressions shape the lives of individual actors who use political violence. It is to constantly query how 'terrorism' became 'disordered' or signified as violence that cannot be understood because it stands so far outside of what is known to be legitimate. The state/non-state binary has resulted in a Manichean binary:

terrorism and terrorists are made to represent a fusion of everything that is bad, while the opposing 'we' takes on the characteristics of everything that is good. (Toros 2008: 409)

In returning to new terrorism, what began as a global theorisation of the next form of terrorist violence quickly became a biased, troubling representation of Islam as a whole, which was used to reconfirm the West as the liberal ideal. This binary representation masked the Western hierarchical violences being committed. It rescued the paragon-like status of the US and allies, thereby posing terrorism as *the* system threat. It was Terrorism Studies scholars, primarily, who did this by bringing new terrorism to government and policy-makers. This is not seen as 'scholarly impact' to Critical Terrorism Studies but as a deep-seated problem.

There is increased pressure on academics to 'engage with, or speak directly to, the powerful' (Jackson 2016: 120). Yet, CTS scholarship lives in a constant tension 'between the contrasting aspirations for policy relevance and access to power, and CTS's commitment to emancipation and critical distance' (Jackson 2016: 120). Furthermore, when terrorism expertise informs or supports counter-terrorism policy, acute tensions arise:

> I would suggest that under these conditions it is virtually impossible to maintain an ethical commitment to human rights, human welfare, non-violence, and progressive politics – that is, emancipation – while simultaneously participating in an inherently violent and counter-emancipatory regime of counterterrorism. (Jackson 2016: 122)

Harmonie Toros (2016: 126) is more optimistic about these collaborations as 'resist[ance to] these logics of brutality . . . can go through an engagement with state power', especially as states are 'capable of change and transformation' (127). Yet, the longer-standing legacies and biases of how people and places become classified as something Other precede 9/11. If this is not recognised the same biases and hierarchies will be continually reinforced, if not magnified, in the relay of information when it moves from the academic community to the 'public realm'.

While these early chapters have focused on the structures the academic subjects of IR and Terrorism Studies are built upon, our theories travel and have force. Whether this is through work with governments or through media engagement, Chapter 3 especially will show how 'public' discourses pick up academic ones. Therefore we have to query what responsibility theorists bear for their work once it is brought out of the ivory tower and into the 'real' world of policy. Piki Ish-Shalom (2009: 303) expresses the problem succinctly:

The lives of theories are tumultuous. Conceived in the serenity of the academy, they are, at times, forced into the real world, where the upheavals of politics dominate. This migration from academy to the real world raises the issue of theorists' social responsibility. Do theorists bear responsibility for the real world's ramifications of their theorising?

Academics do not bear 'blame responsibility', but they do bear a 'social responsibility for the actions or effects that derive from their theorising' (Ish-Shalom 2009: 303). While Ish-Shalom (2009) is mainly focused on the slice of the social sciences dedicated to the works that lead to a grand theory, like the democratic peace thesis, his argument has a bearing on the less grand and more nitty-gritty theories that have influenced Terrorism Studies, like the new terrorism thesis, or as will be explored in the following chapters, suicide terrorism, radicalisation, identity extremism and misogynistic terrorism.

Theories are meant to possess 'rhetorical capital' as they are 'inherent[ly] . . . persuasive resources' (Ish-Shalom 2009: 308). Additionally, they 'function' to offer explanations – conceivably explanations in a (neo-)positivist realm that are objective and free from 'political partisanship, moral convictions, and ideological persuasions' (Ish-Shalom 2009: 308). They must also be accessible, allowing them to have ramifications outside of the academy: accessible theories 'migrat[e] well' (Ish-Shalom 2009: 308). Herein lies the challenge:

> As theorising is carried out in the public sphere and as theories are freely circulated, they become highly accessible to the public. This accessibility enables the theories' migration to the public sphere and is a major source of rhetorical capital. (Ish-Shalom 2009: 308)

Yet, when these migrations happen, they lose 'the cautiousness and sense of criticism that is built into academic discourse and conduct' (Ish-Shalom 2009: 308). In doing so, they become 'absolute, law-like statements' that are 'simplistic' and 'highly susceptible to rhetorical excess and political mobilisation' instead of the nuanced and attenuated theories that they were meant to be (Ish-Shalom 2009: 308–9).

Therefore, for Ish-Shalom (2009: 307), the real problem lies in how theories are 'translat[ed.] . . . into publicly debated items, . . . distorting them into political representations'. While 'it is the politicians who have abused or used the theories who are to be blamed or praised', the fact that 'these abuses are a recurrent pattern in the interaction of theory and politics' makes demands on the theorists (Ish-Shalom 2009: 307).

Ish-Shalom (2009: 307) identifies this as a 'social responsibility produced by an ethical obligation to address present social and political problems'. Thus, what responsibility do Terrorism Studies scholars bear when their theories, which are dependent upon structural, epistemological violences, get translated into policy?

To elaborate on this, Dag Tuastad (2003) does an impeccable job of tracing out how the new barbarism thesis, as articulated by Daniel Pipes and Bernard-Henri Lévy and joined by Samuel Hungtington's 'clash of civilisations' (1993; 1996), worked to justify the neo-Orientalist response to 9/11. Even though Huntington at the very least had been heavily critiqued for his Islamophobia in the thesis, once 9/11 happened it was widely embraced. This Islamophobic perspective existed already, finding fidelity with the policy world particularly in its discursive relationship to Pipes' own work. This significant discourse joined with the emerging new terrorism thesis, especially as it was produced by Bruce Hoffman, a Georgetown professor with an affiliation with the largest terrorism think-tank, RAND, and the School of IR at St Andrews.

Hoffman holds the immense privilege of being invited to give testimony before the House of Representatives Subcommittee on Terrorism and Homeland Security on 26 September 2001. Hoffman contributes to the nascent narrativising of 9/11 as a significant shift in American and global politics:

> The enormity and sheer scale of the simultaneous suicide attacks of September
> 11th dwarf anything we have previously seen. . . . Accordingly, . . . the events
> of September 11th argue for nothing less than a re-configuration of both
> our thinking about terrorism and our national security architecture as well.
> (Hoffman 2001: 1)

Additionally, he begins to hint at the new terrorism thesis, that bin Laden had a 'flair for self-promotion to meld together the disparate strands of Islamic fervour, Muslim piety, and general enmity towards the West into a formidable force' (Hoffman 2001: 4). Yet, in reading some of Hoffman's publications that follow after this particular testimony, new terrorism emerges more forcefully.

In one article, the 'spectacular' mass casualties of 9/11 are significant departures from previous terrorist attacks, as 'no single terrorist operation had ever killed more than 500 persons at one time' (Hoffman 2002: 304). Yet, what really sets apart 9/11 was the 'patience' shown by the hijackers alongside 'their religious imperative' (Hoffman 2002: 304). Hoffman's descriptions of the religious imperative are demonstrative of how new terrorism slides, messily and all too easily, into neo-Orientalism. One element of neo-Orientalism is representing Islam and other 'eastern' religions as mystical, otherworldly: Other. Thus, when Hoffman (2002: 303) describes bin Laden as 'A tall skinny man with a long, scraggly beard, wearing . . . the headdress of a desert tribesman, with an AK-47 assault rifle at his side, . . . before a rocky backdrop' – it has impact and meaning. He continues to drive the point home,

> The scion of a porter turned construction magnate whose prowess at making money was perhaps matched only by his countless progeny and devout religious piety, the young Osama pursued studies not in theology . . . but business and management. (Hoffman 2002: 307)

In one well organised sentence, Hoffman manages to both underscore the assumptions of neo-Orientalist hypersexuality of men alongside implications of religious extremism. Perhaps the slide of new terrorism into neo-Orientalism was unintentional; perhaps the coincidences between the two were simply that, coincidences. Yet, one has to ask: what responsibility do Hoffman and other new terrorism proponents have for the Islamophobia that followed in the United States (Kishi 2017)?

While it can certainly be argued that new terrorism did not intend to single out Muslims, the linkage of new terrorism with radical Islamism meant that as the public picked up on this theorisation, particularly with the narrativising of 9/11 as exceptional, Muslims and all of Islam became seen as anti-American and as terrorists (see Ahmed 2004: 76). Indeed, the US became so hyper-focused upon the radical Islamist threat that it has failed to investigate or take as seriously other violences, such as the rising tide of white supremacist/alt-right violence (Reitman 2018). Additionally, the stickiness of Islam/Muslim/terrorist was used as a campaign technique by Trump, who played on the racist hatred towards this group of people. That one of his first policies as president was to issue the executive order that became known as the Muslim ban is simply not surprising – regrettable, disgusting and sad, but not surprising.

Conclusion

This chapter has parsed out how terrorism has been conceived of as both irrational and immoral. These claims have traction and deeper hidden meanings given their relationship with gendered assumptions and racial bias. Because of these hard 'truths', scholars of Terrorism Studies must ask themselves what harm our work may do – not just in reifying and spreading messages, but how these can be problematically applied through counter-terrorism policies. Therefore, there are 'real world' implications for our theorising. The implications of these theories are explored in the next three chapters.

The next chapter looks at how individual terrorists are constructed, examining the information supplied about them through the intersectional lens of asking the other question. It shows that there are adjectives and misnomers repeatedly used to describe terrorist actors from a variety of backgrounds, but as these adjectives are applied, they intersect with other identifiers, shifting the meaning and intent of these discursive labels. Chapter 4 looks at how counter-terrorism responses focused on radicalisation undermine any ideas of terrorism as a rational activity. This then combines in gendered and racialised ways in counter-terrorism initiatives, such as the London Metropolitan Police's Prevent Tragedies programme and the FBI's deflection from white supremacy to 'Black Identity Extremism'. Finally, Chapter 5 looks at violence that lies outside of orthodox Terrorism Studies, misogynistic terrorism, and makes the case that orthodox Terrorism Studies should do a better job of including this violence in its canon, even if it turns the typical counter-terrorism figure of a white, Western man into the terrorist.

Notes

1. Chapter 4 goes into a more extensive conversation about rationality and the social sciences, introducing both 'bounded' and 'thin' rationality.
2. Within process theory, individual motivation is often attributed to the elements of a person's life that would be considered linked to emotion: family, friends, belief systems and the events that impact these objects (Taylor and Horgan 2012 and 2006; Horgan 2008; see also McCauley and Moskalenko's [2016 and 2008] work on political mobilisation).
3. There is a convergence of work here, where I started using gendered neo-Orientalism in several publications (Gentry 2016a and 2016d) and by Narozhna and Knight's (2016) excellent work on women and suicide terrorism.

References

Abrahms, Max (2008), 'What Terrorists Really Want: Terrorist Motives and Counterterrorism Strategy', *International Security*, 32(4): 78–105.

Ahmed, Sara (2004), *The Cultural Politics of Emotion* (Edinburgh: Edinburgh University Press).

Akram, Susan Musarrat (2000), 'Orientalism Revisited in Asylum and Refugee Claims', *International Journal of Refugee Law*, 12(1): 7–40.

Arendt, Hannah (1970), *On Violence* (New York: Houghton Mifflin Harcourt).

Atran, Scott (2003), 'Genesis of Suicide Terrorism', *Science*, 299(5612): 1534–9.

Brown, Chris (2002), *Sovereignty, Rights and Justice: International Political Theory Today* (London: Polity Press).

Brunner, Claudia (2007), 'Occidentalism Meets the Female Suicide Bomber: A Critical Reflection on Recent Terrorism Debates', *Signs: Journal of Women in Culture and Society*, 32(4): 957–71.

Brunner, Claudia (2015), 'Knowing Suicide Terrorism? Tracing Epistemic Violence Across Scholarly Expertise', Centre for Peace Research and Peace Education, <http://www.uni-klu.ac.at/frieden/downloads/knowing_suicide_terrorism_brunner_2015(1).pdf> (last accessed 22 November 2018).

Connell, Robert W., and James W. Messerschmidt (2005), 'Hegemonic Masculinity: Rethinking the Concept', *Gender and Society*, 19(6): 829–59.

Crenshaw, Martha (1981), 'The Causes of Terrorism', *Comparative Politics*, 13(4): 379–99.

Crenshaw, Martha (1987), 'Theories of Terrorism: Instrumental and Organisational Approaches', *The Journal of Strategic Studies*, 10(4): 13–31.

Crenshaw, Martha (1990), 'The Logic of Terrorism: Terrorist Behaviour as a Product of Strategic Choice', in Walter Reich (ed.), *The Origins of Terrorism: Psychologies, Ideologies, Theologies, States of Mind* (Washington, DC: Woodrow Wilson Press), pp. 7–24.

Crenshaw, Martha (2000), 'The Psychology of Terrorism: An Agenda for the 21st Century', *Political Psychology*, 21(2): 405–20.

De Carvalho, Benjamin, Halvard Leira and John M. Hobson (2011), 'The Big Bangs of IR: The Myths that Your Teachers Still Tell You About 1648 and 1919', *Millennium*, 39(3): 735–58.

Enloe, Cynthia (2000), *Manoeuvres: The International Politics of Militarising Women's Lives* (Berkeley: University of California Press).

Foley, Richard (1991), 'Rationality, Belief, and Commitment', *Synthese*, 89(3): 365–92.

Fricker, Miranda (2007), *Epistemic Injustice: Power and the Ethics of Knowing* (Oxford: Oxford University Press).

Fromkin, David (1975), 'The Strategy of Terrorism', *Foreign Affairs*, 53(4): 683–98.

Galván-Álvarez, Enrique (2010), 'Epistemic Violence and Retaliation: The Issue of Knowledges in "Mother India"/*Violencia y Venganza Epistemológica: La Cuestión de las Formas de Conocimiento en "Mother India"'*, *Atlantis*: 11–26.

Gentry, Caron E. (2014), 'Epistemic Bias: Legitimate Authority and Politically Violent Nonstate Actors', in Caron E. Gentry and Amy E. Eckert (eds), *The Future of Just War: New Critical Essays* (Athens: University of Georgia Press), pp. 17–29.

Gentry, Caron E. (2015), 'Anxiety and the Creation of the Scapegoated Other', *Critical Studies on Security*, 3(2): 133–46.

Gentry, Caron E. (2016a), 'The Mysterious Case of Aafia Siddiqui: Gothic Intertextual Analysis of neo-Orientalist Narratives', *Millennium*, 45(1): 3–24.

Gentry, Caron E. (2016b), 'Gender and Terrorism', in Simona Sharoni, Julia Welland, Linda Steiner and Jennifer Pederson (eds), *Handbook on Gender and War* (Cheltenham: Edward Elgar Publishing), pp. 146–68.

Heinze, Eric, and Brent Steele (eds) (2009), *Ethics, Authority, and War: Non-State Actors and The Just War Tradition* (Basingstoke: Palgrave MacMillan).

Held, Virginia (2008), *How Terrorism Is Wrong: Morality and Political Violence* (Oxford: Oxford University Press).

Hoffman, Bruce (1999), 'Terrorism Trends and Prospects', in Ian Lesser, John Arguilla, Bruce Hoffman, David F. Ronfeldt, Michele Zanini (eds), *Countering the New Terrorism* (Santa Monica, CA: RAND), pp. 7–38.

Hoffman, Bruce (2001), 'Rethinking Terrorism in Light of a War on Terrorism', Testimony Before the Subcommittee on Terrorism and Homeland Security, US House of Representatives, 26 September, <https://www.rand.org/content/dam/rand/pubs/testimonies/2005/CT182.pdf> (last accessed 22 November 2018).

Hoffman, Bruce (2002), 'Rethinking Terrorism and Counterterrorism Since 9/11', *Studies in Conflict and Terrorism*, 25(5): 303–16.

Horgan, John (2008), 'From Profiles to Pathways and Roots to Routes: Perspectives from Psychology on Radicalisation into Terrorism', *The Annals of the American Academy of Political and Social Science*, 618(1): 80–94.

Huntington, Samuel (1993), 'The Clash of Civilizations?', *Foreign Affairs*, 72(3): 22–49.

Huntington, Samuel (1996), *The Clash of Civilizations and the Making of a New World Order* (New York: Simon and Schuster).

Ish-Shalom, Piki (2009), 'Theorising Politics, Politicizing Theory, and the Responsibility That Runs Between', *Perspectives on Politics*, 7(2): 303–16.

Jackson, Richard D. (2005), *Writing the War on Terrorism: Language, Politics, and Counterterrorism* (Manchester: Manchester University Press).

Jackson, Richard D. (2012), 'Unknown Knowns: The Subjugated Knowledge of Terrorism Studies', *Critical Studies on Terrorism*, 5(1): 11–29.

Jackson, Richard D. (2015), 'The Epistemological Crisis of Counterterrorism', *Critical Studies on Terrorism*, 8(1): 33–54.

Jackson, Richard D. (2016), 'To be or Not to be Policy Relevant? Power, Emancipation and Resistance in CTS Research', *Critical Studies on Terrorism*, 9(1): 120–5.

Jarvis, Lee (2009), *Times of Terror: Discourse, Temporality, and the War on Terror* (Basingstoke: Palgrave MacMillan).

Kishi, Katayoun (2017), 'Assaults Against Muslims in US Surpass 2001 Level', *Pew Research Centre*, 15 November, <http://www.pewresearch.org/fact-tank/2017/11/15/assaults-against-muslims-in-u-s-surpass-2001-level/> (last accessed 22 November 2018).

Kochi, Tarik (2009), *The Other's War: Recognition and the Violence of Ethics* (London: Birkbeck Law Press).

Laqueur, Walter (1996), 'Postmodern Terrorism', *Foreign Affairs*, 75(5): 24–36.

Laqueur, Walter (1999), *The New Terrorism: Fanaticism and the Arms of Mass Destruction* (Oxford: Oxford University Press).

Lesser, Ian, John Arguilla, Bruce Hoffman, David F. Ronfeldt and Michele Zanini (eds) (1999), *Countering the New Terrorism* (Santa Monica, CA: RAND).

Lum, Cynthia, Leslie W. Kennedy and Alison Sherley (2006), 'Are Counter-Terrorism Strategies Effective? The Results of the Campbell Systematic Review on Counter-Terrorism Evaluation Research', *Journal of Experimental Criminology*, 2(4): 489–516.

McCauley, Clark, and Sophia Moskalenko (2008), 'Mechanisms of Political Radicalisation: Pathways Toward Terrorism', *Terrorism and Political Violence*, 20(3): 415–33.

McCauley, Clark, and Sophia Moskalenko (2011), *Friction: How Conflict Radicalises Them and Us* (Oxford: Oxford University Press).

McCormick, Gordon H. (2003), 'Terrorist Decision Making', *Annual Review of Political Science*, 6(1): 473–507.

Merari, Ariel (1990), 'Suicidal Terrorism', in Walter Reich (ed.), *The Origins of Terrorism: Psychologies, Ideologies, Theologies, States of Mind* (Washington, DC: Woodrow Wilson Press), pp. 192–210.

Mills, Charles (1997), *The Racial Contract* (Ithaca, NY: Cornell University Press).

Muro-Ruiz, Diego (2002), 'The Logic of Violence', *Politics*, 22(2): 109–17.

Nader, Laura (1989), 'Orientalism, Occidentalism, and the Control of Women', *Cultural Dynamics*, 2(3): 323–55.

Narozhna, Tanya, and W. Andy Knight (2016), *Female Suicide Bombings: A Critical Gender Approach* (Toronto: University of Toronto Press).

Nussbaum, Martha C. (2003), *Upheavals of Thought: The Intelligence of Emotions* (Cambridge: Cambridge University Press).

Pape, Robert A. (2003), 'The Strategic Logic of Suicide Terrorism', *American Political Science Review*, 97(3): 343–61.

Pape, Robert A. (2006), *Dying to Win: The Strategic Logic of Suicide Terrorism* (New York: Random House).

Pateman, Carole (1980), '"The Disorder of Women": Women, Love, and the Sense of Justice', *Ethics*, 91(1): 20–34, 26.

Peterson, V. Spike (2010), 'Gendered Identities, Ideologies, and Practices in the Context of War and Militarism', in Laura Sjoberg and Sandra Via (eds), *Gender, War, and Militarism: Feminist Perspectives* (Denver, CO: Praeger), pp.17–29.

Post, Jerrold M. (1990), 'Terrorist Psycho-Logic: Terrorist Behaviour as a Product of Psychological Forces', in Walter Reich (ed.), *The Origins of Terrorism: Psychologies, Ideologies, Theologies, States of Mind* (Washington, DC: Woodrow Wilson Press), pp. 25–42.

Rasmussen, David M. (2003), 'Reasonability, Normativity, and the Cosmopolitan Imagination: Arendt, Korsgaard, and Rawls', *Continental Philosophy Review*, 36(2): 97–112.

Reich, Walter (ed.) (1990), *The Origins of Terrorism: Psychologies, Ideologies, Theologies, States of Mind* (Washington, DC: Woodrow Wilson Press).

Reitman, Janet (2018), 'US Law Enforcement Failed to See the Threat of White Nationalism. Now They Don't Know How to Stop It', *The New York Times*, 3

November, <https://www.nytimes.com/2018/11/03/magazine/FBI-charlottesville-white-nationalism-far-right.html> (last accessed 24 November 2018).

Richter-Montpetit, Melanie (2007), 'Empire, Desire, and Violence: A Queer Transnational Feminist Reading of the Prisoner "Abuse" in Abu Ghraib and the Question of "Gender Equality"', *International Feminist Journal of Politics*, 9(1): 38–59.

Richter-Montpetit, Melanie (2014), 'Beyond the Erotics of Orientalism: Lawfare, Torture and the Racial–Sexual Grammars of Legitimate Suffering', *Security Dialogue*, 45(1): 43–62.

Said, Edward (1978), *Orientalism* (New York: Pantheon Books).

Shepherd, Laura J. (2006), 'Veiled References: Constructions of Gender in the Bush Administration Discourse on the Attacks on Afghanistan Post-9/11', *International Feminist Journal of Politics*, 8(1): 19–41.

Silke, Andrew (2009), 'Contemporary Terrorism Studies: Issues in Research', in Richard D. Jackson, Marie Breen Smyth and Jerone Gunning (eds), *Critical Terrorism Studies: A New Research Agenda* (Abingdon: Routledge), pp. 34–48.

Sjoberg, Laura (2009), 'Feminist Interrogations of Terrorism/Terrorism Studies', *International Relations*, 23(1): 69–74.

Sjoberg, Laura (2013), *Gendering Global Conflict* (New York: Columbia University Press).

Sjoberg, Laura, and Caron E. Gentry (2008a), 'Profiling Terror: Gendering the Strategic Logic of Suicide Terror and Other Narratives', *Austrian Journal of Political Science*, 2: 181–96.

Sprinzak, Ehud (2009), 'Rational Fanatics', *Foreign Policy*, 20 November, <https://foreignpolicy.com/2009/11/20/rational-fanatics/> (last accessed 25 November 2018).

Stampnitzky, Lisa (2013), *Disciplining Terrorism: How 'Experts' Invented Terrorism* (Cambridge: Cambridge University Press).

Steele, Brent J., and Jacque L. Amoreaux (2009), '"Justice is Conscience:" Hizbollah, Israel, and the Perversity of Just War', in Eric A. Heinze and Brent J. Steele (eds), *Ethics, Authority, and War: Non-State Actors and the Just War Tradition* (Basingstoke: Palgrave MacMillan), pp. 177–204.

Taylor, Max, and John Horgan (2006), 'A Conceptual Framework for Addressing Psychological Process in the Development of the Terrorist', *Terrorism and Political Violence*, 18(4): 585–601.

Taylor, Max, and John Horgan (2012), 'A Conceptual Framework for Addressing Psychological Process in the Development of the Terrorist', in John Horgan and Kurt Braddock (eds), *Terrorism Studies: A Reader* (Abingdon: Routledge), pp. 130–44.

Third, Amanda (2010), 'Imprisonment and Excessive Femininity: Reading Ulrike Meinhof's Brain', *Parallax*, 16(4): 83–100.

Tickner, J. Ann (1992), *Gender in International Relations: Feminist Perspectives on Achieving Global Security* (New York: Columbia University Press).

Toros, Harmonie (2008), '"We Don't Negotiate with Terrorists!": Legitimacy and Complexity in Terrorist Conflicts', *Security Dialogue*, 39(4): 407–26.

Toros, Harmonie (2016), 'Dialogue, Praxis, and the State: A Response to Richard Jackson', *Critical Studies on Terrorism*, 9(1): 126–30.

Vitalis, Robert (2015), *White World Order, Black Power Politics: The Birth of American International Relations* (Ithaca: Cornell University Press).

Walzer, Michael (1977), *Just and Unjust Wars: A Moral Argument with Historical Illustrations* (New York: Basic Books).

Wilson, Timothy (2012), Untitled Talk, *Handa Centre for the Study of Terrorism and Political Violence*, University of St Andrews, 19 April 2012.

Yeğenoğlu, Meyda (1998), *Colonial Fantasies: Towards a Feminist Reading of Orientalism* (Cambridge: Cambridge University Press).

CHAPTER 3

Strange Bedfellows: What Happens When We Ask the Other Question?

Within discourse analysis it is known that discursive labels are used to fix something, to uphold a dominant way of being. Yet, these discursive labels are also never as stable as the one speaking or labelling would like them to be; they shift and move as culture, time and history unfold (see Hansen 2013: 98, 128; Milliken 1999: 230). All academic work is part of a discursive process – it joins with other discourse production, creating 'grids of intelligibility' (Milliken 1999: 230). Terrorism Studies has created its own grids of intelligibility, yet all grids are 'unstable grids, requiring work to "articulate" and "rearticulate" their knowledges and identities (to fix the "regime of truth")' (Milliken 1999: 230). This chapter looks at how discursive narratives within (or that inform) Terrorism Studies travel beyond the academy, situating terrorist actors in particular lights that produce the subject in particular way, reproducing grids of intelligibility that shift to home in on different actors in different ways.

It is my contention that the discursive hierarchy of terrorism is not simply dependent upon the state and its agents. Instead, the discourse is enabled by fears, prejudices and biases that exist on a personal level. As pointed out in Chapter 2, the Westphalian myth is not just about Western pre-eminence; it is also masculinist and white. Therefore, harm does not just remain between states or non-state actors – protection/harm impacts individuals as well. In order to get below the abstractions that occur when IR and Terrorism Studies becomes hyper-focused on state-level activities, feminism urges us to look at the complexity of individuals (Sylvester 2013 and 2010; Tickner 1992).

Therefore, how do the racialised, gendered, heteronormative biases embedded in the Westphalian/imperialism narrative bleed downwards?

How do they impact not only our understanding of the violence and of the organisations labelled as terrorist, but our thinking on those individuals that are labelled as terrorists? An intersectional analysis helps to bring these to the forefront, forcing us to recognise that there has always been a power-over between the researcher and her subject that have tended to follow race, class, gender and religious lines. By looking at how these biases have been levelled at different actors from different locales, groups and ideologies, we can see how the easy marks of routinely held identity prejudices provide a 'narrative fidelity' for the disorder, irrationality and immorality of terrorist violence.

This chapter will provide an intersectional analysis of eight well-known politically violent actors from a range of locations, ideologies and time periods. These actors were chosen as 'iconic' or exemplars given the amount of publicity paid to them, but also because of the discursive convergence between them. The chosen actors include Andreas Baader of the West German Red Army Faction, Bernardine Dohrn of the Weather Underground, Leila Khaled of the Popular Front for the Liberation of Palestine, José 'Pepe' Mujica of the Tupamaros of Uruguay, Dhanu of Sri Lanka's Liberation Tigers of Tamil Eelam (LTTE), 'self-radicalised' lone gunmen Anders Breivik and Nidal Hasan, and Aafia Siddiqui, who is accused of aiding al Qaeda.

Each profile plays on what is 'known' before proceeding to ask the other question. In doing so, unusual patterns emerge. Where we might have thought hypersexuality was only implicated in neo-Orientalism, it is clear that it was a narrative that formed attitudes towards those involved in left-wing terrorism in the 1960s. Furthermore, these snapshots will illustrate how perspectives on terrorism shifted; where once some forms of ethno-nationalist terrorism were seen as more legitimate as part of the post-colonial, self-determination process, now forms of ethno-nationalist terrorism, particularly those stemming from areas associated with Islam, are seen as without any legitimacy. While some of this has to do with methods and tactics – from preserving life to killing indiscriminately – much of it has to do with the overwhelming neo-Orientalist discourse that pervades reporting and policy-making on terrorism. Even this, though, maintained a form of narrative fidelity in keeping with a coloniality of racism. Whereas the main groups in the 1960s were left-wing Marxist-Leninist groups – populated by upper-middle-class and predominantly well-educated individuals – the 1970s and 1980s saw a rise in right-wing and religiously motivated terrorism, often with less well educated and more working-class members. With this rise came a racialised element, like the one that has infiltrated the new terrorism thesis. Therefore, this chapter looks for hidden continuities that speak to the hidden structures that shape and inform Terrorism Studies and the narratives that it replicates as a means of creating coherency within a chosen audience.

Before conducting these profiles, this chapter will first examine the intersectional studies on terrorism that do exist. For the most part, these studies may not be explicitly intersectional, yet they examine facets that are at play in these reifying structures. Furthermore, most of these articles and books were written by feminist and other critical scholars. Only a few of them come from Terrorism Studies scholars per se; some of these scholars may have no, or very little, affiliation with orthodox or Critical Terrorism Studies.

Dissecting Terrorism Studies through Intersectionality

This section looks at the literature available for the more prominent intersectional identifiers, including gender, broken down into femininities and masculinities, racism and neo-Orientalism, sexuality/queer theory, and classism and Marxism. As such, it inherently draws upon work that is already rooted in critical, and more particularly, feminist and/or queer theory. Therefore, this section does less evaluation of the problems that exist in Terrorism Studies; instead it is a peek inside the literature that was some of the first to point out the fallacies within Terrorism Studies.

Gender

The feminist scholars focused upon terrorism and political violence that emerged in the mid-2000s are highly critical of Terrorism Studies' gender-essentialising frames (see Gentry and Sjoberg 2015; Sjoberg and Gentry 2011 and 2007; Parashar 2014 and 2009; Alison 2009; Cunningham 2003; Dwyer 1998). As gender consists of both the sex/gender and masculine/feminine logocentric binaries, any suggestion of a 'female terrorist' suggests that the non-gender-specified terrorist is both the norm and male (see Sjoberg and Gentry 2008a) and any suggestion of a terrorist suggests a counter-terrorist. Therefore, in these binaries of (male) terrorist/female terrorist and counter-terrorist/terrorist, the first term is the superior and the 'inferior marks a fall' or a negation (Culler 1982 as cited in Krishna 1993: 385). In such a co-constitutive relationship, any demarcation of one part of the binary interpellates the opposite. While the second binary as gendered – and raced – is alluded to in the previous chapters, in the gendered dynamic between states and terrorist groups, how gender demarcates the male/female terrorist is equally important. Furthermore, when masculinity is investigated in relation to terrorism and political violence, it indicates a different dynamic between the terrorist, who is made out to be hypersexual and hyperviolent, and the counter-terrorist, who is made out to be fully in control of 'his' baser 'instincts'.

Agency and political activity have long been intertwined, and as such agency has been seen as a deeply public and therefore masculine attribute. The feminist literature on women's involvement in political violence has in some way been to complicate the assignment, or lack thereof, of agency to said women by Terrorism Studies (see Gentry and Sjoberg 2015; Third 2010; Åhäll 2012; Auchter 2012). For instance, most of the early literature was led by gender essentialisation, believing that men and women act from inherent and instinctive reasons that tie them to gender-ideal types. One of the first pieces on women and terrorism described these women as not 'rational' but 'emotional' (Anonymous 1976: 245). Therefore, their 'violence will in all probability stem not from dedication to the particular cause . . . but from blind obedience to another more personal cause' (Anonymous 1976: 245). H. H. A. Cooper's (1979: 153–4) work compares them to the Gorgons of Greek mythology and describes them as 'childish' imitators of the men. Female terrorists are 'obsessive' and 'pathological' and, hence, 'it is useless to inquire why women become terrorists' (Cooper 1979: 153–4). As a radical feminist, Robin Morgan believes that violence is innately patriarchal, therefore she argues that female terrorists are in the 'harem' of male terrorists – that the primary reasons for their involvement are the sexual attraction between (weak, apolitical) women and the ultimate bad boy male terrorist (Morgan 1989). One of the West German GSG-9's commands (the SWAT-team like unit created to combat the Marxist-Leninist Red Army Faction) was 'shoot the women first' (MacDonald 1991). This stemmed from a belief that the women revolutionaries were unpredictable and more prone to violence than the men revolutionaries (MacDonald 1991).

Thus, the main argument in my books with Laura Sjoberg (Sjoberg and Gentry 2007; Gentry and Sjoberg, second edition, 2015) retheorises agency via a relational autonomy framework, one that takes into account individual choice within structural constraints. For instance, the Chechen women who acted as suicide bombers in 2005 often had their actions attributed to dishonour, which led their families to sell them to Chechen extremist groups, or to 'zombiefication', where women were drugged into acting (see Gentry and Sjoberg 2015: 130–1; Gentry and Whitworth 2011: 156). This indicates a resistance to seeing women as fully capable of making the same strategic and logical choices that (male) terrorists make. As such, this is a long-standing echo of the tensions that Elshtain (1981) and Pateman (1980) pointed out nearly forty years ago.

This is a similar tension to that Amanda Third (2010) picks up on in her article on Ulrike Meinhof, one of the three leaders of the first generation of the West German Red Army Faction. Meinhof committed suicide in prison in 1976 (although her compatriots maintained that she had been murdered by the West German state). Without asking her family, West Germany 'decapitated' Meinhof (Third 2010: 96), removing her brain for study, determined to prove there was something pathologically wrong with her (brain). Utilising Hélène Cixous' theory on the metaphorical decapitation of women through their essentialisation as unreasonable and irrational, Third (2010: 85) suggests

> As a terrorist then, Meinhof represents a necessary site of containment – a figure that must be controlled in order to shore up the threat to the order of the everyday and deliver the promise of freedom. In this respect, it is not surprising that the West German state sought to annul the threat she posed. However, this in itself does not adequately explain why such efforts would continue beyond her death in prison. Nor does it explain why the state's posthumous strategies of containment focused specifically on her brain. Tackling these questions requires specific attention to the fact of her gender. Whilst, as a terrorist, Meinhof threatens life and property, as a *female* terrorist, she threatens the very basis upon which freedom is postulated.

If we return to Pateman (1980), we know that a democratic society is dependent upon the rational capability of its citizens and that women have been excluded from this project historically. In needing to dissect Meinhof's brain, yet another study is done in order to demonstrate women's incapacity to act as political subjects in the deeply masculine politics of Western liberal democratic thought.

Interrogating this dichotomisation between women and political violence versus the possession of agency is key to most feminist work on women and terrorism, and has been for a decade. Therefore it is quite surprising that the need to divide women from their agency continues in the recent work on women and Da'esh (see Loken and Zelenz 2018 for a discussion of this work). While this might indicate to some the failure of feminist work to make an impact, I think instead it indicates quite the opposite: the failure of mainstream Terrorism Studies to take the critique and knowledge of feminism and gender studies seriously (see also Henshaw 2016: 3). It says to me that the feminist scholars who have worked on women and terrorism for a decade are not included as 'experts' when these journals seek peer-reviewers. This means the same problems that existed in the 1970s exist in literature from 2017. This is a problem – and it shows us that Terrorism Studies has a gender problem.

This gender problem is also demonstrated when one considers what the opposite of a female terrorist is: a 'male' terrorist. As there are very few studies that look at masculinity and terrorism, it is argued that the 'normal' terrorist is assumed to be male (see Sjoberg and Gentry 2008a). Yet, very rarely does the 'normal' terrorist stand against 'female terrorists', but against counter-terrorists. Indeed, the counter-terrorist/terrorist binary is best seen in light of hegemonic masculinity. Hegemonic masculinity holds that there is an idealised masculine type (Connell and Messerschmidt 2005) – one that is often context-specific. Those that fit this type are automatically conferred with a certain amount of power and privilege, subordinating men that do not exactly fit this type, as well as all women.

While counter-terrorist marks the superior term, since terrorist is inherently a discrediting pejorative, Terrorism Studies never quite defines what a counter-terrorism agent is. It is populated as a term by what it is not: the terrorist. Even though counter-terrorism has been examined in academic literature (see Crelinsten 2011; Ganor 2005), a counter-terrorism agent may be a law enforcement official, military personnel or, conceivably, in some instances, a teacher or school administrator (see for instance the UK laws that obligate university lecturers to report a student for radicalisation). As agents of the state – particularly in the case of law enforcement and military personnel – an automatic assumption of rationality and responsibility is present, as noted in the previous chapter. In this, competing masculinities begin to assert themselves on that afore- and oft-mentioned fulcrum of rationality.

When one begins to investigate the scholarship that looks specifically at terrorism and masculinity, the essentialised linkage between masculinity and violence becomes more pronounced with few exceptions. For instance, White's 1990 article flips the agency and performativity question on its head by arguing that feminist literature often conflates masculinity with the desire to engage politically and, in this case, violently, without questioning this gendered depiction of men's agency. Nevertheless, such a conflation continues, especially outside of feminist literature. Kimmel (2003) investigates how masculinity is redeployed by societies that are harmed by globalisation. The harm results in these financially vulnerable men asserting their masculinity via radical Islamist violence. Similarly, in their investigation of evolutionary biology and 'Islamic suicide terrorism', Bradley Thayer and Valerie Hudson (2010) conclude that suicide attacks are a way for non-alpha males to participate in a resource-scarce environment. In other words, in societies where 'beta males' may not be able to contribute socially and economically, terrorism provides them with an answer. David Duriesmith (2017) has begun publishing on toxic masculinity and its relationship to actors in the New Wars, war violence which is often seen as outside of 'normal' traditional warfare. Others (Kimmel and Wade 2018; Sculos 2017) have begun to connect toxic masculinity with the white nationalism/supremacy on the rise in the West – from Germany and Scandinavian states to the United States.

Race and Neo-Orientalism

Much of the literature on race and terrorism, from a critical perspective, centres on neo-Orientalism. While this is crucially important to explore, it fails to recognise the long-standing racial divides and tensions that have informed Terrorism Studies since its inception. However, there is still scholarship that does look at racialisation separately from neo-Orientalism. The first is the scholarship highlighted in the previous two chapters by Tarak Barkawi and Mark Laffey (2006 and 2002) and Barkawi alone (2010).

Working within Critical Race theory, Sentas (2006) flips the Westphalian-state-as-counter-terrorist script by posing state counter-terrorism policy as a form of terrorism that maintains white supremacy and seeks to harm and police non-white bodies. Arguing that 'the racial violence of white supremacy is integral to liberal democracy', 'counterterrorism is presented as a state investment in the future of white supremacy' (Sentas 2006: 2). While Sentas (2006: 6) is concerned with the emergence of post-9/11 Islamophobia, there is a realisation that this is just the latest iteration of racialised policing and counter-terrorism, particularly as 'Aborginal[s] or non-white others' are viewed as 'transgressions or intrusions into national space' (Sentas 2006: 3). These transgressions are criminalised:

> Crime has long operated as a proxy force for race, while contemporary law is deployed as race neutral and democratic. Security policing is central to processes of criminalisation of indigenous and migrant communities, at the

front end of the criminal justice system. Constructions of criminality have been extended in the war on terror to target ethnic and religious practice. (Sentas 2006: 6)

By seeing counter-terrorism, with its targeting of suspect communities and racial profiling, as a form of terrorism, this begins to queer terrorism and counter-terrorism practices. It sees what is conventionally known as the good, state-affiliated counter-terrorist in a problematic light, helping to highlight how counter-terrorism often contravenes normative and legal practices.

As noted in Chapter 1, neo-Orientalism rather problematically entered the counter-terrorism discourses post-9/11 and became central to CTS literature. Two key texts emerged from an *International Feminist Journal of Politics* 2006 special issue. Meghana Nayak's (2006) contribution examines the how the US discursively shaped and then fought the War on Terror, particularly through the construction of the US self as a Western, white saviour versus a heavily Orientalised enemy Other that was infantilised, demonised and dehumanised. Laura J. Shepherd's (2006) article looks more specifically at how these discursive identities played out as a triad – the US's hegemonic masculinity, the victimised femininity of Afghan women, the hypermasculinity of the 9/11 hijackers and Afghan men – in order to understand how such gendered structuring impacts the international system and justifies war. Building upon both of these, my own interest in Aafia Siddiqui (see Gentry 2016a), as explored later in this chapter, is also dependent upon an intersectional analysis of how gender, neo-Orientalism and geopolitics combined to impact our understanding of this one woman accused of working for al Qaeda.

Bringing together Sentas's (2006) argument with neo-Orientalism is particularly helpful in considering the past eighteen years of counter-terrorism practices, which have come to be hyper-focused on Muslims or other individuals somehow associated with Islam. The conflation of 'terrorist' with such specific identity traits has impacted counter-terrorism measures and policies, mainly in the West, meaning that other acts of violence that could/should be seen as terrorist violence go unobserved and ignored (see Githens-Mazer and Lambert 2010). It has led to the creation of 'suspect communities' (see Heath-Kelly 2012) and to laughably ignorant declarations by US President Trump that certain areas of the UK were 'no-go' areas because they were controlled by radical Islamists (Horton 2018). This problem will be picked up again in Chapter 4.

In querying this conflation, Dwyer, Shah and Sanghera (2008) utilised ethnographic research in Muslim communities in the Midlands.

They were concerned with how young Muslim men were being conceived as at odds with a British identity:

> Newspapers and politicians demanded young Muslims demonstrate that they were not 'the enemy within'. Media accounts of the lives of young Muslim men in the aftermath of the bombings in London reanimated earlier academic arguments about a generation gap and cultural conflict to emphasise the alienation of young Muslim men and thus the likelihood that they might succumb to extremist forms of Islam. (Dwyer et al. 2008: 117)

What they found is that Muslim masculine identity in these locations is comprised of a series of contestations that are not just built on a racialised religious identity. Instead, these young men have to wrestle with gender and class issues as well. Recognising these complexities makes it clear that young Muslim men are so much more than just possible terrorist suspects. An additional newer study also examines the nexus of class and race, arguing that lack of opportunity is something that needs to be addressed instead of radicalisation (Aslam 2012). Yet, such assumptions are at the heart of UK Prevent, the counter-radicalisation element of its counter-terrorism platform.

Queer Theory

The hypermasculinising of radical Islamist actors is particularly picked upon by queer theorists. As an emerging theoretical approach to the problematic binaries that dominate IR, queer theory is uniquely poised to move IR and Terrorism Studies beyond logocentric fallacies. Weber's (2016) scholarship looks at how this governing dichotomy impacts the considerations of terrorist/counter-terrorist. In queer theory scholarship on terrorism, particularly the War on Terror, the authors argue that performing hetero- and homonormativity are important to understanding how the War on Terror was constructed (Weber 2016; Puar 2017).

Heteronormativity is the essentialist belief that people fall into one of two natural ways of being (male or female) that are complementary. As a way of making homosexuality more palatable and compatible with heteronormativity's governing structure, Lisa Duggan (2003: 179) defines homonormativity as

> politics that does not contest dominant heteronormative assumptions and institutions – such as marriage, and its call for monogamy and reproduction – but upholds and sustains them while promising the possibility of a demobilised gay constituency and a privatised, depoliticised gay culture anchored in domesticity and consumption.

Thus, to look at terrorism and terrorist actors through queer theory is to examine how they are presented not necessarily as either/or but through 'queer logics', using 'and/or' to demonstrate how 'such "truths"', for instance, terrorist/counter-terrorist, 'are never stable and their representation is never guaranteed' (Weber 2014: 598).

Sexuality is central in the narratives of the 9/11 hijackers and the raid of the bin Laden compound in May 2011. The 9/11 hijackers supposedly were frequent visitors of strip clubs and purchased porn on their hotel televisions. The debunked assertion that porn was found at the bin Laden compound still circulates (Schmidle 2011). These narratives are used to paint these religious extremists as non-credible – how can they claim purity when they are tainted by 'perverted' sexual desire? This helps to constitute terrorists in this neo-Orientalist moment as hypersexualised and, therefore, those that counter them as pure (or appropriately sexualised). Yet this is a false dichotomy, particularly noted in the aftermath of the sexualised torture that took place at Abu Ghraib (see Richter-Montpetit 2014). It is one built upon notions of appropriate sexual behaviour in (Western, rational) individuals, as elaborated upon by Jasbir Puar and Amit Rai (2002), and notions of innocence (Weber 2002).

For instance, Puar and Rai (2002) explore how sexuality establishes a hierarchical dynamic within the War on Terror by presenting a Foucauldian genealogy of the conflation of 'the monster' with 'the homosexual', particularly in the Victorian era. This conflation re-emerges in how terrorists are presented post-9/11. For them it showcases the logocentrism of the perverse monster/terrorist and the 'aggressive' masculinity of a good hetero-patriot in the US. In a related way, Weber (2002: 131) looks at the 9/11 attack as a loss of American innocence, and considers how this discourse is supported by a 'moral grammar' that has sexuality at its core. Once again, the terrorist's sexuality is presented as deviant whereas Western actors remain pure.

In later work, both Puar (2017) and Weber (2016) go on to complicate these claims. In Weber's 2016 book, chapter 4 locates the 'terrorist' in IR as the uncivilisable and undevelopable figure. All things non-Western, including heteronormativity and cisgender, are invested in this figure, placing the terrorist as the ultimate threat to Western hegemonic order. In Puar's 2017 (first published in 2007) book, she conducts an intersectional analysis that places an emphasis on sexuality, this time focusing on queered patriotic identities in the US post-9/11, particularly in the co-opting of homonormativity to support the war on terror.

Classism and Marxism

There are several ways of thinking about class in IR, particularly the work on development and dependency as well as the extension of Marxism into world systems theory. While some of the work highlighted above, particularly Kimmel (2003) and Dwyer et al. (2008), speaks to class, there are few works that actually provide an intersectional critique of how class functions within Terrorism Studies. By that I mean a sense of positional self-reflexivity: that academics often come from middle- or upper-class backgrounds that lend certain perspectives. If Terrorism Studies emerged in the 1960s – as 'modern' terrorism was taking hold worldwide, primarily in Western states with Marxist-Leninist groups often coming out of a university setting – surely these academics were familiar with the groups and the people within them. How did this shape perceptions? What tensions existed and still possibly do? With a few exceptions, there is not enough information to answer this question. Robin Morgan (1989), the feminist mentioned above, considered join- ing the Weather Underground. A former childhood television star and a university student in New York, she was put off by their sexism. Lou- ise Richardson, author of *What Terrorists Want* (2006), who is a former Vice-Chancellor of St Andrews and current Vice-Chancellor of Oxford, has publicly stated as well as discussed in her book that she would have joined the IRA 'in a heartbeat' (*Belfast Telegraph* 2009).

Otherwise, the literature that looks at political violence or terrorism from a class/economic perspective takes its starting points from T. R. Gurr's *Why Men Rebel* (1970). In this seminal text he argues that politi- cal violence, particularly sub-state political violence, is owed to relative deprivation, or the 'perceived discrepancy between men's [sic] value expectations and their value capabilities' (Gurr 1970: 13). Basically, vio- lence happens when people feel there is a significant and drastic differ- ence between what their potential to earn and gain is and what they will actually earn and gain. Other, more recent work builds upon the 'greed and grievance' debate: do people act violently for economic reasons (greed) or for political reasons (political) (Henshaw 2016)?

One excellent piece that focuses on terrorism argues that 'warfare' is a 'different expressio[n] of the expansion of the capitalist-world-economy' (Flint and Radil 2009: 155). Using a Marxist-Leninist argument that imperialism is a class issue, thus ignoring the gendered and racialised argument used in this book, 'warfare was . . . a feature of the expansion of the capitalist system . . . through Western exploration, imperialism, and colonialism' (Flint and Radil 2009: 155). Terrorism is a response to this warfare and imperial violence: 'Terrorism is a form of warfare that has changed with the changing structure of the modern social-system' (Flint and Radil 2009: 155). Additionally, 'terrorism [is] a reaction to marginalisation' (Flint and Radil 2009: 156). Drawing upon the work of others, including Bergesen and Lizardo (2004) and Flint and Taylor (2007), Flint and Radil (2009: 157) are able to quantitatively demonstrate that terrorism happens within semi-peripheral states, where 'social struggles are most intense and the role of the state as an interventionist organ of economic development is most pronounced'. An additional World Bank report finds that high-income developing countries experience higher rates of terrorism (Blomberg and Hess 2005).

Intersectional work has been done, but there is still so much more to do in bringing together these disparate ideas, looking to see where there is overlap or where there is tension. This will take more than one single book. Yet it is crucially important work to do: we must keep uncovering how these various intersecting structures form competing and harmful relationships. It is particularly important to look at how scholarship and policy relies upon racial, gendered and heteronormative structures to create a 'natural' or 'normal' approach to those we see as credible/non-credible or legitimate/illegitimate, as these would reify the relationship between counter-terrorist and terrorist.

The Profiles

When teaching my Gender and Terrorism class, I found myself recalling different stories about some of the individuals in these profiles and including some of the more anecdotal material as if by rote. And what I noticed, and what some of my students pointed out to me, is how some of the men were feminised, such as the focus on Andreas Baader's clothing, whereas I had really only been paying attention to the treatment of women – of how narratives that focus on their 'broken' femininity dismisses or diminishes their agency (see Gentry and Sjoberg 2015). This was a great *learning* moment for me – whereas I have recognised how *men* and women associated with radical Islam are scripted within neo-Orientalism (see Gentry 2016a; Gentry 2015) – I have never noticed how *all* actors labelled within terrorism are scripted in different, yet related, ways that work towards minimising their credibility and, potentially, their morality. Such a discourse continues to secure 'terrorism' as illegitimate and immoral – what was codified at the level of the state trickles down, allowing for discursive coherency and fidelity.

Furthermore, whereas the hypersexuality that surrounded the men involved with radical Islamism is seen as novel, perhaps it is not. While such an observation in no way lessens the need to deconstruct hyper-sexuality, neo-Orientalism, and radical Islamic actors, what I bring out below demonstrates that (hyper)sexuality has long been used to discredit actors. This works within the observations that Kapoor (2015: 1611) made about the 'queerness' of Third World actors: of 'grouping them in their common inheritance of subjugation and disparagement'. The profiles below attempt to bring out more of these identifying oppressors, ones that are threaded throughout the discourse on individual terrorist actors throughout the forty years of Terrorism Studies.

The profiles were created in part by drawing upon cultural knowl-edge gathered from magazines and newspapers, but mainly from sources that are closely related to or entrenched within Terrorism Stud-ies. This approach is intended to show the reifying relationship that exists between those who 'own' the knowledge on terrorism and those who 'consume' the knowledge on terrorism. For this reason, I have also included anecdotes that have been told to me in passing: ones that can-not be verified via research but ones that have been brought to my atten-tion, feeding into the lore of the titillating terrorist.

The profiles are ordered by the years that they were active and include biographical information as well as information on the group and its ideological and political purpose. While writing and researching, I actively asked the other question: for instance, where the references to Baader's class are close to the surface, his masculinity is overt and hyperviolent; where the sexualisation of Bernardine Dohrn is readily apparent, class falls to the background. And for both, as they are white, which is often coded as 'normal', whiteness does not protect them from the use of hypersexuality to suggest irrationality. Yet, the sexuality of Dohrn, which she is in control of, contrasts with Dhanu's, where any suggestion of sexuality undermines the necessity of submissiveness and purity. I have put the two profiles of Breivik and Hasan together, as it is impossible to show the intersectional dimensions of how the Lone Wolf is constructed (or not) without placing them in direct contrast and comparison.

Andreas Baader

Andreas Baader is best known as one of the three leaders of the first-generation West German Red Army Faction, otherwise known as Baader-Meinhof. The other two leaders were women: Ulrike Meinhof and

Gudrun Enslinn, Baader's girlfriend. Given the usage of 'Baader-Meinhof', many assume that Baader and Meinhof were the main leaders, but this is not the case. Alfred Klaus, lead of the Special Commission on Terrorism, labelled Meinhof the head, Baader the engine and Enslinn the soul (Aust 1987: 267). The first generation operated from 1970 until the time of their arrest in 1972. They tried to maintain some control and leadership from prison until their suicides in 1976, which were staged to look like they were murdered by agents of the West German state. When looking specifically at Baader, several elements emerge: his family of origin, his affinity for violence, and his class. Yet there is also a significant subtext that revolves around sexuality.

There is a rather infamous West German psychological study of the members of the Red Army Faction. Published in the 1970s, the multiple-volume study came to several conclusions, one of which included the notion that members were often raised in female-headed households, leading the subjects to a weak sense of self (Post 1990: 28). This captures Baader's own family of origin. He was raised by his mother and grandmother after his father died in World War II and was therefore seen as 'spoiled', 'lazy' and 'strong-willed' (Aust 2008: 9). This was used to explain his often aggressive, demeaning (particularly toward Meinhof) and egotistical behaviour. While this may be true for Baader, the psychological study did not have a control group. To pinpoint the lack of a father figure as leading to terrorist behaviour is thus hard to verify, especially in West Germany after WWII, where surely many households were headed by women.

This also leads quickly to the class issue. Whereas many of the Red Army Faction members were from the middle class, often recruited out of the student movement on university campuses, Baader did not attend university; he became associated with the student movement by meeting people socially at pubs (Aust 2008: 18–19, 30–1). Accordingly, Michael 'Bommi' Baumann, who led a smaller politically violent group, the 2nd June, found Baader to be a boorish 'chain smoker' and 'speed addict' (Aust 2008: 131). Baader would 'needle people in bars, letting the argument come to the point of physical violence. It was usually the other person who walked away, giving Baader a "certain authority"' (Aust 1987: 47). He was additionally described as 'aggressive' and 'contemptuous'; 'he spat venom until he was foaming at the mouth' (Aust 1987: 66); 'He was deaf to rational argument' (Aust 1987: 92). This also speaks to the association of violence with the lower class (Moran 2000: 206).

Yet there is a 'hidden in plain sight' sexualised element to descriptions of Baader that helps to answer the other question. It is well known that the entirety of the Baader-Meinhof leadership was obsessed, rather hypocritically, with the finer things: buying clothing from nice boutiques and stealing BMWs (in part because of the 'BM' for Baader-Meinof) (Mair 2013: 79). Baader too was known for dressing in tight trousers; for instance, when Baader-Meinhof went to train with the Fateh in the Jordanian desert, it was difficult for him to manoeuvre because his velvet trousers were 'skin tight' (Aust 2008: 67). Additionally, the group's time in the camp was tenuous in part because they did not respect customs, and sunbathed naked on the roofs of the camp buildings (Aust 2008: 70). Finally, there is Hoffman's suggestion that Baader had an almost sexual relationship with his gun (as noted in Chapter 1). While this was not relevant to what I was researching at the time, it stuck with me. I began to recognise it as a gendered statement, used to discredit him as unstable, when it cohered with the use of sexuality to undermine the 9/11 hijackers (their purchasing of porn in their hotel rooms and visits to strip joints while at flying school in Florida [Chesler 2015]). When discussing Baader with another academic expert on terrorism, I found that he was also familiar with the sexual undertones.

Bernardine Dohrn

Sexuality also comes through when one begins to look at Bernardine Dohrn. Dohrn was one of several leaders of the Weather Underground, a contemporary of the Baader-Meinhof Group that grew out of the main organisation of student movements in the United States, the Students for a Democratic Society (SDS). Like the Red Army Faction, the Weather Underground membership was also close to fifty-fifty male/female. Additionally, the leadership was also shared between men and women, even if both groups continued to have problems with male dominance and masculine behaviour.

In the contemporaneous descriptions of Dohrn, her sexuality was often emphasised. One of the most formative actions for the Weather Underground were the riots in downtown Chicago known as the 'Days of Rage'. Dohrn was arrested for her participation and much was made of what she wore: a 'tight mini-skirt' and knee- or thigh-high 'Italian leather boots' at the height of the sexual revolution (Collier and Horowitz 1996: 73, 96). Additionally, she is described as a 'radical pinup' (Collier and Horowitz 1996: 68), wearing a button declaring 'Cunnilingus is Cool, Fellatio is Fun' and was referred to as 'Las Pasionaria of the Lunatic Left' by J. Edgar Hoover (Kolbert 2001: 49). Yet, it is necessary to note that sexuality and sexual politics were used by the Weather Underground leadership to maintain control (Gitlin 1987: 165–6; Ayers 2002: 105; Morgan 1989: 219). The male leadership, who travelled the country visiting the various cells, were known for sleeping around. All cells practised 'smashing monogamy', which rejected monogamous relationships and enforced 'free love' (Gentry 2004: 289). Thus, for Dohrn to be singled out for her sexuality is a gendered dynamic that certainly secured her reputation as a leader within the group to the policing community (see for instance the aforementioned scholarship published in the 1970s lamenting the connections between the sexual revolution and women's involvement in terrorism [Cooper 1979; Anonymous 1976]).

Class and education are another part of Dohrn's story. Before she joined the SDS and before it split into the Weather Underground, she was a lawyer. Thus, she was slightly older than some of her contemporaries. She also came from a well-off background, as did her now husband and fellow leader of the Weather Underground, Bill Ayers. Both of them have downplayed the wealth of their families of origin; yet, Dohrn's father was a white-collar worker (Collier and Horowitz 1996: 72–3) and Ayers's father was Chicago Chairman of the Board for Commonwealth Edison (Jacobs 1997: 7). In the 1970s, after a series of failures for the Weather Underground, most of the leadership went underground and relatively inactive. Dohrn and Ayers were in New York running a children's nursery (Kolbert 2001). After a series of events, they came above ground, both of them landing positions at universities in the Chicago area. Dohrn retired in 2013 from the Children and Family Justice Centre in the Bluhm Legal Clinic at Northwestern Law School, which she founded and directed.

Yet two angles still remain in telling her story: that she is either an unreformed, unrepentant radical, or a *reforming* presence on Ayers as his wife. The first, the radical, works well with her aforementioned 'warped' psychology. For instance, on the night the Weather Underground broke away from the SDS, effectively ending the SDS, Dohrn glorified violence and expressed a desire to emulate the Charles Manson murders of Sharon Tate and others that had just happened in Los Angeles (Kengor 2017). When she came above ground, she defended her actions; Dohrn was one of the only members who faced legal consequences, three years' probation and a $1,500 fine (Jacobs 1987: 184). In this context, 'radical' is often associated with the disconnected or disenchanted hippie activist from the late 1960s who followed Timothy Leary's 'turn on, tune in, and drop out'. Here, radical is counter-cultural and discrediting, yet discrediting in a different way from the 'radicalisation' now associated more frequently with radical Islamist terrorism.

More recent attention focuses on Dohrn's status as Bill Ayers's wife and not necessarily a co-founder of the Weather Underground (Kengor 2017). Ayers came back into the limelight when Barack Obama ran for president the first time. Obama was charged by the Republicans as associating with terrorists because Ayers and Dohrn (who was less of a focus) held a fundraiser for him at their brownstone in Hyde Park, Chicago (Kengor 2017). Morgan (1989: 186–9), a radical feminist, conceptualises Marxist-Leninist *male* terrorists as the logical next step in the Jungian hero journey: he is a modern Jason chasing his golden fleece: 'the terrorist . . . [,] the ultimate sexual ideal of a male-centred tradition [,] . . . is the logical extension of the patriarchal hero . . .' Owing to her brush with the highly gendered Weather Underground, Morgan has a difficult time removing the sexuality and gender politics from her evaluation of why men and women become involved in terrorism. She argues, for instance, that women are 'token-terrorists' who have given up their femininity and female-centred perspective of the world to serve in the harem of the 'demon lover', or the male terrorist (Morgan 1989: 186–9). Thus to situate Dohrn-as-wife minimises her agency and highlights that of her husband's. In spite of this minimisation, it is striking that Dohrn and another Weather Underground woman, Kathy Boudin, are *the only members* who have served time (although Boudin's incarceration was owed to her violence with a group related to the Black Panthers [Kolbert 2001]). This is joined by the hypersexualisation of Dohrn's involvement, when the men do not receive the same treatment.

Leila Khaled

Leila Khaled is a renowned leader within the Palestinian Resistance Movement based in Amman, Jordan. She was born in Haifa, and remembers hiding under the stairs during the IDF shelling of the city. Her family escaped to Beirut, where they lived for a number of years. Her siblings were early members of the Palestinian Resistance Movement, and Leila attended meetings as a young teenager. While at the American University, Beirut, Leila was captivated by the Palestinian hijackings and eventually joined the Popular Front for the Liberation of Palestine as a committed Marxist-Leninist. For the PFLP, Khaled hijacked two planes. The first mission was 'successful', but the second mission ended in the death of her partner and a three-week detention for Khaled in the UK (Khaled 1973). After this, Khaled became too recognisable to participate in further activities, and she eventually moved to the Central Committee of the PFLP, where she continues to serve (Lerner 2017).

The early reaction to Khaled – and her fame – tends to be due to her gender. She is seen as an anomaly; a Palestinian woman who is also violent is seen as antithetical. Yet, there is evidence of women's participation in the PRM, and of other women participating in violence and leadership (see Peteet 1991; Gentry 2011a). Within this gendered and racialised response, there are two elements. The first focuses on her beauty, which is captured perfectly in this *Guardian* article:

> The iconic photograph of Leila Khaled, the picture which made her the symbol of Palestinian resistance and female power, is extraordinary in many ways: the gun held in fragile hands, the shiny hair wrapped in a *keffiah*, the delicate Audrey Hepburn face refusing to meet your eye. But it's the ring, resting delicately on her third finger. To fuse an object of feminine adornment, of frivolity, with a bullet: that is Khaled's story, the reason behind her image's enduring power. Beauty mixed with violence. (Viner 2001)

The second focuses on her relationships with men. Morgan also directed the label of 'token terrorist' at Leila Khaled because she has 'never spoke[n] about women' and she 'has not survived being female', because Khaled once said, 'When I speak at an international conference . . . I represent Palestinians, not women' (Morgan 1989: 210–11).

Behind this early reaction is a substantial absence: a discussion of class. Palestinian resistance can be divided into at least three generations: the first, the PRM, was dominated by university students and university-educated leadership who adopted either a non-secular (the Palestinian Liberation Organisation), or a Marxist-Leninist (the PFLP, amongst others) position; the second, emerging close to the first intifada, was led by Hamas, inserting religion into the resistance; the third coincided with the second intifada, bringing a more militarised and organised element to the resistance, and most especially, introducing suicide attacks into the fray. Class is often noted in the first generation: the PRM began amongst those mobile enough to leave what is now Israel, and wealthy enough to not end up in the UN-run camps. Khaled falls into this category: her family was wealthy enough to live in Beirut and send their children to American University, Beirut (AUB) for either all four years or for two, as in Leila's case (Khaled 1973).

Beyond this silence, there are two rumours that come up in spoken discussions but rarely or ever in publication, which are also strong identifiers: religion and sexuality. It is fairly well known that George Habash, one of the early PRM leaders who founded the PFLP, was a Christian (Levy 2018). After conference presentations on Khaled, I have been told, in passing and with something of a wink, that Khaled is a Christian. Being told in this way, after questions and discussion, in the intimacy of one-on-one conversations, it is as if the person is telling me something that Khaled does not want known. It seems to me that this stems from an assumption that Palestinian violence is *religious* violence, instead of seeing Palestinian violence as anti-colonial. Thus, to point Khaled out as Christian somehow discredits her activism, even though as a firmly committed Marxist (having dropped the Leninism after the dissolution of the Soviet Union), religious belief would not be a problem anyway.

The second has come up several times, but most strongly by a woman who approached me after I presented my interview with Khaled (see Gentry 2011a) at a 2007 conference in San Francisco. The woman introduced herself as a peer of Khaled's in that she had grown up in the same neighbourhood as Khaled in Beirut. She led with Khaled's Christian background as a challenge to her activism. She then addressed one of the more well-known of Khaled's own anecdotes: that, due to Khaled's young age, her mother had forbidden her attending the PRM meetings that her older brothers and sisters were able to go to. Therefore, much to the embarrassment of the family and the ire of the leadership, Khaled snuck out in her pyjamas. The woman in San Francisco told me that Khaled was not sneaking out to go to PRM meetings, but to meet her 'lesbian girlfriends'. On some level this works like the accusations of hypersexuality against Baader, the 9/11 hijackers and Dohrn: it makes Khaled less credible because of some sense of abnormality tied to homosexuality (see Sjoberg and Gentry 2008b: 14).

José 'Pepe' Mujica

José 'Pepe' Mujica is a former president of Uruguay and a former Tupamaro. The Tupamaros were an urban guerrilla group that operated from 1967 until 1972, inspired by the success of the Cuban revolution, hoping to bring about economic and social change in Uruguay (Telesur 2016). In the earlier part of the twentieth century, Uruguay was a thriving South American powerhouse, exporting meat and wool to the United States. When this trade ceased in the late 1960s and 1970s, Uruguay experienced skyrocketing inflation, creating extreme economic inequality and exacerbating pre-existing social class divisions (see Tremlett 2014). The Tupamaros strove to address these via armed robberies of particular individuals and companies. As a response, the Uruguayan political elite securitised the country against the Tupamaros, using the threat to bring an authoritative government into power for eighteen years – a government associated with other Southern Cone *juntas* that participated in Operation Condor, in which the torture of political prisoners and extreme government and military responses to the resistance were acceptable practices (Telesur 2016; Fairbanks 2015; Tremlett 2014).

Mujica was one of these political prisoners. While his current narrative – as the former president of Uruguay – centres around his Marxist politics, painting him as chivalrous, generous and humble, the narrative of him as a terrorist actor centres on his charm, looks and use of violence only when necessary. The image of Mujica as a modern Robin Hood romanticises him. He was known for reassuringly flirting with women while holding them at gunpoint (Tremblett 2014). Adding to this romanticism, one journalist wrote that '[i]n Uruguay, Mujica's personal austerity made him an object of fascination' (Fairbanks 2015). Mujica, at eighty-three, resigned as senator early (after serving as president) and turned down his owed pension (and he only took 10 per cent of his salary [Tremlett 2014]) (BBC 2018). He explained the reason for his retirement as 'tiredness after a long journey' (BBC 2018).

There are hidden aspects to Mujica's narrative. The role of his wife is downplayed in many of the more recent accounts of Mujica. Even though Mujica himself grew up in relative poverty, thus making him an insider to the very social conditions the Tupamaros were battling, his wife, Lucía Topolanksy, grew up in relative privilege (Tremlett 2014). The farm that they live on – the farm that most news accounts use to point to his chivalry as 'he' charges minimal rent – was inherited from her family. Additionally, one of the rumours I encountered when living in Uruguay's capital city, Montevideo, was that Topolanksy was also a Tupamaro (something that is widely acknowledged). Apparently, she was also a member of their death squad. Yet, it is difficult to find this information, which is oddly gender-confirming by making women out to be 'more' intense than the men as described earlier but also by working with Morgan's 'demon lover'. Therefore, writing Mujica as a charming and chivalrous Robin Hood who remains true to his politics throughout his life and minimising, if not ignoring, the politics of his wife (who is now the vice president of Uruguay after serving as a senator), writes Mujica as the ultimate political hero and his wife as a 'token' – someone just hanging on to his coattails.

One more element to investigate is how Mujica's experience of torture is discussed, as it contributes to the mysterious romanticism of Mujica as a Robin Hood. After escaping from Punta Carretas prison along with a hundred other prisoners (Telesur 2016) – the prison is, incidentally, located in one of the nicer neighbourhoods in Montevideo and has since been turned into a high end shopping mall – Mujica, along with others, was re-imprisoned. They were all kept in isolation in various camps, something Mujica struggled with the most:

> [T]he hostages could only communicate by tapping Morse Code on their cell walls. Allowed to use the toilet just once a day, they urinated into their water bottles, allowing the sediment to settle and drinking the rest – because water was also scarce. It was even worse for Mujica, whose bullet wounds had seriously damaged his guts. Solitary confinement drove them half-mad. Pepe became convinced that a bugging device was hidden in the ceiling. Its imaginary static deafened him. 'He would put stones in his mouth to stop himself from screaming.' (Tremlett 2014)

While this may not have been physical torture like that possibly experienced by Aafia Siddiqui (as explored later), the isolation, lack of stimulation and poor conditions were torturous to Mujica. After yelling and disrupting an event, thereby embarrassing the camp's governor, Mujica was able to negotiate for a potty – something he carried from camp to camp (Tremlett 2014). About his time in prison, he has said:

> I've no doubt that had I not lived through that I would not be who I am today. Prison, solitary confinement had a huge influence on me. I had to find an inner strength. I couldn't even read a book for seven, eight years – imagine that! (Bartlett 2014)

Mujica has survived his time remarkably well, but it is fascinating how this narrative confirms Morgan's description of the male terrorist as a Jungian ideal, a new Jason.

Dhanu

The Liberation Tigers of Tamil Eelam (LTTE) was one of the most well-organised and well-trained 'terrorist' organisations globally and historically. It was led by Velupillai Prabhakaran, beginning in 1975, with the aim of setting up a separate state of Tamil Eelam in Sri Lanka. The Tamils were a politically marginalised Hindu minority in Sri Lanka, where the Sinhalese, who are Buddhists, ruled. By the early

2000s, LTTE membership was 8,000–10,000 strong, with 3,000–6,000 of those trained as soldiers (Van de Voorde 2005: 185–6). Women comprised one-third of the LTTE, and conducted 30 to 40 per cent of the suicide attacks (Alison 2003: 39). The suicide bombers were known as Black Tigers, and the female suicide bomber brigade were known colloquially as the Black Tigresses. Between 1987 and 2005, the Black Tigers had committed 200 attacks, aiming for high-ranking government officials and landmarks (*Al Jazeera* 2009; Van de Voorde 2005: 187).

Dhanu (Thenmozhi Rajaratnam) was the twenty-four-year-old assassin of Rajiv Gandhi on 21 May 1991 in Tamil Nadu, India. It was a suicide attack. Her father was one of Prabhakaran's advisors, who was 'honoured' by Prabhakaran 'posthumously with a "gold medal"' for Dhanu's actions (*India Today* 1992). Dhanu had a middle-school level of education (*India Today* 1992), which was unusual, as in 2012 only 17 per cent of Sri Lankan women attained this level of education (Department of Census and Statistics 2014: 18). Yet, this historical understanding – her strong family ties to the LTTE and relatively high level of education – fades to the background when Dhanu is discussed.

The gendering of her story is particularly apparent. According to Robert Pape (2005: 226):

> For Dhanu, a remarkably beautiful woman in her late twenties, motivation probably came directly from revenge: reportedly her home in Jaffna was looted by Indian soldiers, she was gang-raped, and her four brothers were killed.

While Pape discusses her membership and training in side-by-side discussion with the training of other Black Tigers/Tigresses, he discusses how Dhanu, in her last three weeks,

> took advantage of her new surroundings. With money and encouragement from the LTTE, she went to the market, the beach, and restaurants every day, enjoying many luxuries rarely found in the jungles of Jaffna. She bought dresses, jewellery, cosmetics, and even her first pair of glasses. In the last twenty days of her life, she took in six movies at a local cinema. (Pape 2005: 230)

Another source says she spent her last night watching a movie and eating ice cream (*Outlook* 2005).

While Mia Bloom (2005a) has attributed women's participation in suicide bombings to the shame of sexual violence, in the case of Dhanu, she argues,

> Allegations of Dhanu's rape have never been proven and sources within the Indian government assert that she was still a virgin at the time of her death. Although such sources have cause to lie, in my interviews with the Tamil Tigers, they too do not think she was actually raped. There have been questions raised about whether her mother might have been the victim of sexual abuse by the Indian Peacekeeping Forces (IPKF) when they intervened in the country in 1987–1990, but the main reason why Dhanu became a Tiger is that her brother was a well-known cadre who had died and she was carrying on the family tradition. (Bloom 2005b)

Yet there is still a gendered dimension: her father was posthumously honoured for her death; she was carrying out a family tradition; she was finding justice/revenge for the death of her brother. In her interviews with fourteen female LTTE members, she found that both political and personal oppression and suffering motivated the women to join (Alison 2003: 40–1). Thus, while Alison (2003: 43) does affirm that sexual violence was part of this suffering, a commitment to the political goals of the group as well as a desire for 'emancipation and increase[ed] life opportunities' was significant. Dhanu's sexuality is still one of innocence and purity – ice-cream eating, movie-watching, sweet femininity – which is in solid contrast to the previous profiles. In the well-received film *The Terrorist* by Santoush Sivan (1998), he memorialises the character based upon Dhanu as both pure and maternal. This is potentially where race enters the picture. While the Tamils were primarily minority Hindu, neo-Orientalism and the racialised structures of imperialism frame women in colonised territories as submissive to domineering men.

Aafia Siddiqui

Whereas the relationship of most people discussed in this chapter with terrorism is clear, there is no clarity when it comes to Aafia Siddiqui. Indeed, there is relatively little that is stable about Siddiqui and the narratives that surround her when it comes to her supposed involvement with al Qaeda (Gentry 2016a). Intersectionality provides one of the best ways of exploring this instability: gender, racialised religion, ethnicity and class all seem to play a part in the mystery of Aafia Siddiqui.

Siddiqui is a Pakistani woman who was educated at MIT and earned a PhD from Brandeis University in the 1990s. While completing her PhD, she married a Pakistani man, an anaesthesiologist at Brigham and Women's Hospital in Boston, and had two children. While she was pregnant with their third child, Siddiqui and her husband returned to Pakistan for a divorce in late 2002. In March 2003, John Ashcroft declared her one of the most wanted people in the US for her alleged support for al Qaeda, which included smuggling conflict diamonds and planning a major attack on the Eastern seaboard. Siddiqui and her children were missing between 2003 and 2008 – some believe she was held and tortured in Bagram during that time, and some believe she married 9/11 'mastermind' Khaled Sheik Mohammad's nephew and was further integrated into al Qaeda. She surfaced in 2008 in Ghazni, Afghanistan, supposedly to plan a suicide attack, and was returned (after a shooting episode) to the US to stand trial, but was never charged with nor found guilty of terrorism. Her youngest son is presumed dead, and her other two children live with her sister in Pakistan (Gentry 2016a). Siddiqui's mental stability is constantly questioned: whether this is owed to her 'radicalisation' and her rejection of the West or the mental illness she is diagnosed with while awaiting her trial in the US is unknown. Just as her narrative is never stable, Siddiqui is an unreliable witness within her own life.

As neo-Orientalism post-9/11 is dependent upon the 'new barbarism' thesis, Siddiqui's 'radicalisation' is linked to her prior family ties to a particular Islamic 'tribe'. Siddiqui's family were Deobandis, a form of political Islam that had supported the *mujahideen* in Afghanistan and then the Taliban (Scroggins 2012: 6); yet they were very well off, and sent all of their children to be educated in the United States. Siddiqui's ex-husband also claims that she was radicalised from the start of their marriage (Scroggins 2012: 24, 46, 70). He claims that Siddiqui had 'a more fiery character than he wished. "She was so pumped up about *jihad*"' (Walsh 2009). To a Pakistani journalist, he said, 'She got hysterical fits when she became angry and would physically attack me', and that 'he found her opinion toward *jihad* to be of an extreme nature that . . . made him uncomfortable' (*Voice of Balistan* 2012).

Divorce lends credibility to Siddiqui's guilt. In 2002, 'Aafia was a scorned and lonely creature, a divorced woman in Pakistan' (Scroggins 2012: 218). In order to explain her disappearance between 2003 and 2008, the audience is meant to believe that Siddiqui marries into one of the most politicised families in Pakistan after her divorce. Divorce coheres with some of the more gendered rationale for women's involvement in terrorism and political violence: that women become involved in terrorism when they have lost their social standing and respect in Islamic societies (Bloom 2005b: 31, 135; Pape 2005: 209). Thus, when the 'scorned' Siddiqui is introduced to Kalid Sheik Mohammad's nephew, she marries him and works with him on planning the Eastern seaboard attacks (Scroggins 2012: 245; Fisk 2010). Neo-Orientalism's assumptions about male domination are still used against her.

Even though she was sentenced to eighty-six years in prison, and is held in Carswell Federal Medical Center because she is unfit to be held in a general prison population, Siddiqui's mental illness is not an explanation of her actions – as it might be in the case of Breivik or Hasan. Instead, it is a by-product of what has happened to her in her life. There are some who argue that Siddiqui was never mentally well – as her former husband maintains – and that mental fragility was present before she left for Pakistan in 2002. But others argue that her mental illness is a result of her being held at Bagram from 2003 to 2008 and tortured by the US military (Walsh 2009). Indeed, it is believed that she was taken from Karachi in March 2003 by Pakistani agents who handed her over to the US and that they took her children in the process, accidentally killing her infant son (Ozment 2004). As a Muslim woman who has seemingly rejected the West and all it offers, the dominating neo-Orientalism framing of women cannot help researchers make sense of Siddiqui (Gentry 2016a).

The Lone Wolves: Anders Breivik and Major Nidal Hasan

Anders Breivik, a white supremacist, was solely responsible for the single largest security event in Norway since World War II on 22 July 2011. He exploded a car bomb in front of a government building in Oslo, killing eight people, and committed a massacre of teenage summer campers, killing sixty-nine victims, of whom thirty-three were under eighteen years old. He wounded another 319. Even in relation to the numerous lone-gunman attacks in the US, this is monumental: Breivik killed and wounded 396 people in one day. He was sentenced to twenty-one years in prison, with the possibility of five-year extensions if he continues to pose a threat to society. Before his spree, he sent a 1,500-page manifesto to a lengthy list of people, claiming that he wanted to protect Norwegian culture from a 'Muslim invasion' (Knausegaard 2015). The attack was purely for publicity:

> 'I was wondering how many people I needed to kill to be read,' he said after he had committed his acts of violence in 2011. He had calculated that he had to kill a dozen people to be noticed. (Seierstad 2016)

His reasoning was a mix of white supremacist Christianity and Odinism (pre-Christian Norse pagan religion), and he ultimately aimed to create the 'Nordic State' (Seierstad 2016).

Norway has never shied away from casting Breivik as a lone wolf terrorist, but this has also led to some existential questioning about Norwegian society and how it fits into the contested notion of 'Europe' as either tolerant and therefore less white, or as a white Christian homeland of sorts (Žižek 2017). Beyond this tension, he becomes a touchstone for another tension: how he not only represents a Norway that would rather be deflected – of intolerance and rigid, right-wing Christianity (quasi- in his mix of Norwegian mythology and Christianity), and of what it means to be a tolerant society and open to immigration and Islam (BBC 2012). Thus, Breivik becomes a way of discussing epistemic ordering of the West over the rest and the need to protect this identity.

Looking at Breivik intersectionally illuminates not just the way in which race and masculinity come together in the growing awareness of alt-right, white nationalism in the US and Europe, but also the tension between, and the complexity of, mental illness and political violence. Breivik was described as deeply troubled as a young child, and

> the court deliberated over whether Breivik was mentally ill and in need of treatment or whether he was a cold-blooded, rational mass killer. Some of the psychiatrists who evaluated Breivik diagnosed him as having narcissistic and antisocial personality disorder. (An earlier group of doctors said he suffered from schizophrenia.) In August 2012, the court sided with the second group and ruled that because he was not psychotic and had understood what he was doing, he was legally accountable for his actions. (Seierstad 2016)

As Breivik was declared competent enough to stand trial, he often falls within the designation of a 'lone wolf'. Lone wolf is a concept related to the new terrorism thesis, in which a terrorist is influenced by social context and terrorist ideology, but who also tend to invent their own ideology (Berntzen and Sandberg 2014). Yet there is also evidence to suggest significant psychological disturbances and mental illnesses amongst those labelled as lone wolves (Spaaij 2010).

Breivik sits at an uncomfortable junction. While he may have been declared legally sane, there is still a significant amount of discussion about his mental illness in the *Telegraph* (2011), the *Guardian* (Beaumont 2012; Orr 2011) and *Psychology Today* (Diamond 2012). White men who commit mass-casualty shootings, like those that are endemic in the United States, are often described as mentally ill, and any link with a political motivation is downplayed and/or dismissed.

However, if a man of colour commits a mass-casualty shooting, he is often painted as a terrorist, whether there are political motivations or not, which denies that mental illness may play any role. This is true of one prominent shooter in the US: Major Nidal Hasan.

On 5 November 2009, Major Hasan entered Fort Hood's Soldier Readiness Processing Centre, shouted 'Allau Akbar' and shot 200 bullets from his high-powered handgun. He harmed forty-five people and killed thirteen. He was sentenced to death in 2013 (Kenber 2013). Hasan was a psychiatrist for the army, and during his time at Fort Hood, he gave a rambling, slightly incoherent talk on the psychic problem facing Muslims serving in the military who are required to kill other Muslims in Iraq and Afghanistan (Hasan 2015). This sparked some concerns from his superiors, which joined 'poor ratings from supervisors and medical school faculty, with documents suggesting military officials overlooked signs he was not fit to be an army doctor' (BBC 2010). Additionally,

> Dr Thomas Grieger, who was training director at the centre while Major Hasan was an intern there, told AP that he had had 'difficulties' that required counselling and extra supervision.
> And in 2007 Major Hasan was cited for unprofessional behaviour, including inappropriately discussing religion. One instructor, Lt Col Donald Lundy, thought Major Hasan risked developing a psychosis, the Associated Press reported. (BBC 2010)

In the literature on Hasan, the terrorism charges lead, even though the evidence suggests mental illness. Hasan was never brought up on terrorism charges, yet an entire panel led and convened by scholars at West Point's Combating Terrorism Centre at the February 2010 International Studies Association Annual Conference seemed dedicated to providing rationale for Hasan as a terrorist. Additionally, debates on whether his actions constituted terrorism appeared in the pages of *Vanity Fair* (Myers 2009), ABC News (Ferran and Meek 2018), *The Washington Post* (Manning 2013) and CNN (Bergen 2017). Several years later, after another attack at Fort Hood in 2014, *The New York Times* deliberated the question once again, engaging fully in the subjectivity of the term:

> The disconnect between how the Army mentioned the word terrorism in relation to one shooting and avoided it in the other underscores the still-unresolved debate over how to define the 2009 shooting and whether it should be considered an act of terror, a debate the attack last week has

rekindled. When President Obama returns to Fort Hood on Wednesday for a memorial service, victims of the 2009 shooting will be listening closely.

'This would be the perfect opportunity to acknowledge that 2009 was terrorism,' said Neal M. Sher, a lawyer representing dozens of victims of the 2009 attack and their relatives in a lawsuit accusing federal and Pentagon officials of providing them with inferior treatment. 'When you juxtapose the 2009 attack by Hasan with what happened this past week, it crystallises the fact that Hasan committed an act of terror.' (Fernandez and Blinder 2014)

While there might be some hints of classism – Hasan was well edu-cated, whereas Breivik has only enrolled at the University of Oslo since his imprisonment (Pickles 2018) – it is *not insignificant* that both men of colour were military personnel, both were mentally ill and both had their violence cast or aligned with a political grievance. Militarised masculinity – even if Breivik never served, he has cast himself in a highly militaristic light – is linked with a level of toxicity that leads to domestic and sexual violence (Goodmark 2015; Baaz and Stern 2009; Myrttinen 2003).

Conclusion

Bringing together these disparate profiles of actors who participated in violent conflict in various locations, with varying ideologies, from multiple decades shows how similar rhetoric is relied upon over and over again. This reliance creates strange bedfellows, bringing together actors in similar but unexpected ways. The most striking is the connec-tion between sexualisation and radicalisation. A more expected aspect is the question of mental health as a motivation for acting. Additionally, and somewhat expected, there is the romanticising of particular figures as popular heroes, along the lines of Robin Hood.

The connection between sexualisation and radicalisation happens in two ways. The first is the connection, as noted, between Andreas Baader and the 9/11 hijackers. Using hypersexuality is one way of minimis-ing access to logic and rationality. Puar and Rai (2002) use Foucault to explain how perverse sexuality and monstrousness were part of Victo-rian culture, leading us to see particular actors in discrediting ways. In their article on the aftermath of 9/11, they pick up on the language that sexualises the 9/11 hijackers *and* the counter-terrorist response to it. For example,

Posters that appeared in midtown Manhattan only days after the attacks show a turbaned caricature of bin Laden being anally penetrated by the Empire State Building. The legend beneath reads, 'The Empire Strikes Back' or 'So you like skyscrapers, huh, bitch?' Or think of the Web site where, with a series of weapons at your disposal, you can torture Osama bin Laden to death, the last torture being sodomy; or another Web site that shows two pictures, one of bin Laden with a beard, and the other without – and the photo of him shaven turns out to be O. J. Simpson. What these representations show, we believe, is that queerness as sexual deviancy is tied to the monstrous figure of the terrorist as a way to otherise and quarantine subjects classified as 'terrorists', but also to normalise and discipline a population through these very monstrous figures. (Puar and Rai 2002: 126)

Therefore, while the queer sexualisation of the 9/11 hijackers is well explored, Baader's sexual deviancy (or the construction of it) is far less explored. Other than to discredit him, what other reason would be needed for discussing his skin-tight velvet trousers or his equation of 'fucking and shooting' (Hoffman 2006: 246)? Real men do not wear velvet, nor do rational men have an erotic relationship with violence.

The connection between Dohrn and Dhanu's radicalisation and sexualisation works differently when intersected with race. Dohrn's command of her sexuality works against her, making her a threatening figure, especially in a country that is in the throes of the sexual revolution. It makes her seem *more* radical, as her sexuality is both angry and confrontational. Dhanu, on the other hand, is a brown woman, and brown women are constructed as submissive and in need of saving (Spivak 1988). Any implication of rape solidifies this submissiveness, and highlights the abusiveness of brown men. Therefore, Dhanu's decision or participation in her own suicide bombing is minimised and explored only in tension with implicit abuse. This is secured when her father, not Dhanu, is posthumously awarded a medal for *her death*.

An implication of mental ill health is almost a given. Terrorism is *terror*ism precisely because the scale and surprising nature of the violence is often hard for the majority of people to understand. In searching for reasons and explanations, the suggestion that terrorists must be unwell is a facile answer. What makes Breivik's violence shocking is both the location (Norway had not seen that level of violence since World War II) and his skin colour; what makes Hasan's violence shocking is both the location – the largest US Army base – and his position as a military doctor, but clearly not his skin colour. With Siddiqui, the question of mental health is settled (she is serving her time at a medical facility), but the reasons behind her ill health are not. It could be a result of her having been tortured; alternatively, a US government-conducted psychological evaluation of her at Carswell in 2009 suggests she has 'Delusional Disorder of the Paranoid type', in which elements of her beliefs are consistent with 'radical political ideology' while others are indicative of deeper instability (Kucharski 2009).

Finally, the last image is one that I thought had disappeared with the Marxist-Leninst groups of the 1960s. Because these groups were conceived of as having (slightly more) legitimacy, the actors were seen as popular heroes. This has not disappeared, but it has stayed stuck to Marxist-Leninist actors such as Khaled and Mujica. Both of them are romanticised, in a way that spurs 'crushes' but not in a way that creates concern over deviant sexuality. This is seen when Khaled is portrayed as a delicate Audrey Hepburn, whereas Mujica is a dashing Robin Hood. The legacies of both Khaled and Mujica are very much tied to class and class struggles – on getting one over on the powers that be, seeing these powers not as legitimate but as exploitative and harmful. This continues to be an interesting twist within terrorism.

References

Al-Jazeera (2009), 'The History of the Tamil Tigers', 28 April, <https://www .aljazeera.com/focus/2008/11/2008112019115851343.html> (last accessed 23 November 2018).

Åhäll, Linda (2012), 'Motherhood, Myth, and Gendered Agency in Political Violence', *International Feminist Journal of Politics*, 14(1): 103–20.

Akram, Susan Musarrat (2000), 'Orientalism Revisited in Asylum and Refugee Claims', *International Journal of Refugee Law*, 12(1): 7–40.

Alison, Miranda (2003), 'Cogs in the Wheel? Women in the Liberation Tigers of Tamil Eelam', *Civil Wars*, 6(4): 37–54.

Aslam, Maleeha (2012), *Gender-Based Explosions: The Nexus between Muslim Masculinities, Jihadist Islamism and Terrorism* (Tokyo: United Nations University Press).

Auchter, Jessica (2012), 'Gendering Terror: Discourses of Terrorism and Writing Woman-as-Agent', *International Feminist Journal of Politics*, 14(1): 121–39.

Aust, Stefan (1987), The Baader-Meinhof Group: The Inside Story of a Phenomenon (London: Bodley Head).Aust, Stefan (2008), *The Baader-Meinhof Complex* (London: Bodley Head).

Ayers, Bill (2002), *Fugitive Days: Memoirs of an Anti-War Activist* (Boston: Beacon Press).

Baaz, Maria Eriksson, and Maria Stern (2009), 'Why Do Soldiers Rape? Masculinity, Violence, and Sexuality in the Armed Forces in the Congo (DRC)', *International Studies Quarterly*, 53(2): 495–518.

Barkawi, Tarak (2010), 'Empire and Order in International Relations and Security Studies', in Bob Denemark (ed.), *The International Studies Encyclopedia* (Hoboken, NJ: Blackwell), pp. 1360–79.

Barkawi, Tarak, and Mark Laffey (2006), 'The Post-colonial Moment in Security Studies', *Review of International Studies*, 32(2): 329–52.

Bartlett, Evan (2014), 'Eight Reasons Why We'll Miss José Mujica, Uruguay's Maverick President', <https://www.indy100.com/article/8-reasons-why-well-miss-jose-mujica-uruguays-maverick-president--e1t_MupEpl> (last accessed 23 November 2018).

BBC (2010), 'Profile: Major Nidal Malik Hasan', 12 October, <https://www.bbc.co.uk/news/world-us-canada-11525580> (last accessed 23 November 2018).

BBC (2012), 'Norway Debates Immigration in Wake of Breivik Killings', 22 January, <https://www.bbc.co.uk/news/world-europe-16636885> (last accessed 23 November 2018).

BBC (2018), 'World's "Poorest" Ex-President Mujica Turns Down Pension', 15 August, <https://www.bbc.co.uk/news/world-latin-america-45195188> (last accessed 23 November 2018).

Beaumont, Peter (2012), 'Anders Breivik and the Trouble with Defining Sanity', The Guardian, 18 June, <https://www.theguardian.com/commentisfree/2012/jun/18/anders-breivik-defining-sanity> (last accessed 23 November 2018).

Belfast Telegraph (2009), '"I'd Have Joined the IRA in a Heartbeat, Says Principal of St Andrews University', 16 April, <https://www.belfasttelegraph.co.uk/news/id-have-joined-the-ira-in-a-heartbeat-says-principal-of-st-andrews-university-28475719.html> (last accessed 23 November 2018).

Bergen, Peter (2017), 'A Pattern in Terror – Second Generation, Homegrown', CNN, 24 May, <https://edition.cnn.com/2017/05/24/opinions/homegrown-terrorism-opinion-bergen/index.html> (last accessed 23 November 2018).

Bergesen, Albert J., and Omar Lizardo (2004), 'International Terrorism and the World-System', Sociological Theory, 22(1): 38–52.

Berntzen, Lars Erik, and Sveinung Sandberg (2014), 'The Collective Nature of Lone Wolf Terrorism: Anders Behring Breivik and the Anti-Islamic Social Movement', Terrorism and Political Violence, 26(5): 759–79.

Bloom, Mia (2005a), 'The Truth about Dhanu', The New York Review of Books, 20 October, <https://www.nybooks.com/articles/2005/10/20/the-truth-about-dhanu/> (last accessed 23 November 2018).

Bloom, Mia (2005b), Dying to Kill: The Allure of Suicide Terror (New York: Columbia University Press).

Blomberg, S. Brock, and Gregory D. Hess (2005), The Lexus and the Olive Branch: Globalization, Democratisation, and Terrorism, November 2005, <https://ssrn.com/abstract=904024> (last accessed 23 November 2005).

Collier, Peter, and David Horowitz (1996), Destructive Generation: Second Thoughts About the Sixties (New York: Simon and Schuster).

Connell, Robert W., and James W. Messerschmidt (2005), 'Hegemonic Masculinity: Rethinking the Concept', Gender and Society, 19(6): 829–59.

Cooper, H. A. A. (1979), 'Women as Terrorist', in Freda Adler and Rita James Simon (eds), The Criminology of Deviant Women (Boston: Houghton Mifflin).

Crelinsten, Ronald (2011), Counterterrorism (London: Polity Press).

Culler, Jonathan (1982), On Deconstruction: Theory and Criticism after Structuralism (Ithaca, NY: Cornell University Press).

Department of Census and Statistics (2014), *The Sri Lankan Woman: Partner in Progress*, <http://www.statistics.gov.lk/Gender%20Statistics/Publications/The%20Sri%20 Lankan%20Woman.pdf> (last accessed 23 November 2018).

Diamond, Stephen A. (2012), 'The Breivik Verdict: Forensic Commentary', *Psychology Today*, 26 August, <https://www.psychologytoday.com/gb/blog/evil-deeds/201208/ the-breivik-verdict-forensic-commentary> (last accessed 23 November 2018).

Duggan, Lisa (2003), *The Twilight of Equality?* (Boston: Beacon Press).

Duriesmith, David (2017), *Masculinity and New War: The Gendered Dynamics of Continued Armed Conflict* (Abingdon: Routledge).

Dwyer, Claire, Bindi Shah and Gurchathen Sanghera (2008), '"From Cricket Lover to Terror Suspect" – Challenging Representations of Young British Muslim Men', *Gender, Place, and Culture*, 15(2): 117–36.

Fairbanks, Eve (2015), 'José Mujica Was Every Liberal's Dream President. He Was Too Good to Be True', *The New Republic*, 6 February, <https://newrepublic.com/ article/120912/uruguays-jose-mujica-was-liberals-dream-too-good-be-true> (last accessed 23 November 2018).

Fernandez, Manny, and Alan Blinder (2014), 'At Ford Hood, Wrestling with Label of Terrorism', *The New York Times*, 8 April, <https://www.nytimes. com/2014/04/09/us/at-fort-hood-wrestling-with-label-of-terrorism.html> (last accessed 23 November 2018).

Ferran, Lee, and James Gordon Meek (2018), 'US Army Officer-Turned-Terrorist Thought Fort Hood Attack Would Save Mother's Soul, Letters Show', *ABC News*, 18 October, <https://abcnews.go.com/US/us-army-officer-turned-terrorist-thought-attack-save/story?id=58585738> (last accessed 23 November 2018).

Fisk, Robert (2010), 'The Mysterious Case of the Grey Lady of Bagram', *The Independent*, 19 March, <https://www.independent.co.uk/voices/commentators/ fisk/robert-fisk-the-mysterious-case-of-the-grey-lady-of-bagram-1923808.html> (last accessed November 2018).

Flint, Colin, and Steven M. Radil (2009), 'Terrorism and Counterterrorism: Situating al-Qaeda and the Global War on Terror within Geopolitical Trends and Structures', *Eurasian Geography and Economics*, 50(2): 150–71.

Flint, Colin, and Peter J. Taylor (2007), *Political Geography: World-Economy, Nation-State, and Locality* (London: Pearson Education).

Ganor, Boaz (2005), *The Counter-Terrorism Puzzle: A Guide for Decision Makers* (London: Transaction).

Gentry, Caron E. (2004), 'The Relationship between New Social Movement Theory and Terrorism Studies: The Role of Leadership, Membership, Ideology and Gender', *Terrorism and Political Violence*, 16(2): 274–93.

Gentry, Caron E. (2011a), 'The Committed Revolutionary: Reflections on a Conversation with Leila Khaled', in Laura Sjoberg and Caron E. Gentry (eds), *Women, Gender, and Terrorism* (Athens: University of Georgia Press), pp. 120–30.

Gentry, Caron E. (2015), 'Anxiety and the Creation of the Scapegoated Other', *Critical Studies on Security*, 3(2): 133–46.

Gentry, Caron E. (2016a), 'The Mysterious Case of Aafia Siddiqui: Gothic Intertextual Analysis of neo-Orientalist Narratives', *Millennium*, 45(1): 3–24.

Gentry, Caron E., and Laura Sjoberg (2015), *Beyond Mothers, Monsters, Whores: Rethinking Women's Violence in Global Politics* (London: Zed Books).

Gentry, Caron E., and Kathryn Whitworth (2011), 'The Discourse of Desperation: The Intersections of Neo-Orientalism, Gender, and Islam in the Chechen Struggle', *Critical Studies on Terrorism*, 4(2): 145–61.

Githens-Mazer, Jonathan, and Robert Lambert (2010), 'Why Conventional Wisdom on Radicalisation Fails: The Persistence Of A Failed Discourse', *International Affairs*, 86(4): 889–901.

Gitlin, Todd (1993), *The Sixties: Years of Hope, Days of Rage* (New York: Bantam Books).

Goodmark, Leigh (2015), 'Hands Up at Home: Militarised Masculinity and Police Officers Who Commit Intimate Partner Abuse', *Brigham Young Law Review*, 5: 1183–1246.

Gurr, Ted Robert (1970), *Why Men Rebel* (Princeton: Princeton University Press).

Hansen, Lene (2013), *Security as Practice: Discourse Analysis and the Bosnian War* (Abingdon: Routledge).

Hasan, Maj. Nidal (2015), 'The Koranic View of the World as It Relates to Muslims in the US Military', <https://unconstrainedanalytics.org/wp-content/uploads/2015/05/nidal-hasan-powerpoint.pdf> (last accessed 23 November 2018).

Heath-Kelly, Charlotte (2012), 'Reinventing Prevention or Exposing the Gap? False Positives in UK Terrorism Governance and the Quest for Pre-Emption', *Critical Studies on Terrorism*, 5(1): 69–87.

Henshaw, Alexis Leanna (2016), *Why Women Rebel: Understanding Women's Participation in Armed Rebel Groups* (Abingdon: Routledge).

Hoffman, Bruce (2006), *Inside Terrorism* (New York: Columbia University Press).

Horton, Helena (2018), '"War Zone" Hospitals, "No-Go" Areas and "Lousy" Locations: What Donald Trump Has Said about Britain', *The Telegraph*, 12 July, <https://www.telegraph.co.uk/news/2018/07/11/war-zone-hospitals-no-go-areas-lousy-locations-donald-trump/> (last accessed 23 November 2018).

India Today (1992), 'Rajiv Gandhi Assassination: Dhanu, the First-Ever Human Bomb in Sri Lanka's History', 31 May, <https://www.indiatoday.in/magazine/special-report/story/19920531-rajiv-gandhi-assassination-dhanu-the-first-ever-human-bomb-in-sri-lankas-history-766314-2013-06-14> (last accessed 23 November 2018).

Jacobs, Ron (1997), *The Way the Wind Blew: A History of the Weather Underground* (New York: Verso Books).

Kapoor, Ilan (2015), 'The Queer Third World', *Third World Quarterly*, 36(9): 1611–28.

Kenber, Billy (2013), 'Nidal Hasan Sentenced to Death for Fort Hood Shooting Rampage', *The Washington Post*, 28 August, <https://www.washingtonpost.com/world/national-security/nidal-hasan-sentenced-to-death-for-fort-hood-shooting-rampage/2013/08/28/aad28de2-0ffa-11e3-bdf6-e4fc677d94a1_story.html?utm_term=.b4d0fdb96c96> (last accessed 23 November 2018).

Kengor, Paul (2017), 'Let's Not Forget Bernardine Dohrn, Bill Ayers, and the Four-Finger Salute', *The Spectator*, 21 November, <https://spectator.org/charles-manson-and-the-weather-underground/> (last accessed 23 November 2018).

Khaled, Leila (1973), *My People Shall Live: The Autobiography of a Revolutionary* (London: Hodder and Stoughton).

Kimmel, Michael S. (2003), 'Globalisation and Its Mal(e) Contents: The Gendered, Moral, and Political Economy of Terrorism', *International Sociology*, 18(3): 603–20.

Kimmel, Michael, and Lisa Wade (2018), 'Ask a Feminist: Michael Kimmel and Lisa Wade Discuss Toxic Masculinity', *Signs: Journal of Women in Culture and Society*, 44(1): 233–54.

Knausegaard, Karl Ove (2016), 'Inside the Warped Mind of a Mass Killer', *The Telegraph*, 22 July, <https://www.telegraph.co.uk/news/2016/07/22/anders-breivik-inside-the-warped-mind-of-a-mass-killer/> (last accessed 23 November 2018).

Kolbert, Elizabeth (2001), 'The Prisoner', *The New Yorker*, 16 July, <https://www.newyorker.com/magazine/2001/07/16/the-prisoner-3> (last accessed 23 November 2018).

Krishna, Sankaran (1993), 'The Importance of Being Ironic: A Post-Colonial View on Critical International Relations Theory', *Alternatives*, 18(3): 385–417.

Kucharski, L. Thomas (2009), 'Forensic Psychological Evaluation of Aafia Siddiqui', Defendant Exhibit DX 1, Aafia Siddiqui Federal Trial 2009, <http://intelfiles.egoplex.com/2009-07-01-Siddiqui-psych-report.pdf> (last accessed 23 November 2018).

Levy, Gideon (2018), 'This Biography Makes It Clear: The Founder of the Popular Front for the Liberation of Palestine Was Right', *Haaretz*, 15 April, <https://www.haaretz.com/middle-east-news/palestinians/.premium-biography-makes-it-clear-this-palestinian-leftist-leader-was-right-1.5994244> (last accessed 23 November 2018).

Loken, Meredith, and Anna Zelenz (2018), 'Explaining Extremism: Western Women in Daesh', *European Journal of International Security*, 3(1): 45–68.

MacDonald, Eileen (1991), *Shoot the Women First* (Washington, DC: Fourth Estate).

Mair, Kimberly (2013), 'Itinerant Memory Places: The Baader-Meinhof-Wagen', in Dariusz Gafijczuk and Derek Sawyer (eds), *The Inhabited Ruins of Central Europe* (New York: Springer Publishing), pp. 79–101.

Manning, Shawn (2013), 'The Fort Hood Attack Was Terrorism. The Army Should Call It That', *The Washington Post*, 7 August, <https://www.washingtonpost.com/opinions/the-fort-hood-attack-was-terrorism-the-army-should-call-it-that/2013/08/07/cfe62210-feb1-11e2-bd97-676ec24f1f3f_story.html?utm_term=.b3a44287e808> (last accessed 23 November 2018).

Milliken, Jennifer (1999), 'The Study of Discourse in International Relations: A Critique of Research and Methods', *European Journal of International Relations*, 5(2): 225–54.

Moran, Leslie (2000), 'Homophobic Violence: The Hidden Injuries of Class', in Sally Munt (ed.), *Cultural Studies and the Working Class: Subject to Change* (London: Continuum), pp. 206–18.

Morgan, Robin (1989), *The Demon Lover: The Roots of Terrorism* (New York: Washington Square Press).

Myers, Dee Dee (2009), 'Is Nidal Hasan a Terrorist or Not?', *Vanity Fair*, <https://www.vanityfair.com/news/2009/11/is-nidal-hasan-a-terrorist-or-not> (last accessed 23 November 2018).

Myrttinen, Henri (2003), 'Disarming Masculinities', *Disarmament Forum*, 4(1): 37–46.

Nader, Laura (1989), 'Orientalism, Occidentalism, and the Control of Women', *Cultural Dynamics*, 2(3): 323–55.

Nayak, Meghana (2006), 'Orientalism and "Saving" US State Identity after 9/11', *International Feminist Journal of Politics*, 8(1): 42–61.

Orr, Deborah (2011), 'Anders Behring Breivik's Not a Terrorist, He's a Mass-Murderer', *The Guardian*, 27 July, <https://www.theguardian.com/world/2011/jul/27/breivik-not-terrorist-insane-murderer> (last accessed 23 November 2018).

Outlook (2005), 'Lady with the Poison Flowers', 25 August, <https://www.outlookindia.com/magazine/story/lady-with-the-poison-flowers/228400> (last accessed 23 November 2018).

Pape, Robert A. (2005), *Dying to Win: The Strategic Logic of Suicide Terrorism* (New York: Penguin).

Pateman, Carole (1980), '"The Disorder of Women:" Women, Love, and the Sense of Justice', *Ethics*, 91(1): 20–34.

Peteet, Julie (1991), *Gender in Crisis: Women in the Palestinian Resistance Movement* (New York: Columbia University Press).

Pickles, Matt (2018), 'Should a University Teach a Killer?', BBC, 2 October, <https://www.bbc.co.uk/news/business-45705939> (last accessed 23 November 2018).

Post, Jerrold M. (1990), 'Terrorist Psycho-Logic: Terrorist Behaviour as a Product of Psychological Forces', in Walter Reich (ed.), *The Origins of Terrorism: Psychologies, Ideologies, Theologies, States of Mind* (Washington, DC: Woodrow Wilson Press), pp. 25–42.

Puar, Jasbir K. (2017), *Terrorist Assemblages: Homonationalism in Queer Times* (Durham, NC: Duke University Press).

Puar, Jasbir K., and Amit Rai (2002), 'Monster, Terrorist, Fag: The War on Terrorism and the Production of Docile Patriots', *Social Text*, 20(3): 117–48.

Richardson, Louise (2006), *What Terrorists Want: Understanding the Enemy, Containing the Threat* (New York: Random House).

Richter-Montpetit, Melanie (2014), 'Beyond the Erotics of Orientalism: Lawfare, Torture and the Racial–Sexual Grammars of Legitimate Suffering', *Security Dialogue*, 45(1): 43–62.

Said, Edward (1978), *Orientalism* (New York: Pantheon Books).

Schmidle, Nicholas (2011), 'Getting Bin Laden', *The New Yorker*, 8 August, <https://www.newyorker.com/magazine/2011/08/08/getting-bin-laden> (last accessed 21 November 2018).

Scroggins, Deborah (2012), *Wanted Women: Faith, Lies, and the War on Terror: The Lives of Ayann Ali Hirsi and Aafia Siddiqui* (New York: Harper Perennial).

Sculos, Bryant A. (2017), 'Who's Afraid of Toxic Masculinity?', *Class, Race, and Corporate Power*, 5(3) (online).

Seierstad, Asne (2016), 'Is Norwegian Mass Murderer Anders Breivik Still a Threat to Europe', *Newsweek*, 13 April, <https://www.newsweek.com/anders-breivik-neo-nazi-suing-norway-asne-seierstad-447247> (last accessed 23 November 2018).

Sentas, Vicki (2006), 'Counterterrorism Policing: Investing in the Racial State', *ACRAWSA E-Journal*, 2(1): 1–16.

Sivan, Santoush (1998), *The Terrorist*, film.

Shepherd, Laura J. (2006), 'Veiled References: Constructions of Gender in the Bush Administration Discourse on the Attacks on Afghanistan Post-9/11', *International Journal of Feminist Politics*, 8(1): 19–41.

Sjoberg, Laura, and Caron E. Gentry (2007), *Mothers, Monsters, Whores: Women's Violence in Global Politics* (London: Zed Books).

Sjoberg, Laura, and Caron E. Gentry (2008a), 'Profiling Terror: Gendering the Strategic Logic of Suicide Terror and Other Narratives', *Austrian Journal of Political Science*, 2: 181–96.

Sjoberg, Laura, and Caron E. Gentry (2008b), 'Reduced to Bad Sex: Narratives of Violent Women from the Bible to the War on Terror', *International Relations*, 22(1): 5–23.

Spaaij, Ramón (2010), 'The Enigma of Lone Wolf Terrorism: An Assessment', *Studies in Conflict and Terrorism*, 33(9): 854–70.

Spivak, Gayatri Chakravorty (1988), 'Can the Subaltern Speak?', in Cary Nelson and Larry Grossberg (eds), *Marxism and the Interpretation of Culture* (Urbana: University of Illinois Press), pp. 271–313.

Sylvester, Christine (2010), 'Tensions in Feminist Security Studies', *Security Dialogue*, 41(6): 607–14.

Sylvester, Christine (2013), 'Experiencing War: A Challenge for International Relations', *Cambridge Review of International Affairs*, 26(4): 669–74.

Telegraph (2011), 'Anders Behring Breivik Still Feels No Remorse', 12 December, <https://www.telegraph.co.uk/news/2016/07/22/anders-breivik-inside-the-warped-mind-of-a-mass-killer/> (last accessed 23 November 2018).

Telesur (2016), 'Uruguay's Tupamaro Prison Break Was Largest, Coolest in History', 6 September, <https://www.telesurenglish.net/news/Uruguays-Tupamaro-Prison-Break-Was-Largest-Coolest-in-History-20160906-0037.html> (last accessed 23 November 2018).

Thayer, Bradley A., and Valerie M. Hudson (2010), 'Sex and the *Shaheed*: Insights from the Life Sciences on Islamic Suicide Terrorism', *International Security*, 34(4): 37–62.

Third, Amanda (2010), 'Imprisonment and Excessive Femininity: Reading Ulrike Meinhof's Brain', *Parallax*, 16(4): 83–100.

Tickner, J. Ann (1992), *Gender in International Relations* (New York: Columbia University Press).

Tremlett, Giles (2014), 'José Mujica: Is This the World's Most Radical President?' *The Guardian*, 18 September, <https://www.theguardian.com/world/2014/sep/18/-sp-is-this-worlds-most-radical-president-uruguay-jose-mujica> (last accessed 23 November 2018).

Van de Voorde, Cecile (2005), 'Sri Lankan Terrorism: Assessing and Responding to the Threat of the Liberation Tigers of Tamil Eelam (LTTE)', *Police Practice and Research*, 6(2): 181–99.

Viner, Katherine (2001), '"I Made the Ring from a Bullet and the Pin of a Hand Grenade'", *The Guardian*, 26 January, <https://www.theguardian.com/world/2001/jan/26/israel> (last accessed 23 November 2018).

Voice of Baltistan (2012), 'Dr Aafia Siddiqui's Husband Breaks His Silence after Six Years', <http://baltistani.com/dr-aafia-siddiquis-husband-breaks-his-silence-after-six-years/> (last accessed 16 November 2012).

Walsh, Declan (2009), 'The Mystery of Dr Aafia Siddiqui', *The Guardian*, 23 November 23, <http://www.theguardian.com/world/2009/nov/24/aafia-siddiqui-al-qaida> (last accessed 23 November 2018).

Weber, Cynthia (2002), '"Flying Planes Can Be Dangerous'", *Millennium*, 31(1): 129–47.

Weber, Cynthia (2014), 'From Queer to Queer IR', *International Studies Review*, 16(4): 596–601.

Weber, Cynthia (2016), *Queer International Relations: Sovereignty, Sexuality, and the Will to Knowledge* (New York: Oxford University Press).

White, Louise (1990), 'Separating the Men from the Boys: Constructions of Gender, Sexuality, and Terrorism in Central Kenya, 1939–1959', *The International Journal of African Historical Studies*, 23(1): 1–25.

Yeğenoğlu, Meyda (1998), *Colonial Fantasies: Towards a Feminist Reading of Orientalism* (Cambridge: Cambridge University Press).

Žižek, Slavoj (2017), 'There's a Dangerous and Popular Fashion in Europe to be Anti-Semitic and Pro-Zionist at the Same Time', *Independent*, 27 October, <https://www.independent.co.uk/voices/antisemitic-zionist-jewish-identity-muslim-islamophobia-immigration-migrants-racism-a8022726.html> (last accessed 23 November 2018).

CHAPTER 4

Ir/rationality: Radicalisation, 'Black Extremism' and Prevent Tragedies

In the seminal text on Critical Terrorism Studies, the editors of the volume state first that 'there are significant weaknesses and problems in current research modes to justify a new approach'; and second, that this 'necessitates the articulation of a new set of ontological, epistemological, methodological, and research commitments that in combination constitute a new analytical approach to the study of political terrorism' (Jackson et al. 2009: 4–5). Jackson particularly has challenged how knowledge has been arrived at as well as conceived within orthodox Terrorism Studies (Jackson 2012). More specifically, CTS is wary of orthodox Terrorism Studies' 'politica[l] bia[s]', which 'performs an ideological function in support of Western states' (Heath-Kelly 2010: 236). The work on

> CTS uncovers state-centrism, deep attachments to the rational-actor model of the subject, and Eurocentric attitudes that are prejudicial towards religion (treating it as less rational and more prone to violence), which have been drawn from the heritage of Western social science. (Heath-Kelly 2010: 242)

Thus, this ontological, epistemological and methodological challenge very much considers social scientific approaches that often dominate North American IR and have come to strongly influence, if not dominate, orthodox Terrorism Studies as well (Rapheal 2009: 50). With them they bring the not-so-neutral concept of rationality. CTS aims are seemingly at odds with 'rationality', a deeply loaded concept tied to gendered and racialised structures stemming from the Western Enlightenment (see also Heath-Kelly 2010: 239).

Imagine my surprise, then, when, attending a recent Critical Terrorism Studies conference, I heard several papers that called for a reclamation of 'rationality' within Critical Terrorism Studies, declaring that this would help us with CTS's stated objectives. While one recent key text looks at a Weberian critique of rationality[1] as essential to a Frankfurtian route to emancipation (Lindhal 2018), it fails to grapple with the discursive structuration of rationality and how embedded it is in gendered and colonial practices. Thus, like previous chapters, it is well and good to critique power structures and hierarchies, but if we cannot articulate what is behind or at the root of the power structures and hierarchies – like gender, race and heteronormativity – then we are bound to repeat the same mistakes as before.

Therefore, the central theme of this chapter is to drill more deeply into rationality as a social construct deriving its sense of meaning from the Western Enlightenment and therefore related to liberalism and modernity (Smith 2012: 61). Rationality stems from a strict duality – Cartesian duality – between the material body, aligned with nature, and the rational, immaterial thinking mind (Smith 2012: 50). It assumes that humans, most especially Western men, have the capacity to sublimate bodily passions and discipline the mind to such an extent that full rationality can be achieved (Elshtain 1981: 24). This leads to another dualism, where rationality, thinking and progressiveness become intrinsic to Western masculinities, leaving irrationality, non-thinkingness and atavism to non-Western and non-masculine individuals. While *how* rationality is conceived has shifted over time (see Toulmin 1982), philosophers note that an emphasis on or a desire for complete rationality is deeply problematic because it denies how humans relate to one another and how they make decisions (Nussbaum 2003; Toulmin 2001). Therefore, Terrorism Studies' expectation of rationality in all people is unachievable, failing to see complexity in the situation and people under study.

That CTS scholars want to invite rationality into the study of CTS means that the stated critiques of power structures and discourse in the earlier CTS scholarship (Jackson et al. 2009) did not go deep enough in exploring what those power structures relied upon and what those discourses pointed to: race, gender, class, heteronormativity, etc. While the founding texts of CTS discuss neo-Orientalism (Jarvis 2009; Jackson 2007; Jackson 2005), neo-Orientalism does not, though accurate and necessary in the post-9/11 context, speak to all colonial violences – nor does it grasp the context of slavery in the US or Latin America, nor the gendered constructs that infiltrate all of these. This chapter will engage in a deeper deconstruction of rationality and how it fed and continues to feed into the gendered, colonial and racial ordering of IR and Terrorism Studies. It will then interrogate how the insistence of mainstream Terrorism Studies supports Western structures. Finally, it will turn to 'radicalisation' and counter-terrorism as the latest way of undermining the 'rationality' of terrorists, reliant upon the hidden gendered and raced structures. To illustrate this, it will look at the racialised counter-terrorism response to the manipulation of British Muslim women's identity in Prevent Tragedies, a Metropolitan Police counter-terrorism initiative, and the FBI response to the white nationalist rally in Charlottesville, Virginia in 2017.

The Problem with Rationality

Chapter 1's discussion of what rationality is and what it expects is simply the beginning of the conversation. In short, contemporary understandings of rationality within the social sciences, where Terrorism Studies is most evidently placed, make the assumption that people make decisions based upon cost-benefit analysis, striving for emotionless objectivity. In North American IR (read the US), the social sciences became tied to neo-positivist work, with the belief in 'scientific rationality as a key to solving collective problems'[2] (Hoppe 1999: 202). Yet, such a determined position did not recognise that even in the 'hard' sciences this idea of rationality is compromised by the researcher's own agendas, biases and limitations (see Toulmin 1982: 95).

For instance, 'scientific rationality has become untenable' because a scientific approach to studying human behaviour and dynamics is one choice amongst many – it provides an incomplete picture of a subject (Hoppe 1999: 203). Scientific rationality within the social sciences is too rigidly connected to an idea of infallibility, where a better notion might be to recognise that for 'rationality' to work it must be 'social, interactive, and dialogic' (Hoppe 1999: 203). It therefore needs to be flexible, cognisant of human fallibility, and open to correction (see also Toulmin 2001). One of the ways that 'rationality' has shifted in the face of these critiques is via an understanding of 'bounded rationality'. Coming out of Economics and dependent upon the work by Amos Tversky and Daniel Kahneman (1974), bounded rationality recognises the limitations of human nature: that we simply are not capable of complete rationality. The originators of bounded rationality found 'that people systematically deviate from the predictions of expected utility-theory and some of the axioms upon which it is based' (Levy 2002: 272).

Bounded rationality is, in part, based upon the notion of 'psychological plausibility' in which

> the goal . . . is to understand how actual humans . . . make decisions, as opposed to heavenly beings equipped with practically unlimited time, knowledge, memory, or other finite resources. The challenge is to base models of bounded rationality on the cognitive, emotional, social, and behavioural repertoire that [humans] actually [have]. (Gigerenzer 2001: 38)

While there are those who are less positive of bounded rationality's impact on the social sciences (Gigerenzer 2001), it is a vision that fits within the philosophical approach of both Stephen Toulmin (2001) and Martha Nussbaum (2001).

Additionally, Tversky and Kahneman's related work on prospect theory has much to contribute to Terrorism Studies, as it holds that

> people define value relative to a reference point (reference dependence) rather than in terms of net assets, based on evidence that people are more sensitive to changes in assets than to net asset levels. People give more weight to losses from that reference point than to comparable gains (loss aversion), and they value what they have more than comparable things not in their possession (the endowment effect), which in turn makes actual losses hurt more than foregone gains. Individuals' strong aversion to losses, particularly to losses that are perceived as certain (as opposed to those that are perceived as probabilistic), induces them to take significant risks in the hope of avoiding loss. (Levy 2002: 272)

Thus, people will not react in the way that a rational choice, cost-benefit model expects them to act. Another approach, then, to consider is 'thin rationality', which does not place a value on an individual's preferences – something that is potentially harder to accomplish in Terrorism Studies, given the loaded nature of the field. Thin rationality

> refers to the behavioural principle stating that rational people act according to their preferences. More precisely, a rational individual chooses A rather than B just in case he/she (hereafter he) prefers A to B. Provided that the individual's preference is a binary, connected and transitive relation over alternative courses of action, we can define a utility function that represents the individual's preferences so that when acting rationally – i.e. in accordance with his preferences – he acts as if he were maximising his utility. (Nurmi 2010: 321)

While some within Terrorism Studies would demonstrate an under-standing of bounded and thin rationality in their discussion (as will be discussed below), it remains crucially important that we recognise 'rationality' as a result of the Enlightenment, all things also connected to imperialism and the racial and gendered structuring of the international system.

Rationality is very much a social construction, and as such has shifted over time (see Toulmin 2001: 5). Intrinsic to rationality's social construc-tion is how it has been used to locate and organise different populations and different people hierarchically. Certain people (white Western men) are imbued with a certain amount of status because of their ability to act and think rationally, whereas those outside of the hegemonic ideal (women and people of colour) are seen as less able to think rationally, thereby removing them from power (Elshtain 1981: 31). From the time of Ancient Greece, women were locked out of the public sphere, based upon the assumption that they have less intellectual capability, which means they have less access to the rationality necessary for public life (Pateman 1980; Elshtain 1987: 4–5). As Jean Bethke Elshtain writes in her classic text *Public Man, Private Woman* (1981: 22),

> The private person or *idiot* [woman or slave] was a being of lower purpose, goodness, rationality, and worth the *polites* or public citizen [male] who belonged to and participated in the city.

Even if this ordering of the world started in Ancient Greece, Greek patri-archal thought had clear influence on Enlightenment thinking, particu-larly on Descartes' dualism between the material body and immaterial mind.

As the Enlightenment was a Western project, it justified colonialism and imperialism. It was at this time that 'race as a rigid and hierarchical category came to dominate identity in the periphery' (Delatolla and Yao 2018: 5). Not only was 'Western reality reified as . . . something "better", reflecting "higher orders of thinking", and . . . less . . . primitive' (Smith 2012: 50–1), such superiority drove imperialism – indigenous people did not properly tend their territorial land (Delatolla and Yao 2018: 9); they were unable to

> use [their] minds or intellects. [They] could not invent things, . . . could not create institutions or history . . . , imagine, . . . or produce anything of value . . . , [they] did not practice the arts of civilisation. (Smith 2012: 26)

Furthermore, scholarship and research were intimately tied to imperialism:

> In the wider Enlightenment context, imperialism becomes an integral part of the development of the modern state, of science, of ideas, and of the 'modern' human person. In complex ways, imperialism was also a mode through which . . . new ideas and discoveries could be made and harnessed, and through which Europeans could develop their sense of Europeanness. (Smith 2012: 23)

Effort was put into bringing order – of a European kind – to the colonised places and people: for instance, it was believed that the 'enlightening forces of rationality [would] sweep away oppressive feudal practices' (Dellatola and Yao 2018: 6–7). Gender, too, was included in this process: gender and the status of women became another way of assessing a colonised society's progressiveness. This particular convergence of rationality and gender is particularly pertinent to problematising the work on radicalisation that connects it to evolutionary biology, especially when considering men, violence against women in Muslim societies and radical Islamism (but not any other form of radicalisation) (Thayer and Hudson 2010).

Women's status within the colonies was manipulated and contrasted to the supposed high status of women in Europe in order to highlight a lack of modernity (Chakrabarty 1992). Spivak (1988), Mutua (2001) and McClintock (2013) argue that progress during colonisation was measured in part by the status of women within the colonies. For instance, women became the 'light that saved' (or justified) colonial practices:

> women's rights stood as exemplars for the progression of the modern individual, freedom, equality, and rights. Women's education and their living conditions became increasingly emphasised, seeing these as necessary for [a colony's] progression into 'modernity'. Yet this is clearly hypocritical and lacking critical self-awareness as 'the women question' was far from settled in the colonising states (and remains unsettled). (Gentry 2017: 114–15)

Additionally, it assumes that women outside of the West are in need of saving by white, Western men, à la Spivak (1988), because they are trapped in non-liberal, non-progressive, non-democratic states. This is an essentialisation of women and their politics: the presumption is that women are natural allies with Western democratic practice, once again believing that women's status in the West is settled and they are secure(d) citizens.[3] When women are seen to reject Western superiority or Western presumptions in their lives, this is seen as rejection of what is natural to them. The rejection becomes an irrational, incomprehensible act – this will be explored below in the context of the work on women's participation in al Qaeda's suicide campaign, and also in how the London Metropolitan Police approached the Prevent Tragedies counter-terrorism project. The essentialisation of women's identity is not the only essentialisation that happened during imperialism; the very purpose of colonisation was to essentialise racial differences.

The construction of indigenous people as 'Other' – as captured so well in Edward Said's *Orientalism* (1978) – is dependent upon the categorisation of difference: difference of history, art and aesthetics, religion and culture, etc. These categorisations supported the 'institutionalisation' of 'academic disciplines', 'learned and scientific societies, and scholarly networks' (Smith 2012: 8). These are codified and transported to and from the colonies in reifying and cyclical patterns:

> The transplanting of research institutions, including universities from the imperial centres of Europe enabled local scientific interests to be organised and embedded in the colonial system. . . . The significance of the travellers' tales and adventurers' adventures is that they represented the Other to a general audience back in Europe which became fixed in the milieu of cultural ideas. Images of the 'cannibal' chief, the 'red Indian', the 'witch' doctor, or the 'tattooed and shrunken' head, and stories which told of savagery and primitivism. (Smith 2012: 8)

The imperial scientific mission owned the narratives of the non-West, but they also took ownership of the people therein.

Himadeep Muppidi's (2006) autobiographical encounter with the Royal Museum of Central Africa in Belgium captures how the imperial research agenda continues to shape social and personal dynamics. This museum was only possible as a colonial collection project with its '350 archives, 8,000 musical instruments, 20,000 maps, 56,000 word samples, 180,000 ethnographic objects, 250,000 rock samples, and 10,000,000 animals' (Muppidi 2006: 53), and, as Muppidi makes clear, humans. Muppidi's visit was deeply, emotionally complex: as he toured the museum, he realised:

> Something seemed amiss, something was out of focus in the long-cultivated relationship between the eyes and the eyed. Try as I might, I couldn't summon the proper academic disposition that this institutional space seemed,

quite silently, to demand. The pressure intensified as I became doubly aware of those around me in that section. I realized I was reflecting on their likely reflections of me walking these corridors – brown imagining white imagining brown eyes seeking traction on brown masks. (Muppidi 2006: 54)

He continues by making his reader acutely aware that colonisation was not just about territorial control, mining of resources, but it was very much a project in hierarchical white ownership, dehumanisation and instrumental control of brown/black bodies:

Understood as a manifestation of the European order of things, the museum made brilliant sense. Here was the trophy room, laboratory, library, school, hospital, and asylum of the colonizer. This was where they – the colonizer's citizen-heirs – repaired to be educated, trained, cultured, and restored to/ into their patrimony. But what was my place and position in such an institution? Where did I fit in an institution displaying the colonizer's collections? In the European order of things, was I, could I be, only another animal-object? (Muppidi 2006: 54–5)

Imperial discourses, as supported through research, knowledge and colonial government practices, contained '[i]deas about what counted as human' (Smith 2012: 26). Thus, the West has embedded 'a cultural system of classification and representation' (Smith 2012: 46) particularly as 'racial difference emerged as a measurable, observable, and therefore scientific truth about global politics' (Delatolla and Yao 2018: 5). Furthermore, 'when race could not be discerned, religious identities' were used instead (Delatolla and Yao 2018: 6).

Therefore, 'Western ways of viewing, talking about, and interacting with the world at large are intricately embedded in racialised discourses' which led to the linking of whiteness with 'human reason' (Smith 2012: 46 and 62). Once it was accepted that (white) 'humans had the capacity to reason' it became possible to discuss 'ideas in *rational* and *scientific* ways' (Smith 2012: 62; emphasis added). Scientific knowledge and progress became tied to 'civilisation', in which the West stood as the paramount example. Thus, all non-white people are civilisation's antithesis: savage, barbarian, fundamental (see also Mutua 2001: 205). Henry Louis Gates echoes Muppidi's own sense of subjectivity by describing how this affects black people:

The salient sign of the black person's humanity . . . would be the mastering of the very essence of Western civilization, the very foundation of the complex fiction upon which white Western culture has been constructed. (as cited in Smith 2012: 60–70)

And this is the very foundation that IR, history, philosophy and the other fields that feed into Terrorism Studies rest upon.

Yet, the social sciences, in their dependence upon universality, are blind to how rationality functions as a discursive ordering structure. It has been argued that when the 'thinkers who shape the nature of social science' create 'theories that embrace the entirety of humanity', these are 'produced in relative, and sometimes ignorance of the majority of humankind', such as those living outside of the West (Chakrabarty 2009: 29). As Ann Tickner (1997: 617) clarified:

> Western theories of universal justice, built on a rather abstract concept of rationality, have generally been constructed out of a definition of human nature that excludes or diminishes women.

Thus, when we hold on to rationality, or use the language of rationality in coded ways, we are upholding a gendered and racialised system of knowledge.

The presumption of rationality is an ontological and epistemological fallacy, one that forces anyone who assesses an Other's reasoning, positionality and values to centre these on Western presumptions. Aníbal Quijano (2007:169) argues that

> the relationship between the European – also called 'Western' – culture, and the others, continues to be one of colonial domination. It is not only a matter of the subordination of the other cultures to the European, in an external relation; we have also to do with a colonization of the other cultures, albeit in differing intensities and depths. This relationship consists, in the first place, of a colonization of the imagination of the dominated; that is, it acts in the interior of that imagination, in a sense, it is a part of it.

It is an epistemic position, if not ontological, that determines how we make sense of all actions of the other. Borrowing from Wittgenstein's 'We create representations of facts for ourselves,' Toulmin (2001: 4) looks at rationality's discursive process 'in which . . . we fashion representations of . . . rational inquiry' to 'hel[p] us find the truth'. These truths are dependent upon the relationship between our assumptions and representations and how these lead us to particular places in our 'investigations' (Toulmin 2001: 4). Rationality joined with whiteness, masculinity, science and order to create a syntagm; it is a signifier of progress and civilisation.

In *Cultural Politics of Emotions*, Sara Ahmed (2004: 13) argues that emotions are only made sense of socially. An individual's emotions can only be known to others through a shared understanding of said emotions; thus, emotions are discursively constructed through common descriptors. As such, accepting or validating another's emotions is also a social construction. In the sharing of emotions, emotions become centred on different objects and ideas; those objects and ideas, now 'stuck' with particular emotions, circulate amongst members of a society or culture. Even if rationality is not an emotion but a supposed characteristic or trait, as a concept it circulates in a similar way. Rationality is stuck to, and thereby circulates with, those terms within its syntagm, becoming stuck to particular bodies and unable to stick to others. Even as rationality has become stuck differently to different bodies, rationality's meaning within the West has shifted multiple times since the Enlightenment. In that regard, Toulmin (2001: 7) questions whether

> it [is] even clear that people from the same culture at the same time are capable of reaching intellectual consensus? In this way the idea of rationality became as open to idiosyncrasy as those of justice or morality.

Even with the arrival of bounded rationality, which thins the concept entirely, if we fail to see how rationality is stuck differently to different bodies, then we perpetuate the myth of Western scientific infallibility. We also perpetuate the logocentrism at the heart of Terrorism Studies, that white men equates to counter-terrorists and that brown/black men equates to terrorists, and that women do not exist in the equation at all.

Rationality and Terrorism Studies

Rationality within Terrorism Studies is located within two different conversations. The first is a debate that has shaped Terrorism Studies:

Should terrorism be conceived as something rational and, therefore, instrumental and exogenous to the terrorist's own mind (Crenshaw 1990, 1987, 1981; Pape 2005, 2003; Hoffman 2011, 2006, 1999; Lake 2002; Fromkin 1975)?

Or: is terrorism a product of multiple psychological forces, whether of mental health, sentimental feelings (such as a need to belong [see McCauley and Moskalenko 2011 and 2008; della Porta 2008; Taylor and Horgan 2006; Peteet 1991]) or radicalisation?

The second is an ongoing conversation:

Is terrorism rational – meaning, does it actually result in benefits (Sprinzak 2009; Pape 2005 and 2003; Crenshaw 1990; Fromkin 1975)?

Or: is terrorism not-rational (but not necessarily irrational either) because it is not efficacious (Chenoweth and Stephan 2011; Stephan and Chenoweth 2008; Abrahms 2004)?

The literature on rationality in the two conversations tends to overlap, and sometimes aim to contribute to both conversations at once. This chapter is more interested in the first question, on how rationality is contrasted with psychological forces that can be (but are not always) related to irrationality and mental health.

According to Stampnitzky's (2013: 65) sociological history of terrorism studies, Terrorism Studies has long been embroiled in the discussion of the rationality or irrationality of terrorism. It was not until the late 1970s that charges emerged equating terrorism with 'a new barbarism' or the belief 'that terrorists can never be depended upon to act rationally', as they are 'fanatics incapable of accommodation' (as quoted in Stampnitzky 2013: 65). This shift in discourse, Stampnitzky (2013: 66–7) found, had everything to do with the perception of the US population as under 'imminent threat' from terrorism and a shift in the 'site of terrorism discourse . . . to a more public realm', flavouring therefore the government and academic discussions.

In some way, the strategic literature has had to work harder for longer to gain traction. The tension between rationality and psychology sets the scene for the debate between Martha Crenshaw and Jerrold Post in *Origins of Terrorism* (Reich 1990). To reiterate from Chapter 1, Crenshaw stood apart in Reich's volume (see Reich's editor's note, p. 7). Whereas the volume focuses on psychological factors in terrorism, Crenshaw defends her long-standing position that terrorist activity is a strategic one. Like other elements within Terrorism Studies, the literature on rationality seems to depend on a few well-cited sources, including Martha Crenshaw's extensive contributions (2014, 1990, 1987, 1981, 1978) as well as the sea-change wrought by Robert Pape's (2005 and 2003) work on suicide terrorism (which is cited by almost every contribution to the field after 2003 [Crenshaw 2014; Hoffman 2011; Kydd and Walter 2006; Abrahms 2004], and both pieces are cited a total of 3,942 times according to Google Scholar).

Within this work, the various definitions and explanations of violence shift between thin and a thicker form rationality. Bruce Hoffman (2011: 259) maintains a thicker form:

> it is . . . widely accepted that terrorist violence is neither irrational nor desperate: but instead is entirely rational and often carefully calculated. Terrorism is thus consciously embraced as a deliberate instrument of warfare; a pragmatic decision derived as a result of a discernibly logical process.

Throughout Crenshaw's many publications, she vacillates between the two versions. On the thicker end, she argues that 'the users of terrorism are strategic or calculating if not purely rational actors and . . . the appropriate level of analysis is that of the group as a collective decision-making actor' (Crenshaw 2014: 558; see also Crenshaw 1987: 13–14); but on the thinner end,

> [g]roups pursuing a strategy of violence against the state are interested in furthering long-term ideological goals – independence, revolution, societal transformation, regime change – at the same time that they seek to promote the success of their own group over rivals. (Crenshaw 2014: 559)

Others follow Crenshaw's lead on holding to a thinner version. For instance, Diego Muro-Ruiz (2002: 114) argues,

> individuals are pictured as given interests, wants, purposes, needs, etc. and constitute independent centres of consciousness, they are independent and rational beings, who are the sole generators of their own wants and preferences, and the best judges of their own interests.

Additionally, Kydd and Walter (2006: 49) argue that

> hijacking planes, blowing up buses, and kidnapping individuals may seem irrational and incoherent to outside observers, but these tactics can be surprisingly effective in achieving a terrorist group's political aims.

While many of these definitions are still problematically masculinist, reifying a form of sovereign autonomy that is as non-existent as pure rationality, and fail to recognise the racial genealogy of rationality, these definitions at least demonstrate the realisation that terrorists-as-humans work from a set of preferences that may not fit into a cost-benefit analysis.

Even if there are those who do not see terrorism as effective, and therefore not strategic, they do not deny the rationality of terrorism. Abrahms' (2004) central argument is that terrorists are not rational in the thickest sense because, relying solely upon the Palestinian struggle, they do not make material gains. Yet, he ends his article with a lengthy discussion of the thin rationality of terrorists, because 'terrorists are [not] devoid of all rational characteristics' (Abrahms 2004: 543). He continues, citing Crenshaw (1981), 'that the outstanding common characteristic of terrorists is their normality' and '[e]ven today's new terrorists' display some attribute of rationality (Abrahms 2004: 544). The thin rationality of terrorists, according to Abrahms (2004: 544) is dependent upon their 'purposiveness', or their 'goal oriented' nature, 'logic', or reliance upon violence as a 'means to ends, which reflects a thought process associated with rational decision makers', and 'timing', where flexibility in type of attack and change of tactic due to developments is rational and strategic.

Nevertheless, academic discussions that centre on the *irrationality* are also present in the literature in different guises. The early work on women, which attempted to address the high level of women's participation in Marxist-Leninist organisations in the late 1960s and 1970s, seems quite fringey now. The work was highly charged, including sentiments such as the idea that female terrorists are 'intractable' and possess a 'cold rage . . . that even the most alienated of men seem quite incapable of emulating' (Cooper 1979: 153); or:

> When [one] is dealing with a female terrorist one is usually dealing not with rational, but with emotional motivation. . . . Thus her violence will in all probability stem not from dedication to the particular cause which she appears to espouse, but from blind obedience to another more personal cause. (Anonymous 1976: 245)

Initially, suicide terrorism was described as stemming from anomie: '[t]errorist suicide, like any other suicide, is basically an individual rather than a group phenomenon: it is done by people who wish to die for personal reasons' (Merari 1990: 206). This separated suicide terrorists from political choice, something that Pape's (2005 and 2003) work changed. Even in Abrahms' (2004) article, which maintains that Palestinians are thinly rational, their choices are framed in animalistic terms; Abrahams (2004: 545) cites Hoffman (1999: 25) saying that when Palestinians learn to shift tactics, they display 'an almost Darwinian principle of natural selection . . . whereby every new terrorist generation learns from its predecessor'. Instead of recognising that (Palestinian) groups learn and are strategic in decision-making, this statement minimises any sense of logic and rationality. It equates the Palestinians with an animalistic process, making their learning less conscious and less about intentional, strategic learning.

Finally, religious terrorism was presented as a long-standing historical dialectic between the (Christian) West and the (non-Christian) Orient (see for instance Ranstorp 1996: 44). While two classic texts on religious terrorism (Stern 2003; Juergensmeyer 2000) look at Christian and Jewish terrorism, there is still an element of resistance to this form of violence, quite possibly because of the Enlightenment's resistance to religious belief, particularly coded as irrational (see also Delatolla and Yao 2018). Other work on radical Islamism treats it as an 'infectious disease', justifying a need to view this form of terrorism from an epidemiological model (Stares and Yacoubian 2007). One of the most influential pieces on religious terrorism, now critiqued for its historical infelicities, is David Rapoport's 1984 article on religious terrorism, in which he investigates the Thugs, Assassins and Zealots. This article is so prominent and respected in the field that it was reprinted in an edited volume in 2012 (Horgan and Braddock 2012). All three of these are located in ancient history and all three are located outside of the West, when, in 1984, the US was in the midst of dealing with Christian white supremacists groups like the Order and the Aryan Nations. In this article, Rapoport (1984: 658–9) makes the argument that terrorism is becoming more prevalent because of modern technology, but choses to look at these groups precisely because of their pre-modern nature. In several respects, Rapoport's article was a precursor to the new terrorism thesis, especially in its contrast between fundamentalist (irrational) groups using contemporary technologies (see Laqueur 1999 and 1996; Hoffman 2002 and 1999). All can conceivably be criticised on the grounds of coloniality – of the persistence of a colonial mindset.

Even if the 'irrationality' scholarship is by and largely marginalised, when one reads deeply into the rationality literature, forms of irrationality can still be located. Boaz Ganor's (2015) recent work explaining to the West how the violence of radical Islamism is also rational makes the same move. In it he explicitly aims to convince his readers that 'Islamist terrorist organisations' are '[f]ar from being irrational or depraved', stating that 'terrorists are rational actors who employ cost-benefit calculations in determining when and how to exert their influence' (Ganor 2015: xi). He continues, echoing Abrahms (2004: 545) and Hoffman

(1999: 25), that 'they are disturbingly normal' and do not 'fi[t] the popularised image of fanatic, insane murderers' because they 'make careful calculations and . . . perpetrate an act of terrorism as a completely rational decision' (Ganor 2015: 99). So far this inclusionary discourse is clear and significant.

Yet, along the way, Ganor's own language begins to unpick this rationality-granting vision. First, he casts some doubt: '[t]he rational choice model *seems* to be the best' (2015: 98) to explain the violence. Second, Ganor (2015) makes it clear that terrorism is not a Western phenomenon, but one that Western 'decision makers' (97) and Western counter-terrorists must confront (98). Third, these Western decision-making, counter-terrorists must not think like Westerners (Ganor 2015: 98) but think like radical Islamists, whose rationality extends only as far as their beliefs allow:

Understanding the rationale of modern terrorist organisations in general, and of radical Islamic terrorist groups in particular, provides a key to understanding their modi operandi, tactics and strategy (Ganor 2015: 97).

Ganor (2015: 100) modifies the cost-benefit decision of a terrorist: 'the choice . . . dictat[ed]' by the terrorist's rational decision is

the result of a subjective judgment, which is influenced by the background of the decision maker who is making that judgment – that is, his [sic] culture, religious beliefs, ideology, experiences, and values. The relative cost or benefit that a terrorist assigns to his various alternatives will depend on the background, the morals it dictates – and his personality. For example, a terrorist leader whose actions are determined by his faith in a supreme protector and in divine or spiritual reward will perform a different cost-benefit analysis than will one who believes only in tangible material rewards. The importance attached to the concept of honour – the honour of women, parents, oneself – is also culture-dependent. For an Islamist terrorist leader, to kill or be killed to protect one's honour may be perfectly acceptable (Ganor 2015: 100).

While I cannot help but applaud Ganor's use of a bounded rationality, this binding rests on differentiating some people from others: leaders are different from followers; radical Islamists are different from Western counter-terrorists. It is like there is a sliding scale of rationality and radical Islamists are on it, but they are not at the top of it, or indeed, on top of their own rationality.

Similarly, when Robert Pape wrote his ground-breaking (yet still problematic) book *Dying to Win* (2005), he changed the script to 'strategic logic', in which he argues that suicide terrorists are rational, political and logical. In most cases where suicide terrorism campaigns have been employed, including Lebanon, the Palestinian Territories, Sri Lanka and Turkey, 'the terrorists' political cause made more gains after the resort to suicide operations' (Pape 2005: 22). An individual's choice to commit a suicide attack, which happens in a complex context of relationships, beliefs and structures, becomes about 'strategic logic'. Yet there is a hidden discourse of Western masculinist universalisation within Pape's work. Strategic logic assumes that this is a universal way of thinking, and that it is superior to other modes of thought (Sjoberg and Gentry 2008a). Utilising a rational analysis and describing a sub- jects' activity with it appears to objective, yet it prioritises rationality and calculation (masculine-related values) over other ways of knowing and making informed decisions (Tickner 1997: 614).

The demographic data in Pape's study shows that suicide terrorists

> have been college educated and uneducated, married and single, men and
> women, isolated and socially integrated; they have ranged in age from fifteen
> to fifty-two. In other words, [they] come from a broad array of lifestyles.
> (Pape 2005: 17)

Furthermore, they are '[p]sychologically normal, have better than aver- age economic prospects for their communities, and are deeply integrated into their social networks' (Pape 2005: 23). But there are those who have more access to rationality than others. This becomes evident in his treatment of women and of followers. Women become martyrs due to rape: 'a stigma that destroys their prospects for marriage and rules out procreation as a means of contributing to the community'. Furthermore, '[a]cting as a human bomb . . . is an understood and accepted offering for a woman who will never be a mother' (Pape 2005: 23).

He also differentiates between leaders and followers. Leaders are the ones who best understand the strategy of suicide terrorism: 'Even if many suicide attackers are irrational or fanatical, the leadership groups that recruit and direct them are not' (Pape 2003: 344). Much of Pape's (2003) discussion in his article centres on how leaders of democracy deal with the coercion nature of terrorism while the leaders of terror- ist groups parse out their strategic path. While the countries he focuses upon are selected as 'democracies', this designation is not only sus- pect in its inclusion of Russia, Israel/Palestine, Sri Lanka and Turkey, but the perpetrators are all outside of the West (Pape 2005 and 2003). Ganor (2005) does this too. Ganor minces no words: the 'emotions and feelings of leaders, terrorist supporters, and activists' are 'irrational' (Ganor 2005: 35–6). Followers in these countries are denied rationality – they are pawns in a game pitted between leaderships. In this sense, narrating non-Western violence as rational, strategic and logical invites the non-West into the fold – it drops the presumptive bias that non-Westerners cannot attain this level of civilisational progress. Yet Pape tempers who belongs to the rationality club, and it just happens to track along gendered and potentially racialised lines.

Therefore, in one sense, Pape and Ganor, amongst others, expect that 'rationality' levels the playing field: it extends to terrorists the same privileges as the counter-terrorist – but only to a point, which is tempered by ideology, gender and lack of status (followers). However, it stands on two significant fallacies. First, it is an expectation that the world and all those in it must emulate Western life and ways of being. Second, it believes that those within the West are *actually capable of complete rationality*, when the reality is that no one can be. These assumptions, then, are further forms of violence. Therefore when a terrorist or a counter-terrorist actor fails to live up to the high bar of rationality, the non-Western terrorist has further to fall because they already fail to meet the ideals of Western, white masculinity, whereas counter-terrorists have all the privilege of the state to catch them.

In Terrorism Studies we are often focused on the Others' emotions and not our own, as we presume Western counter-terrorist identity within Terrorism Studies. This is precisely because in a Western political context, the assumption is that we act rationally and logically, bound or unbound. It is always the terrorists' emotions that are in play, not the counter-terrorists. Indeed, if counter-terrorists are also not always totally the rational, logical beings that they would like to be, perhaps a bounded view of rationality goes some way in explaining how race and gender become stuck to terrorism by admitting that our own prejudices and biases play a role in the construction of terrorism. In a post-9/11 America, anxiety and fear became centred on terrorism, which had already become stuck with 'Arab', 'Muslim' and 'Islam' (Gentry 2015; Ahmed 2004: 76; see also Massumi 2005). Yet, again, this does not go far enough to look at the relationship between terrorism and *race* more generally.

This is evident in the work on radicalisation, as it is the antithesis to (any form of) rationality and the syntagm it signifies. Radicalisation is a problematic phrase, indicative of extremism, fundamentalism, irrationality and all things at odds with masculine Westernness. Thus, by turning radicalisation inside out, by parsing out its discursive phrasing and finger-pointing, it becomes clear that 'radicalisation' is built upon the fears of what *must* be excluded from Western life: anything that will undermine the racial and gendered 'progressive' vision of Western modernity. This becomes clear as we turn to look at how threats are constructed in current events.

Radicalisation and the Countering of *Some* Terrorism

When I teach radicalisation in my Critical Terrorism Studies course, I begin with a word game: what is synonymous with 'radicalisation'? Students will often answer: fundamental, extremists, politicised, violent. Some will almost immediately leap to the point I am making and volunteer, 'irrational'. They have already received some Critical Discourse Analysis methods: they know that discourse is opaque and that meaning is hidden, coded within our words and sentences. Thus, once 'irrational' is injected into the conversation, they refer back to other lectures, associating 'irrational' with gender if not racialisation. This begins my critique of radicalisation literature: it is a code for delegitimising terrorist activity in a way that is central to maintaining a vision of Western modernity as civilised and progressive.

Defining Radicalisation

Like 'terrorism', radicalisation is also shakily defined (Heath-Kelly 2013: 398). Broadly, radicalisation seeks to understand what attracts people to an ideology that supports extremist political viewpoints (Volintiru 2010: 7). It claims to look at the dynamic interaction between person and environment (Borum 2012a: 38). Therefore, radicalisation takes into account an individual's psychology, personal grievances and social and cultural environment, including status and reputation (McCauley and Moskalenko 2011). It is an ongoing thought process of becoming more and more convinced of an extremist viewpoint; yet being an extremist does not constitute being a terrorist. Therefore, it is one way, amongst others, of becoming involved in terrorism and political violence (Borum 2012b: 8–9).

There is an element of the 'unknown' within radicalisation. Multiple models depend upon different, yet quite similar, visualisations of what happens when someone moves from being simply radicalised to being a violent actor. The moment that separates an extremist from a terrorist is conceived of as a line within them (almost quite literally a line in the sand), such as a 'trigger' (Volintiru 2010: 15). Yet these do not, and cannot, clarify why one person crosses that line and another person does not. There is a lack, therefore, in this 'why' that goes unanswered and it is a lack that points at the pathologisation of something within the individual's brain (personality, chemistry, psychopathy) that helped them over this line – particularly as there are others who experience the same socialisation, same cognitive processes, same facilitation, but do not cross the line. As Anthony Richards (2011: 143) critiques, 'We don't know – nor, it appears, are we ever likely to know – why some young men [sic] resort to violent extremism and others do not.'

Radicalisation also takes place within a much larger context. As Randy Borum (2012c: 1) explains:

> Over the course of the past decade, the United States and its international partners have vacillated between waging war on al Qaeda, waging war on terrorism, combating violent extremism, engaging in a battle of ideas, and attempting to win hearts and minds.

When radicalisation becomes the disposition that reveals an internal struggle between being Western or non-Western, as instrumental in winning hearts and minds, it harks back to Huntington's civilisational clash. The loaded nature of radicalisation comes through even further when looking at this definition:

> Extremism can be used to refer to political ideologies that oppose a society's core values and principles. In the context of liberal democracies this could be applied to any ideology that advocates racial or religious supremacy and/ or opposes the core principles of democracy and universal human rights. The term can also be used to describe the methods through which political actors attempt to realise their aims, that is, by using means that show disregard for the life, liberty, and human rights of others. (Neuman 2010, as cited in Borum 2012c: 10)

It is the West that must win certain hearts and certain minds before they are given over to the radical Islamism of al Qaeda or, now, Da'esh. There is a certain element of a zero-sum battle being fought, but additionally of an absolute, age-old game between the West and non-West. If radical Islamism (or another ideology opposed to Western-ness) wins these people, 'civilisation' might be 'lost'.

Some of the recent theorising on radicalisation takes this civilisational framework to heart. Explicitly refuting the sentiment that terrorists are 'disturbingly normal', this work argues that radicalisation is related to personal or developmental disorders (Palermo 2013; Weenink 2015) or, more problematically, to evolutionary biology (Thayer and Hudson 2010). One study refutes that 'terrorists are seemingly normal' by looking at those on file with the Netherlands police who are, or are thought, to be 'radicalised' (Weenink 2015). The author argues that

> identity problems and grievances in immigrant youth, and differentiating between roles, phases, and motivations can assist policymakers in responding more adequately to radicalization. (Weenink 2015)

Already, the first clue is dropped as to who is included in 'radicalisation': immigrants, even though the history of terrorist attacks in the Netherlands varies significantly by ideology and there is a 'slight rise' in neo-Nazi activity there (Simpson-Baikie 2018). Weenink (2015) then makes the central argument clearer: 'we think the evidence for "normality" in radical Islamist terrorists is less unambiguous than currently accepted'. To ascertain what is 'normal', Weenink (2015) looked for 'problematic' behaviours in the police files on 140 suspected and known radicals, including 'unstable' relationships with family and friends, failure to finish school, unemployment, diagnosed mental health issues and homelessness. The study found that 6 per cent of the sample had a 'diagnosed mental health problem' and 46 per cent 'displayed problem behaviour', both of which are disproportionately large to the rest of the Netherlands population. Yet this study fails to contextualise 'problem behaviours' within a socio-political context: it only sees these as evidence of 'problems', and possible mental health problems at that, and not as ones of poverty, social marginalisation and economic disenfranchisement. It also fails to differentiate between being a Muslim and a migrant: it does not set the sample against the migrant population as a whole, nor the Muslim population in the Netherlands as a whole. Thus, the study is reliant upon several unspoken biases, biases that confirm longer legacies about rationality, intelligence and progressivism.

No less problematic is the argument

> that the life sciences can offer insights into suicide terrorism in the Islamic context. We argue that suicide terrrorism as a cultural practice could not exist without it intersecting at some point with evolutionary motivations. (Thayer and Hudson 2010: 37)

Thayer and Hudson (2010: 40–2) use conventional security – anarchy, 'US hegemonic involvement in Islamic states', and 'fundamentalist

Islamic belief system' (Thayer and Hudson 2010: 42) – to situate radical Islamist terrorism. Yet these are 'augment[ed]' by 'explanations grounded in the life sciences' (Thayer and Hudson 2010: 42). For Thayer and Hudson (2010), human behaviour, and particularly a belief in religion, can be explained via evolutionary theory. How this impacts any other religious (or secular) group beyond (radicalised) Muslims is unclear. Instead, the sexual drive of Muslim men, as divided into alpha and non-alpha males, is understood in connection with 'social mammals' (Thayer and Hudson 2010: 43). All male mammals 'seek to maximise their individual reproductive success', which happens via dominance. Therefore,

> The logic is inescapable, non-alpha males are the prime candidates for reproductive failure, and thus are the prime candidates for social unrest in any human group. (Thayer and Hudson 2010: 44)

The tension between alpha and non-alpha males is resolved via 'male bonding' and alpha males redirect the non-alpha males, guiding the violent impulses of non-alpha males 'toward out-groups, not in-groups (and especially not targeted toward the alphas)' (Thayer and Hudson 2010: 45). The violence becomes even more acute when there is a scarcity of females for reproduction.

According to Thayer and Hudson (2010: 47), 'masculinity' has more 'traction' in Muslim societies than Western ones (which is laughable in the current context of Trump and toxic masculinity). Therefore,

> For some non-alpha males, becoming a *shaheed* [suicide bomber] is the most effective response to the human evolutionary conundrum produced by male dominance hierarchies, high levels of gender differentiation, and the scarcity of females. (Thayer and Hudson 2010: 50)

Even if this problematic pathologisation of radicalisation and terrorist violence can someday be proven 'true', the fact that this study focuses on the animalistic tendencies – which removes reason and rationality – of Muslim men highlights more than anything else the need to differentiate between non-Muslims and Muslims (and presumably other people of colour). It reproduces colonial mentalities: people of colour are closer to animals, whereas Westerners have the ability to reason or sublimate their animal impulses.

As Daniel Bell (2015: x) argues in his deconstruction of the deployment of the social sciences by IR scholars, 'The language of science is one of the most powerful ideological weapons' – therefore, when this is invoked against Islam in literature on terrorism, it is 'performative'. It helps to 'support an American imperial order to secure global peace' (Bell 2015: 123). While I will be hard pressed to agree with an evolutionary position that does not take into account socio-political hierarchies, Thayer and Hudson (2010) could have easily complicated their argument by looking at the 'radicalised' white men in the US. These men too draw upon the evolutionary theory of alpha and beta males and sexual urges to explain their violence towards women (further discussed in the next chapter). While media and academic focus on this community has been more recent, the community of men's rights activists pre-dates Thayer and Hudson's work. However, Hudson's work absent Thayer, such as *Sex and World Peace* (2012), has focused more on 'Muslim states' than any other 'type' of state (see Gentry 2017), which confirms the sense that a bias is at play.

Historical Usage of Radicalisation

'Radicalisation' is not the most historic nor the most popular framework within Terrorism Studies. Two relatively recent handbooks do not even address radicalisation. John Horgan's edited volume from 2011 has a chapter on process theory, not radicalisation.[4] The 2018 *Oxford Handbook on Terrorism* (Chenoweth et al.) also does not contain a chapter solely on radicalisation. *Contemporary Debates on Terrorism* (Jackson and Sinclair 2011) does not mention radicalisation, but the 2018 edition (Jackson and Pisoiu) has a chapter debating the utility of 'counter-radicalisation'. As one of the authors of this debate, Charlotte Heath-Kelly (2013: 399) argues elsewhere, '[i]n contrast to long-established literatures' 'the concept of "radicalisation" has only recently gained prominence – its usage escalating after the emergence of "home-grown terrorism"' after the London bombings in July 2005. CTS thus critiques the usage of radicalisation for re-inventing an already well-established and well-respected wheel, which includes work on social movements and mobilisation by scholars like Donatella della Porta (2008) or Julie Peteet (1991), or scholars who theorise reasons behind violence more generally (see Muro-Ruiz 2002: 109).

It has been well documented that terrorism literature exploded post-9/11 (Silke 2009); the same is true when focusing specifically on radicalisation. As Heath-Kelly (2013: 399) notes, the radicalisation literature grew enormously after 2005. Tables 1 and 2 show that radicalisation and mobilisation are terms with historical trajectory in Terrorism Studies. Yet, in searching the contents of one of the leading journals, *Terrorism*

Table 4.1 Google Results for 'radicalisation terrorism' and 'mobilisation terrorism' between 1965 and 2018 (searched 18 October 2018).

	radicalisation terrorism	mobilisation terrorism
1965–1974	102	525
1975–1984	295	1,430
1985–1994	682	4,010
1995–2004	2,070	14,200
2005–2018	30,200	49,400
Total	31,600	87,600

Table 4.2 Keyword search of *Terrorism and Political Violence* for 'radicalisation' and 'mobilisation' (searched 18 October 2018).

	radicalisation	mobilisation
1988–1998	38	131
1999–2009	32	157
2010–2018	227	290
Total	297	578

Table 4.3 Keyword search of *Terrorism and Political Violence* (searched 31 October 2018).

	'Islam radicalisation'	'Muslim radicalisation'	'Neo-Nazis radicalisation'	'white supremacy radicalisation'	'Marxism radicalisation'
Total	237	222	35	28	59
Post-2005	206	194	20	21	39
Percentage Post-2005	86.9%	87.4%	57.1%	75%	66.1%

and *Political Violence*, by decade, the quantity of references to radicalisation began to grow most quickly during the last decade (2009–18). Digging into this more deeply, Table 3 displays an additional keyword content search in *Terrorism and Political Violence*, this time determining which terms radicalisation is tied to more: 'Islam', 'Muslim', 'white supremacy', 'neo-Nazis' (related to white supremacy) and 'Marxism'. In all of them, there is a significant surge in the use of 'radicalisation' post-2005; nevertheless, there were far more returns for 'Islam' or 'Muslim' than any of the other terms combined.[5]

Table 4.4 Google results of 'radicalisation terrorism' between 1965 and 2018 (searched 19 October 2018).

	radicalisation terrorism
1965–1974	701[i]
1975–1984	111
1985–1994	132
1995–2004	111
2005–2018	176

[i] Google did not provide the exact number, but there were seven pages with an average of eleven hits per page.

A further Google search of 'radicalisation terrorism' (on 23 October 2018) brought back 'about 1,540,000' results total. Table 4 demonstrates that using Google for an exercise such as this will not provide a clear response. Even though the total on the table does not equate to 1,540,000 results, it does show an increase over time. When I controlled for the UK, the only choice under 'Country' other than 'All', there were twenty pages of results for 2005–18; therefore returning only somewhere around 220 hits. Many of these results related to Islamist terrorism, radicalisation of Muslim youth, and EU and UK counter-terrorism policy. Indeed, radicalisation is very much tied to counter-terrorism and counter-radicalisation efforts, supporting the claim that 'radicalisation . . . performs a political function', one that supports securitising various communities (Heath-Kelly 2013: 398).

Counter-terrorism: Prevent Tragedies and 'Black Extremism'

The UK's counter-terrorism strategy, CONTEST, has been through various iterations since its implementation in 2003, including ones in 2008, 2011 and 2018. Its stated core values are human rights, rule of law, prosecution and counter- and de-radicalisation. There are four pieces to its framework:

Pursue: to stop attacks
Prepare: where an attack cannot be stopped, to mitigate its effects
Protect: to strengthen protection against attacks
Prevent: to stop radicalisation

The fourth, Prevent, is the main focus here, as its stated aim is to stop radicalisation, thereby reducing support for terrorism and discouraging people from becoming terrorists.

According to the UK Prevent Strategy (Home Office 2011a: 8), radicalisation is a 'process', a way of drawing people into violent extremism that often stems from outside the UK. There are five main objectives: to challenge the ideology behind violent extremism; disrupt those who promote extremism; support individuals who are vulnerable; increase resilience within communities; and address grievances. While there is some discussion of the UK's historical context, particularly the history of Irish political violence, the main contextualisation of these aims and objectives is radical Islamism, Middle East terrorism, and the UK's history with the Middle East. For instance, the 2011 Strategy (Home Office 2011a) document mentions Irish terrorism three times, some variation of the IRA (like the Real IRA) twelve times, and Loyalist groups once, whereas 'Muslim' is in the document 112 times, 'al Qaeda' ninety-eight times, 'faith' ninety-two times and 'Islam' seventy-nine times. Thus, the discourse construction of Prevent is to deflect away from non-religious extremist groups and towards a racialised religious bias concentrated on radical Islamism.

While the 2011 document claims that

> Previous Prevent work has sometimes given the impression that Muslim communities as a whole are more 'vulnerable' to radicalisation than other faith or ethnic groups.
>
> Much more needs to be done in this critical area. But it must be proportionate and focused. It must not imply a need to change the attitudes of most people in this country towards terrorism. It must not seem to pass judgement on faith or to suggest only a particular kind of faith is appropriate or acceptable. It must be done in conjunction with communities here and overseas who are often better able than Government itself to disprove the claims made by terrorist groups and to challenge terrorist and associated extremist ideologies. (Home Office 2011a, 7)

It additionally claims that there is no evidence that Muslim communities are being targeted (Home Office 2011a: 23). Yet, a Home Office review of counter-terrorism policies presented to Parliament reports that between April 2009 and March 2010, of stops and searches, 59 per cent were white, 17 per cent were Asian and 10 per cent were black (Home Office 2011b: 15). These stops and searches are suspiciously disproportionate, as the 2011 census shows that 87.1 per cent of the UK population was white, whereas only 6.9 per cent was Asian and 3 per cent was black (see also Vertigans 2010: 33).

This hyper-focus on Muslims has resulted in the largest critique of Prevent, the creation of suspect communities. While 'suspect communities' is a term that originated from work on Northern Ireland and UK counter-terrorism efforts there, it has become pertinent to the Prevent critique. Muslims from all walks of life have become the ones who bear the brunt of Prevent's objectives:

> Contemporary counterterrorism fixes Muslim communities in its gaze as risky locales from which threats may emerge and directs large policy responses towards the pre-emptive governance of Muslim communities. (Heath-Kelly 2012: 70)

Prevent and its element of suspicion 'ha[ve] become a tool of power exercised by the state and non-Muslim communities against, and to control, Muslim communities' (Githens-Mazer and Lambert 2010: 901). Muslims have a one in 500 chance of being referred to Prevent, which is forty times higher than any other UK population group (Versi 2017). Rather interestingly, while Prevent has led to the creation of 'Muslim Contact Units' in the UK, there has been no such roll out of a 'Loyalist' or 'Republican Contact Unit' in Northern Ireland (see Versi 2017). According to a *Guardian* article,

> A government official is reported to have told Gavin Robinson MP: 'Don't push the issue too far. It is really a counter-Islamic strategy,' after he asked why Northern Ireland was not included. (Versi 2017)

Returning to the argument posed at the end of Chapter 2, what responsibility then does orthodox Terrorism Studies have for the use of radicalisation by the policy world, especially if it is not the most favoured approach? While Critical Terrorism Studies scholars have been active in posing a critique of the hyper-focus on radical Islamism and radicalisation (Brown 2013; Heath-Kelly 2013; Githens-Mazer and Lambert 2010), if orthodox Terrorism Studies is also reluctant to use the term, then the policy world is intrinsically misguided in its usage of it.

Prevent Tragedies and Logics of Gender
In January 2016, the London Metropolitan Police Force launched a new counter-recruitment programme that they named 'Prevent

Tragedies'. It is comprised of a website, video and pamphlet (UK Police and Partners 2015) translated into multiple languages. The website explains that it

> was created because of the increasing concern about the worrying numbers of young people who are putting themselves at risk by travelling to Syria and other conflict zones and to help the numbers of families that have been torn apart by fear when their loved ones travel. (Prevent Tragedies 2015a)

In the next paragraph, however, it clarifies that it has a more specific agenda:

> We care deeply about the well-being of women and girls throughout the world. We reject the degrading treatment of women by terrorist organisations. We seek to prevent the tragedies caused by it.
> We declare that women and girls should not be subject to forced or bogus marriage, rape, held in slavery, denied education or encouraged to put themselves and their children in danger. Men and women who do these things to others are to be condemned. (Prevent Tragedies 2015a)

The pamphlet has a similar gendered focus: the young women who are going to Syria 'have been preyed upon, manipulated and persuaded to travel to Syria' (UK Police and Partners 2015). It continues, echoing other suggestions that young women are being 'groomed' to join:

> Glamorised images and propaganda being promoted online, coupled with the twisted words of those who seek to radicalise vulnerable and impressionable young people in our communities, are encouraging some women and girls to travel to Syria. In some cases the appeal may be the 'glamour' of marrying a fighter, or they may be confused about how to reconcile their religion with modern life, and feel compelled to follow their perceived religious obligation by joining those in Syria.

It sees these young women in the light of gender and not in the light of complicated political agency (Sjoberg and Gentry 2016; Gentry and Sjoberg 2015). Given there is no discussion of the boys and men leaving for Syria, they must be of little or no concern.

Prevent Tragedies is 'for women by women', meaning that the video and website features three Syrian 'mothers' who have settled in the UK to escape the violence. They tell mothers in the UK about their experience in Syria and why UK mothers should prevent their *daughters* from going to Syria. The page, titled 'Syrian Mothers [sic] Open Letters', which is questionably absent from the navigation bar, features these videos. At the very top of the page is a quote:

> Please tell your daughter my story so that she can understand that Syria is a dangerous place to live and no place to bring up children. (Prevent Tragedies 2015b)

It then features 'Open Letters' from these mothers, warning about the dangers of life in Syria under Da'esh. Two different letters play into neo-Orientalist tropes. One letter juxtaposes life in the UK versus life in Syria, clarifying why life in the UK is better:

> The things that you take for granted everyday in this country are things we cannot do in Syria. The reality of life in my country means that just going out of the house brings danger – people feel they have to disguise their roots, change the way they dress so that they are not treated badly just because of their religion. My husband and I were threatened just leaving our home to take our son to hospital for treatment he badly needed. My husband's brother got arrested for no reason. This was our reality. (Prevent Tragedies 2015b)

Another continues along this theme, highlighting what life under Da'esh looks like:

> If I could put myself in a young Muslim girl's shoes I would say to myself – I live in a peaceful, developed country. Why would I want to go to Syria where ISIS are taking people back hundreds of years. They are preventing people from educating themselves, making them illiterate. My sister told me of a family where all the women – including a four-year-old girl – were forced to wear full coverings. They were not allowed to walk by themselves, or do anything by themselves. This is not the Syria I know.

There is no denying the reality of these women's experiences; nor their desire to warn other women about the dangers of life in Syria; nor that life in the UK is better than in a war-torn country. What is interesting, and what needs interrogating, is how the Metropolitan Police are using this to reify a message about life in the West and to play on assumptions about (British) Muslim women's identities and values.

While the Prevent Tragedies approach may seem innovative and rather innocuous, this contributes to the creation of British Muslim communities as suspect (Heath-Kelly 2013; Smyth 2009: 194–215). Furthermore, UK counter-terrorism policy has targeted women in these suspect communities, assuming that the women will be natural allies, supportive of the policing and monitoring of *their own* communities by the government (Rashid 2013). Thus, Prevent Tragedies' targeting of Muslim 'mothers' to stop their daughters from joining is part of a longer tradition that posits women as a stopgap measure in the 'radicalisation' process (Brown 2013 and 2008). This positioning of women as civilising forces, of course, is nothing new, as discussed above in the decolonial discussion of rationality.

Even though the use of 'rationality' or even 'radicalisation' is at a minimum on this website and in these pamphlets, the intellectual trajectory is present. As discussed above, women's status and empowerment has stood as a way in which the West measures progress. Furthermore, it seems untenable to speculate that women actually choose this pathway for complicated reasons, including both political and emotion ones, but being fully aware of what it entails. For instance, Laura Sjoberg and I attempted to combat the incredulity that women's political violence is met with in the first edition of *Mothers, Monsters, Whores* (2007). Yet, when Tasheen Malik participated in a radical Islamist shooting at an office Christmas party in San Bernardino in 2015, a Brookings Institute counter-terrorist expert expressed shock over a woman's choice to be violent (Easton 2015; see also Glenza et al. 2015). This is in part driven by the essentialisation of women's nature – peaceable and nurturing. This was particularly true in the case of Malik as she was a mother with a young infant when she committed the attack and died. It is in part based on a neo-Orientalist bias that intersects with biological essentialism. In it, Muslim men are portrayed as hyper-masculine and therefore hyper-dominant, -violent, and -sexual – perhaps this is why they do not factor into Prevent Tragedies? Do neo-Orientalist attitudes towards Muslim men mean they are already 'lost' (disposable, unimportant) to the UK? Therefore, Muslim women are abused, forced into submission, and possess no political agency (Shepherd 2006: 25). The final part, then, stems from the assumption that Muslim (all) women who have access to the West and all of the apparent opportunity this brings for women would not want to betray this wealth of privilege (see Gentry 2011b).

A similar process of agency-removal is happening in Prevent Tragedies, where women's nature is essentialised and the seduction of the West is overplayed. In Prevent Tragedies and in other Prevent programmes, women are portrayed as natural allies with the law enforcement community. They are seen as the stopgap for their children's involvement in 'homegrown' terrorism or flight to Syria. It assumes that British Muslim women are *not* swayed by radical Islamist terrorism and that they desire, over any other conviction or loyalty, a liberal progressive vision for their own lives and for the lives of their children (see Brown 2013). This rather problematically places British Muslim women at odds with the premises about their own community, because their community is already perceived as untrustworthy interlopers in a liberal, progressive state. If British Muslim women are assumed to desire Western values, and if these values are seen as at odds with (radical) Islam(ism), then these women are being pitted against their faith and/or culture as well as members of their family. When women are presumed to be ready partners, this sets them up as willing to inform or defect from their 'suspect' communities (see Sjoberg and Gentry 2016). It therefore assumes that British Muslim men *should be* suspected because they are inherently untrustworthy. If one is concerned with a sense of alienation as a 'radicalising' force, maybe thinking about the message that is being sent would be the first step.

'Black Identity Extremism' and the Logics of Race

Dominant systems, like patriarchy or white supremacy, require those within the system to uphold them or risk a cost (see for instance Manne's [2018a: xxi] discussion of misogyny). Critiquing the dominant belief engenders a feeling of doubt. Alternatively, it is inordinately difficult to stay focused. In this section, I argue that the FBI, even as it recognises that white supremacist violence is rising in the US, published a report on 'Black Identity Extremism' (BIE) a month after the Charlottesville violence in July 2017 as a way of re-centring the dominant way of being. In other words, to acknowledge the rise of white supremacy poses a critique to the dominant way of being. Yet, publishing an FBI report on violent Black Identity Extremism in the months following the Charlottesville violence, which was one of the largest public demonstrations of white supremacy in recent memory, in July 2017 re-establishes the dominant social order in the US. In writing on this report, I found myself also off-centre. Even though I am very clear about the problems of white supremacist misogyny in the US (as I am in the following chapter, and as I have been in other publications [Gentry 2018b]), I found I was constantly sidetracked in critiquing the dominant paradigm.

The FBI report (2017) was driven by the 'judge[ment]' that the high volume of black people killed by law enforcement officers would lead to retaliatory actions by 'Black Identity Extremists' (see also Capehart 2017).

Membership in groups organised around black identity is growing, from 113 groups to 180 groups in 2015 (Sullivan 2016). The FBI report cobbles together groups as dissimilar as the People's New Black Panther Party and the Moorish Nation and even tacitly brings Black Lives Matter into the discussion. However, there are significant differences between these groups and it must be recognised, particularly by law enforcement, that Black Lives Matter is committed to non-violence.

The Southern Poverty Law Centre (SPLC) designates the People's New Black Panther Party as an extremist hate group that is 'virulently racist and anti-Semitic'. The former members of the (older) Black Panthers denounce it for its racist stance. It is a separatist group, demanding its own nation for all black people into which black prisoners can be released. It is known for its anti-police violence and its desire to kill all white people (SPLC 2018a). The People's New Black Panther Party also believes, strangely, like some white supremacists, that Jews were behind the 9/11 attacks, hence the need to also eliminate Jews (SPLC 2018a).

The people within the Moorish Nation consider themselves 'sovereign citizens' and refuse to obey US state and federal laws (SPLC 2018b; see also CBS News 2013). According to their ideology,

> African Americans constitute an elite class within American society with special rights and privileges that convey on them a sovereign immunity placing them beyond federal and state authority. (SPLC 2018b)

Unlike either Black Panther Party, the Moorish Nation can trace its roots back to the early 1900s and the Moorish Science Temple of America. The Washitaw Nation is related to Moorish sovereignty as those in the Washitaw Nation believe that there is a group of black people who are indigenous to the US. Therefore, they are persuaded by the sovereignty argument. The Moorish Nation's belief in their own sovereignty has led to violence, including 'shootings, bank robberies, murders, and armed confrontations with law enforcement' (SPLC 2018b). They are also 'known to produce fraudulent legal documents which they use against perceived enemies – especially publicly elected officials they view as corrupt' (SPLC 2018b).

The FBI (2017: 4–5) believes six BIE attacks have taken place since 2014, including Micah Johnson's snipe attack on Dallas police officers, Zale Thompson's hatchet attack on New York Police in Queens, and other attacks linked to the 'Moorish Nation'. Moorish sovereignty is an entity that should create concern, but it is nothing related to or linked with the attacks perpetrated by Johnson nor Thompson. Therefore, these linkages need to be unpicked and rethought, particularly because it creates a rather problematic connection between Black Lives Matter and the Moorish Nation.

It is imperative to recognise that Micah Johnson, at the very least, was mentally disturbed, having been dishonourably discharged from the US military over his mental health, and having planned his shootings to coincide with the BLM march as a matter of convenience. (There are echoes here with Major Nidal Hasan's Fort Hood shooting, explored in the previous chapter.) There was nothing to show that Johnson had any formal connection with BLM and his actions were not sanctioned by the BLM organisers or leaders. He did, admittedly, attend a few meetings of the People's New Black Panther Party, but this does raise once again the tension between mental health, race and lone wolf terrorism.

One of the key contentions of those critiquing the report argue that there is no such thing as a Black Identity Movement and that the FBI report attempts to lump together various disparate groups and in so doing, create a violent threat where one does not exist. Indeed, it is claimed that the FBI would not group neo-Nazis, the alt-right and white supremacists under the umbrella of 'White Identity Extremists' (Winter and Weinberger 2017). Yet, that is precisely what the law enforcement and counter-terrorism experts (scholars and policymakers) ostensibly do. All of those are classified under far-right or extreme-right activity, even if this is very loose. All of those are concerned with protecting the rights and 'purity' of white society, with clearly defined threats to it, whether that is the Zionist Occupation Government (ZOG)/globalists, people of colour, feminism or some other cultural identity threat.

For instance, the START (National Consortium for the Study of Terrorism and Responses to Terrorism) database defines far right as follows:

There exists a broad range of far right beliefs and actors (often overlapping movements), including both reactionary and revolutionary justifications of violence. In its modern manifestation in the United States, the ideology of the far right is generally exclusivist and favours social hierarchy, seeking an idealised future favouring a particular group, whether this group identity is racial, pseudo-national (e.g., the Texas Republic) or characterised by individualistic traits (e.g., survivalists). The extremist far right commonly shows antipathy to the political left and the federal government. As a result of this heterodoxy, this category includes radical individuals linked to extremist religious groups (e.g., Identity Christians), non-religious racial supremacists (e.g., Creativity Movement, National Alliance), tax protesters, sovereign citizens, militias and militant gun rights advocates. (START 2018)

While there is grounds for a critique of the FBI's BIE report, it needs to be made on a concrete basis that demonstrates how these two 'sides' are treated differently.

Thus, while the FBI produced a BIE report post-Charlottesville, there was not a similar response to white supremacy, even though white supremacists killed a woman and harmed dozens more. Indeed, in the aftermath of Charlottesville, a Gainesville, Florida police officer began to investigate the threat of white supremacy. Lieutenant Dan Stout recounted his frustration in a *New York Times* article:

> There were no current intelligence reports he could find on the alt-right, the sometimes-violent fringe movement that embraces white nationalism and a range of racist positions. The state police couldn't offer much insight. Things were equally bleak at the federal level. Whatever the FBI knew (which wasn't a lot, Stout suspected), they weren't sharing. The Department of Homeland Security, which produced regular intelligence and threat assessments for local law enforcement, had only scant material on white supremacists, all of it vague and ultimately not much help. Local politicians, including the governor, were also in the dark. This is like a Bermuda Triangle of intelligence, Stout thought, incredulous. He reached out to their state partners. 'So you're telling us that there's nothing? No names we can plug into the automatic license-plate readers? No players with a propensity for violence? No one you have in the system? *Nothing?*' (Reitman 2018, emphasis original)

Moreover, the violence perpetrated by white supremacist groups is not just high, it is growing. The Extremist Violence Crime Database has found that between 12 September 2001 and 2014, radical Islamists committed twenty-eight events in the US resulting in fifty-one deaths, whereas the far-right extremists committed eighty-one events resulting in 131 deaths. Yet, between 2015 and 2016 (preliminary data), radical Islamists committed three events resulting in sixty-eight deaths whereas there were eight far-right extremist events. Although the radical Islamist events resulted in more deaths – sixty-eight compared with twenty-seven – forty-nine of those were from the Pulse nightclub shooting alone (START 2017). White supremacy has found itself back in a culture of acceptance (seemingly). Socio-culturally, it is being legitimised through President Trump's own inflammatory language, as seen most particularly in the autumn of 2018, when within the space of two weeks a shooting took place at a Pittsburgh synagogue and fourteen pipe bombs were sent to Democrats, including Barack Obama and the Clintons, that Trump had declared as 'enemies'. Yet we should also be wary of giving Trump too much credit, because by doing so, we fail to look at the larger historical racist legacies which Trump is simply playing with but far from responsible for.

Finally, discussing the groups that may or may not comprise BIE re-centres the discussion in the way that a white supremacist system wants. It deflects away from white people, mainly men, who commit violence (which is often dismissed as mental illness or downplayed in some other way) and keeps reflecting back who we in the West expect to see violence from: people of colour who do not have a legitimate claim. Therefore, it is necessary to use intersectionality to interrogate this conversation. How do we keep protecting mainly white men? Where is 'toxic masculinity' within this; thus, how do ideas about masculinity drive the violence?

Conclusion

How the West constructs the Self connotes rationality, impassivity and legitimacy. The state and its agents are signified as counter-terrorists with full access to these attributes. Additionally, the relationship between the masculinisation and Westernisation of rationality means we expect certain things of certain bodies. This is why it is so difficult for the FBI to be focused on white supremacy and right-wing terrorism. The inability of law enforcement and counter-terrorists to be suspicious of right-wing/ white supremacists is telling and problematic. It is known that many right-wing sub-state armed groups have a relationship with the state and with law enforcement. It is well known that the paramilitaries in Mexico and Colombia recruit and receive funding from the law enforcement communities.

If masculinity works with rationality and assertiveness, women are nonviolent and nurturing. It is very hard to see them in a different light. This is why law enforcement can rely upon them to 'prevent' their children from going astray. We assume women never deviate – or if they do, there is something deeply broken within them (Gentry and Sjoberg 2015). It is far easier to see mothers as compliant and supportive of the state than to see them working against it. This is how their role has been constructed from the beginning – to be the Beautiful Souls that are deeply enmeshed with upholding state and political structures (Elshtain 1987, introduction and chapter 1).

Radicalisation serves as discursive mechanism for coloniality and for never being able to see brown bodies as anything but subversive and harmful. It works behind the rhetorical scenes to subtly undermine these actors: radicalisation is implicated in deviant thought, behaviour and violence. Without having to write, speak or assign 'irrationality', writing, speaking or assigning 'radicalised' does this for counter-terrorists, law enforcement and government officials. It spurns a new level of governmentality: teachers and university lecturers are meant to look for signs of radicalisation in their students. We are meant to scan our trains and buses for the 'unusual'. Yet, here, 'unusual' is tied to particular bodies and particular ways of being. Awareness enforces compliance, but not all things can be made to comply, and in this we have a problem.

Notes

1. Max Weber's critique of rationality holds that while rationalisation – systematic, efficient automated conditions – makes sense in streamlining bureaucracy and business practices, attempting to conform human relationships to this idea of rationality is ultimately alienating and erases social and moral normative customs, leading to a shift in perspectives on authority (Turner 2009: xxvi–xxvii). Weber clearly ties capitalism, modernity and rationality together as significant forces for social change. Wary of all three, there were clear limits to the utility of rationality and rationalisation in the social environment (Turner 2009: xxx).
2. Scientific rationality is identified as an ontological perspective: 'Many scientists, philosophers, and laypersons have regarded science as the one human enterprise that successfully escapes the contingencies of history to establish eternal truths about the universe, via a special, rational method of inquiry' (Nickles 2017).
3. This is the central point of 'feminisation' within the decline of violence thesis as articulated mainly by Stephen Pinker (2011) and Joshua Goldstein (2012). The thesis holds that violence in the world is declining in part because of the rise of Western civilisation, with its emphasis on democracy, civil rights and liberties, and the equality of women within it (see also Gentry 2017).
4. Instead of focusing on individual psychology and morality, process theory asks: what are the factors in a person's life that lead to radicalisation? Process refers to a sequence of events in a person's life that leads to the radicalised point, but not in a deterministic or standardising way. It looks at the 'push/pull' factors in an individual's life. Push factors are those that alienate a person from mainstream society, including lack of education, lack of access, low socio-economic status, low job prospects, ideology, friends/family network. Pull factors attract individuals to terrorist groups, and can including money, status and group acceptance (Taylor and Horgan 2006; see also McCauley and Moskalenko 2011 and 2008).
5. I did not separate out repeated articles, so there is some overlap between the various keyword searches.

References

Abrahms, Max (2004), 'Are Terrorists Really Rational? The Palestinian Example', *Orbis*, 48(3): 533–49.

Ahmed, Sara (2004), *The Cultural Politics of Emotion* (Edinburgh: Edinburgh University Press).

Anonymous (1976), 'The Female Terrorist and Her Impact on Policing', *Top Security Project*, 2(4): 242–5.

Bell, Duncan (2015), 'In Biology We Trust', in Daniel Jacobi and Annette Freyberg-Inan (eds), *Human Beings in International Relations* (Cambridge: Cambridge University Press), pp. 113–31.

Borum, Randy (2012a), 'Radicalisation into Violent Extremism I: A Review of Social Science Theories', *Journal of Strategic Security*, 4(4): 7–36.

Borum, Randy (2012b), 'Radicalisation into Violent Extremism II: A Review of Conceptual Models and Empirical Research', *Journal of Strategic Security*, 4(4): 37–62.

Borum, Randy (2012c), 'Rethinking Radicalisation', *Journal of Strategic Security*, 4(4): 1–6.

Brown, Katherine (2008), 'The Promise and Perils of Women's Participation in UK Mosques: The Impact of Securitisation Agendas on Identity, Gender and Community', *British Journal of Politics and IR*, 10(3): 472–91.

Brown, Katherine (2013), 'Gender, Prevent, and British Muslims', 16 December, <http://www.publicspirit.org.uk/gender-prevent-and-british-muslims-2/> (last accessed 24 November 2018).

Capehart, Jonathan (2017), 'Trump's War on the American People', *The Washington Post*, 9 October, <https://www.washingtonpost.com/blogs/post-partisan/wp/2017/10/09/trumps-war-on-the-american-people/> (last accessed 24 November 2018).

CBS News (2013), 'Moorish Nationals: Religious Group or Opportunists?', 25 March, <https://www.cbsnews.com/news/moorish-nationals-religious-group-or-opportunists/> (last accessed 24 November 2018).

Chakrabarty, Dipesh (1992), 'Provincialising Europe: Post-coloniality and the critique of history', *Cultural Studies*, 6(3): 337–57.

Chakrabarty, Dipesh (2009), *Provincialising Europe: Post-colonial Thought and Historical Difference-New Edition* (Princeton, NJ: Princeton University Press).

Chenoweth, Erica, and Maria J. Stephan (2011), *Why Civil Resistance Works: The Strategic Logic of Nonviolent Conflict* (New York: Columbia University Press).

Chenoweth, Erica, Richard English, Andreas Gofas and Stahis N. Kalyvas (eds) (2019), *The Oxford Handbook of Terrorism* (Oxford: Oxford University Press).

Cooper, H. A. A. (1979), 'Woman as Terrorist', in Freda Adler and Rita James Simon. *The Criminology of Deviant Women* (Boston: Houghton Mifflin).

Crenshaw, Martha (1981), 'The Causes of Terrorism', *Comparative Politics*, 13(4): 379–99.

Crenshaw, Martha (1987), 'Theories of Terrorism: Instrumental and Organizational Approaches', *The Journal of Strategic Studies*, 10(4): 13–31.

Crenshaw, Martha (1990), 'The Logic of Terrorism: Terrorist Behaviour as a Product of Strategic Choice', in Walter Reich (ed.), *The Origins of Terrorism: Psychologies, Ideologies, Theologies, States of Mind* (Washington, DC: Woodrow Wilson Press), pp. 7–24.

Crenshaw, Martha (2014), 'Terrorism Research: The Record', *International Interactions*, 40(4): 556–67.

De Carvalho, Benjamin, Halvard Leira and John M. Hobson (2011), 'The Big Bangs of IR: The Myths that Your Teachers Still Tell You About 1648 and 1919', *Millennium*, 39(3): 735–58.

Delatolla, Andrew, and Joanne Yao (2018), 'Racialising Religion: Constructing Colonial Identities in the Syrian Provinces in the Nineteenth Century', *International Studies Review*, doi: https://doi.org/10.1093/isr/viy060.

Della Porta, Donatella (2008), 'Research on Social Movements and Political Violence', *Qualitative Sociology*, 31(3): 221–30.

Easton, Nina (2015), 'How ISIS is Recruiting Women – and Turning Them into Brutal Enforcers', *Fortune*, 5 May, <http://fortune.com/2015/05/05/isis-women-recruiting> (last accessed 24 November 2018).

Elshtain, Jean Bethke (1987), *Women and War* (Chicago: University of Chicago Press).

Elshtain, Jean Bethke (1981), *Public Man, Private Woman: Women in Social and Political Thought* (Princeton, NJ: Princeton University Press).

FBI (2017), 'Black Identity Extremists Likely Motivated to Target Law Enforcement Officers', 3 August, <https://www.documentcloud.org/documents/4067711-BIE-Redacted.html> (last accessed 24 November 2018).

Fromkin, David (1975), 'The Strategy of Terrorism', *Foreign Affairs*, 53(4): 683–98.

Ganor, Boaz (2002), 'Defining Terrorism: Is One Man's Terrorist Another Man's Freedom Fighter?', *Police Practice and Research*, 3(4): 287–304.

Ganor, Boaz (2005), *The Counter-Terrorism Puzzle: A Guide for Decision Makers* (London: Transaction).

Gentry, Caron E. (2011b), 'The Neo-Orientalist Narratives of Women's Involvement in al-Qaeda', in Laura Sjoberg and Caron E. Gentry (eds), *Women, Gender, and Terrorism* (Athens: University of Georgia Press), pp. 176–94.

Gentry, Caron E. (2015), 'Anxiety and the Creation of the Scapegoated Other', *Critical Studies on Security*, 3(2): 133–46.

Gentry, Caron E. (2016a), 'The Mysterious Case of Aafia Siddiqui: Gothic Intertextual Analysis of neo-Orientalist Narratives', *Millennium*, 45(1): 3–24.

Gentry, Caron E. (2017), 'The "Duel" Meaning of Feminisation in International Relations: The Rise of Women and the Interior Logics of Declinist Literature', *Global Responsibility to Protect*, 9(1): 101–24.

Gentry, Caron E. (2018b), *This American Moment: A Feminist Christian Realist Intervention* (New York: Oxford University Press).

Gentry, Caron E., and Laura Sjoberg (2016), 'Female Terrorism and Militancy', in Richard D. Jackson (ed.), *Routledge Handbook of Critical Terrorism Studies* (Abingdon: Routledge), pp. 145–56.

Githens-Mazer, Jonathan, and Robert Lambert (2010), 'Why Conventional Wisdom on Radicalisation Fails: The Persistence of a Failed Discourse', *International Affairs*, 86(4): 889–901.

Gigerenzer, Gerd (2001), 'The Adaptive Toolbox', in Gerd Gigerenzer and Reinhard Selten (eds), *Bounded Rationality: The Adaptive Toolbox* (Cambridge, MA: MIT Press), pp. 37–50.

Glenza, Jessica, Tom Dart, Andrew Gumbel and Jon Boone (2015), 'Tasheen Malik: Who was the "Shy Housewife" Turned San Bernardino Killer?', *The Guardian*, 6 December, <http://www.theguardian.com/us-news/2015/dec/06/tashfeen-malik-who-was-the-shy-housewife-turned-san-bernardino-killer> (last accessed 22 November 2018).

Goldstein, Joshua S. (2012), *Winning the War on War: The Decline of Armed Conflict Worldwide* (New York: Plume Books).

Heath-Kelly, Charlotte (2010), 'Critical Terrorism Studies, Critical Theory, and the "Naturalistic Fallacy"', *Security Dialogue*, 41(3): 235–54.

Heath-Kelly, Charlotte (2012), 'Reinventing Prevention or Exposing the Gap? False Positives in UK Terrorism Governance and the Quest for Pre-Emption', *Critical Studies on Terrorism*, 5(1): 69–87.

Heath-Kelly, Charlotte (2013), 'Counterterrorism and the Counterfactual: Producing the "Radicalisation" Discourse and the UK PREVENT Strategy', *The British Journal of Politics and International Relations*, 15(3): 394–415.

Hoffman, Bruce (1999), 'Terrorism Trends and Prospects', in Ian Lesser, John Arguilla, Bruce Hoffman, David F. Ronfeldt and Michele Zanini (eds), *Countering the New Terrorism* (Santa Monica, CA: RAND), pp. 7–38.

Hoffman, Bruce (2002), 'Rethinking Terrorism and Counterterrorism Since 9/11', *Studies in Conflict and Terrorism*, 25(5): 303–16.

Hoffman, Bruce (2006), *Inside Terrorism* (New York: Columbia University Press).

Home Office (2011a), *Prevent Strategy*, June <https://assets.publishing.service.gov.uk/government/uploads/system/uploads/attachment_data/file/97976/prevent-strategy-review.pdf> (last accessed 24 November 2018).

Home Office (2011b), 'Review of Counterterrorism and Security Findings', <https://assets.publishing.service.gov.uk/government/uploads/system/uploads/attachment_data/file/97972/review-findings-and-rec.pdf> (last accessed 24 November 2018).

Hoppe, Robert (1999), 'Policy Analysis, Science and Politics: From "Speaking Truth to Power" to "Making Sense Together"', *Science and Public Policy*, 26(3): 201–10.

Hudson, Valerie, Bonnie Ballif-Spanvill, Mary Caprioli and Chad F. Emmett (2012), *Sex and World Peace* (New York: Columbia University Press).

Jackson, Richard D. (2005), *Writing the War on Terrorism: Language, Politics, and Counterterrorism* (Manchester: Manchester University Press).

Jackson, Richard D. (2007), 'Constructing Enemies: "Islamic Terrorism" in Political and Academic Discourse', *Government and Opposition*, 42(3): 394–426;

Jackson, Richard D. (2012), 'Unknown Knowns: The Subjugated Knowledge of Terrorism Studies', *Critical Studies on Terrorism*, 5(1): 11–29.

Jackson, Richard D., and Daniela Pisoiu (eds) (2018), *Contemporary Debates on Terrorism* (Abingdon: Routledge).

Jackson, Richard D., and Samuel Justin Sinclair (eds) (2011), *Contemporary Debates on Terrorism* (Abingdon: Routledge).

Jarvis, Lee (2009), *Times of Terror: Discourse, Temporality, and the War on Terror* (Basingstoke: Palgrave MacMillan).

Juergensmeyer, Mark (1999), *Terror in the Mind of God: The Global Rise of Religious Violence* (Berkeley: University of California Press).

Kydd, Andrew H., and Barbara F. Walter (2006), 'The Strategies of Terrorism', *International Security*, 31(1): 49–80.

Lake, David A. (2002), 'Rational Extremism: Understanding Terrorism in the Twenty-First Century', *Dialogue IO*, 1(1): 15–28.

Laqueur, Walter (1996), 'Postmodern Terrorism', *Foreign Affairs*, 75(5): 24–36.

Laqueur, Walter (1999), *The New Terrorism: Fanaticism and the Arms of Mass Destruction* (Oxford: Oxford University Press).

Levy, Jack S. (2002), 'Daniel Kahneman: Judgment, Decision, and Rationality', *PSOnline*, <https://pdfs.semanticscholar.org/47b0/312fb97a83e3f9bb639f3309e960e5037664.pdf> (last accessed 24 November 2018): 271–3.

Lindhal, Sondre (2018), *A Critical Theory of Counterterrorism: Ontology, Epistemology, and Normativity* (Abingdon: Routledge).

Massumi, Brian (2005), 'Fear (the Spectrum Said)', *positions: east asia cultures critique*, 13(1): 31–48.

McCauley, Clark, and Sophia Moskalenko (2008), 'Mechanisms of Political Radicalisation: Pathways toward Terrorism', *Terrorism and Political Violence*, 20(3): 415–33.

McCauley, Clark, and Sophia Moskalenko (2011), *Friction: How Conflict Radicalises Them and Us* (Oxford: Oxford University Press).

McClintock, Anne (2013), *Imperial Leather: Race, Gender, and Sexuality in the Colonial Contest* (Abingdon: Routledge).

McCormick, Gordon H. (2003), 'Terrorist Decision Making', *Annual Review of Political Science*, 6(1): 473–507.

Merari, Ariel (1990), 'Suicidal Terrorism', in Walter Reich (ed.), *The Origins of Terrorism: Psychologies, Ideologies, Theologies, States of Mind* (Washington, DC: Woodrow Wilson Press), pp. 192–210.

Muppidi, Himadeep (2006), 'Shame and Rage: International Relations and the World School of Colonialism', in Robin L. Riley and Naeem Inayatullah (eds), *Interrogating Imperialism* (Basingstoke: Palgrave Macmillan), pp. 51–61.

Muro-Ruiz, Diego (2002), 'The Logic of Violence', *Politics*, 22(2): 109–17.

Mutua, Makau (2001), 'Savages, Victims, and Saviours: The Metaphor of Human Rights', *Harvard International Law Review*, 42(1): 201–45.

Nayak, Meghana (2006), 'Orientalism and "Saving" US State Identity after 9/11', *International Feminist Journal of Politics*, 8(1): 42–61.

Neuman, Peter R. (2010), 'Prisons and Terrorism Radicalisation and De-radicalisation in 15 Countries', *International Centre for the Study of Radicalisation and Political Violence*, <https://www.clingendael.org/sites/default/files/pdfs/Prisons-and-terrorism-15-countries.pdf> (last accessed 26 November 2018).

Nickles, Thomas (2017), 'Historicist Theories of Scientific Rationality', *Stanford Encyclopaedia of Philosophy*, <https://plato.stanford.edu/entries/rationality-historicist/> (last accessed 24 November 2018).

Nurmi, Hannah (2010), 'Thin Rationality and Representation of Preferences with Implications to Spatial Voting Models', in Salvatore Greco, Ricardo Alberto Marques Pereira, Massimo Squillante, Ronald R. Yager and Janusz Kacprzyk (eds), *Preferences and Decisions: Studies in Fuzziness and Soft Computing* (New York: Springer), pp. 321–37.

Nussbaum, Martha C. (2003), *Upheavals of Thought: The Intelligence of Emotions* (Cambridge: Cambridge University Press).

Palermo, Mark T. (2013), 'Development Disorders and Political Extremism: A Case Study of Asperger Syndrome and the Neo-Nazi Subculture', *Journal of Forsenic Psychology Practice*, 13(4), 341–54.

Pape, Robert A. (2003), 'The Strategic Logic of Suicide Terrorism', *American Political Science Review*, 97(3): 343–61.

Pape, Robert A. (2006), *Dying to Win: The Strategic Logic of Suicide Terrorism* (New York: Random House).

Pateman, Carole (1980), '"The Disorder of Women:" Women, Love, and the Sense of Justice', *Ethics*, 91(1): 20–34.

Peteet, Julie (1991), *Gender in Crisis: Women in the Palestinian Resistance Movement* (New York: Columbia University Press).

Pinker, Stephen (2011), *The Better Angels of Our Nature: A History of Violence and Humanity* (New York: Penguin).

Post, Jerrold M. (1990), 'Terrorist Psycho-Logic: Terrorist Behaviour as a Product of Psychological Forces', in Walter Reich (ed.), *The Origins of Terrorism: Psychologies, Ideologies, Theologies, States of Mind* (Washington, DC: Woodrow Wilson Press), pp. 25–42.

Prevent Tragedies (2015a), 'About', <http://www.preventtragedies.co.uk/about/> (last accessed 24 November 2018).

Prevent Tragedies (2015b), 'Syrian Mothers Open Letters', <http://www.preventtragedies .co.uk/syrianmothers/> (last accessed 24 November 2018).

Ranstorp, Magnus (1996), 'Terrorism in the Name of Religion', *Journal of International Affairs*, 50(1): 41–62.

Rapheal, Sam (2009), 'In the Service of Power: Terrorism Studies and US Intervention in the Global South', in Richard D. Jackson, Marie Breen Smyth and Jerone Gunning (eds), *Critical Terrorism Studies: A New Research Agenda* (Abingdon: Routledge), pp. 49–65.

Rapoport, David C. (1984), 'Fear and Trembling: Terrorism in Three Religious Traditions', *American Political Science Review*, 78(3): 658–77.

Rapoport, David C. (2012), 'Fear and Trembling: Terrorism in Three Religious Traditions', in John Horgan and Kurt Braddock (eds), *Terrorism Studies: A Reader* (Abingdon: Routledge), pp. 3–26.

Rashid, Naaz (2013), 'Giving the Silent Majority a Stronger Voice? Initiatives to Empower Muslim Women as Part of the UK's "War on Terror"', *Ethnic and Racial Studies*, 37(4): 589–604.

Reich, Walter (ed.) (1990), *The Origins of Terrorism: Psychologies, Ideologies, Theologies, States of Mind* (Washington, DC: Woodrow Wilson Press).

Reitman, Janet (2018), 'US Law Enforcement Failed to See the Threat of White Nationalism. Now They Don't Know How to Stop It', *The New York Times*, 3 November, <https://www.nytimes.com/2018/11/03/magazine/FBI-charlottesville-white-nationalism-far-right.html> (last accessed 24 November 2018).

Richards, Anthony (2011), 'The Problem with "Radicalisation": The Remit of "Prevent" and the Need to Refocus on Terrorism in the UK', *International Affairs*, 87(1): 143–52.

Said, Edward (1978), *Orientalism* (London: Vintage).

Silke, Andrew (2009), 'Contemporary Terrorism Studies: Issues in Research', in Richard D. Jackson, Marie Breen Smyth and Jerone Gunning (eds), *Critical Terrorism Studies: A New Research Agenda* (Abingdon: Routledge), pp. 34–48.

Shepherd, Laura J. (2006), 'Veiled References: Constructions of Gender in the Bush Administration Discourse on the Attacks on Afghanistan Post-9/11', *International Journal of Feminist Politics*, 8(1): 19–41.

Simpson-Baikie, Shai (2018), 'The Netherlands' Surprise New Best Seller: Hitler's "Mein Kampf"', *Haaretz*, September 28, <https://www.haaretz.com/world-news/europe/.premium-the-netherlands-surprise-new-best-seller-hitler-s-mein-kampf-1.6512781> (last accessed 21 July 2019).

Sjoberg, Laura, and Caron E. Gentry (2008a), 'Profiling Terror: Gendering the Strategic Logic of Suicide Terror and Other Narratives', *Austrian Journal of Political Science*, 2: 181–96.

Sjoberg, Laura, and Caron E. Gentry (2008b), 'Reduced to Bad Sex: Narratives of Violent Women from the Bible to the War on Terror', *International Relations*, 22(1): 5–23.

Smith, Linda Tuhiwai (2012), *Decolonising Methodologies: Research and Indigenous Peoples* (London: Zed Books).

Smyth, Marie Breen (2009), 'Subjectivities, "Suspect Communities", Governments, and the Ethics of Research on "Terrorism"', in Richard D. Jackson, Marie Breen Smyth and Jerone Gunning (eds), *Critical Terrorism Studies: A New Research Agenda* (Abingdon: Routledge), pp. 194–215.

Southern Poverty Law Centre (2018a), 'New Black Panther Party', <https://www.splcenter.org/fighting-hate/extremist-files/group/new-black-panther-party> (last accessed 24 November 2018).

Southern Poverty Law Centre (2018b), 'Moorish Sovereign Citizens', <https://www.splcenter.org/fighting-hate/extremist-files/group/moorish-sovereign-citizens> (last accessed 24 November 2018).

Spivak, Gayatri Chakravorty (1988), 'Can the Subaltern Speak?', in Cary Nelson and Larry Grossberg (eds), *Marxism and the Interpretation of Culture* (Urbana: University of Illinois Press), pp. 271–313.

Sprinzak, Ehud (2009), 'Rational Fanatics', *Foreign Policy*, 20 November, <https://foreignpolicy.com/2009/11/20/rational-fanatics/> (last accessed 25 November 2018).

Stampnitzky, Lisa (2013), *Disciplining Terrorism: How 'Experts' Invented Terrorism* (Cambridge: Cambridge University Press).

Stares, Paul B., and Mona Yacoubian (2007), 'Terrorism as a Disease: An Epidemio-logical Model for Countering Islamist Extremism', Matthew B. Ridgeway Cen-tre for International Security Studies, <https://pdfs.semanticscholar.org/3a62/c0105444e2739f40357091f76db6c74f2eff.pdf> (last accessed 26 November 2018).

START (2017), 'Islamist and Far-Right Homicides in the United States', <https://www.start.umd.edu/pubs/START_ECDB_IslamistFarRightHomicidesUS_Infographic_Feb2017.pdf> (last accessed 24 November 2018).

START (2018), 'PIRUS: Frequently Asked Questions', <https://www.start.umd.edu/pirus-frequently-asked-questions#q7> (last accessed 22 November 2018).

Stephan, Maria J., and Erica Chenoweth (2008), 'Why Civil Resistance Works: The Strategic Logic of Nonviolent Conflict', *International Security*, 33(1): 7–44.

Stern, Jessica (2003), *Terror in the Name of God* (New York: Ecco).

Sullivan, Kevin (2016), 'The Rise of Black Nationalist Groups that Captivated Killers in Dallas, Baton Rouge', *The Washington Post*, 23 July, <https://www.washingtonpost.com/national/inside-the-black-nationalist-groups-that-captivated-killers-in-dallas-baton-rouge/2016/07/23/e53aef66-4f89-11e6-a422-83ab49ed5e6a_story.html?utm_term=.c7c4f3fded39> (last accessed 24 November 2018).

Taylor, Max, and John Horgan (2006), 'A Conceptual Framework for Addressing Psychological Process in the Development of the Terrorist', *Terrorism and Political Violence*, 18(4): 585–601.

Thayer, Bradley A., and Valerie M. Hudson (2010), 'Sex and Shaheed: Insights from the Life Sciences on Islamic Suicide Terrorism', *International Security*, 34(4): 37–62.

Tickner, J. Ann (1997), 'You Just Don't Understand: Troubled Engagements Between Feminists and IR Theorists', *International Studies Quarterly*, 41(4): 611–32.

Toulmin, Stephen (1982), 'The Construal of Reality: Criticism in Modern and Postmodern Science', *Critical Inquiry*, 9(1): 93–111.

True, Jacqui (2015), 'Winning the Battle but Losing the War on Violence: A Feminist Perspective on the Declining Global Violence Thesis', *International Feminist Journal of Politics*, 17(4): 554–72.

Turner, Bryan (2009), 'Preface', in Max Weber, *Essays in Sociology* (Abingdon: Routledge), pp. ix–xii.

Tversky, Amos, and Daniel Kahneman (1974), 'Judgment Under Uncertainty: Heuristics and Biases', *Science*, 185(4157): 1124–31.

UK Police and Partners (2015), 'Working with Mothers to Prevent Tragedies', <http://www.preventtragedies.co.uk/wp-content/uploads/2015/03/CT_A5_4PP_Online-usage.pdf> (last accessed 24 November 2018).

Versi, Miqdaad (2017), 'The Latest Prevent Figures Show Why the Strategy Needs an Independent Review', *The Guardian*, 10 November, <https://www.theguardian.com/commentisfree/2017/nov/10/prevent-strategy-statistics-independent-review-home-office-muslims> (last accessed 24 November 2018).

Vertigans, Stephen (2010), 'British Muslims and the UK Government's "War On Terror" Within: Evidence of a Clash of Civilizations or Emergent De-Civilizing Processes?', *The British Journal of Sociology*, 61(1): 26–44.

Volintiru, Clara (2010), 'Towards a Dynamic Model of Terrorist Radicalization', European Institute of Romania, Bucharest, <https://www.econstor.eu/bitstream/10419/140677/1/642367078.pdf> (last accessed 26 November 2018).

Weenink, Anton W. (2015), 'Behavioural Problems and Disorders among Radicals in Police Files', *Perspectives on Terrorism*, 9(2), <http://www.terrorismanalysts.com/pt/index.php/pot/article/view/416/html> (last accessed 21 July 2019).

Winter, Jana, and Sharon Weinberger (2017), 'The FBI's New US Terrorist Threat: "Black Identity Extremists"', *Foreign Policy*, 6 October, <https://foreignpolicy.com/2017/10/06/the-fbi-has-identified-a-new-domestic-terrorist-threat-and-its-black-identity-extremists/> (last accessed 24 November 2018).

CHAPTER 5

What Does Not Get Counted:
Misogynistic Terrorism

In the wake of the #metoo movement and the election of Trump, feminist public figure Rebecca Solnit (CBC 2018) stated in a radio interview:

> I wish we talked about misogyny as a kind of terrorism or hate group or something like that . . . Misogynist violence is so pervasive now. You know as Kim Wall's[1] killers [sic] [was] just sentenced, as we wait to hear the jury verdict on Bill Cosby,[2] as we deal with so many other stories like this one . . . or [any other] stories of hatred and violence against women.

What Solnit may not be aware of is that there is a way of talking about misogynistic violence as terrorism – it just has not been accepted by mainstream Terrorism Studies, nor has it filtered from some circles of feminism into the larger public. Therefore, there are two concurrent trends this chapter wishes to interrogate and bring together.

The first is to elaborate upon long-standing scholarship on what is termed by different scholars as patriarchal, intimate or everyday terrorism, which looks at domestic violence as terrorism. I build upon these forms and align them more substantially with what feminists outside of IR and Terrorism Studies call 'misogynistic terrorism', which expansively includes mass shootings and sexual violence. In doing so, a second trend is equally important: to look at how white supremacy has come back out of the shadows, and how misogyny is as central as the racism. This can be seen within the thinking on 'misogynoir', or the way black women are emotionally, physically and structurally harmed by the raced and gendered narratives particular to them (see Bailey and

Trudy 2018). It captures the continued frustration with the erasures committed by white feminism and black (male) activism:

> [M]isogynoir lives in a realm apart from general-use sexism – which often acts as a placeholder for strictly white women's experiences with misogyny – and anti-Black racism that targets Black men. Misogynoir acknowledges that while white women have been fighting for the chance to prove themselves in the workplace, Black women are considered the workhorse of both white and Black America. (Jackson 2014)

In order to bring these together, it is important to see how thinking on this violence as 'terrorist' has evolved and to envision where it needs to go next.

As stated, mainstream Terrorism Studies has been somewhat resistant to the inclusion of violence against women as a form of terrorism. None of the main Terrorism Studies journals have ever published a piece on patriarchal/intimate/everyday terrorism, nor have any of the edited volumes ever dared to include a chapter on it. Instead, the work that has been done on it has been included in *Studies on Critical Terrorism*, or journals in human geography, sociology and psychology. When I went to publish an article on why orthodox Terrorism Studies should consider a more direct inclusion of 'patriarchal terrorism' in the literature, I received two desk rejects from orthodox Terrorism Studies journals. Clearly, the article may not have been that great, but at the same time, the editors cited that 'it had already been done'. Instead, *Studies on Critical Terrorism* has been the academic home to this work within the Terrorism Studies stream, having published an excellent article linking patriarchal politics, political violence and domestic abuse in Spain (Ortbals and Poloni-Staudinger 2014) and a special issue I edited with Laura Sjoberg on 'everyday terrorism' (2015).

This reluctance stems from several places. First, IR literature tends to point to domestic violence as something that is declining in the West as it is seen as an aberration to the aspirational rationality of Western democratic order. Whether one relies upon the Democratic Peace thesis or the Decline of Violence thesis (see Gentry 2017; True 2015), war is considered an unfortunate failure, and violence within a society is evidence of socio-political ills. Within this thinking, war and indeed individual violence are declining in the West due to civilisational trends, including the rise of liberal democracy concurrently with rights (Goldstein 2012; Pinker 2011).

Second, to see violence against women as a form of terrorism within the West means seeing those who are typically aligned with counter-terrorists as suddenly aligned with the terrorists themselves:

Naming domestic abuse as terrorism applies to white and non-white perpetrators. While men of colour are more likely to be labelled violent in white western societies, in reality they, and women of colour, are at heightened risk from a range of violences. A significant literature, still often overlooked in policy and academic work, has highlighted the universalism and whiteness of mainstream theories of and responses to everyday terrorism. (Pain 2014: 534)

To reiterate, the mainstream has assumed normalcy and authority resides within the white male figure – the counter-terrorist – while deviancy becomes aligned with the non-white Other. On some level, this chapter then aims to use queer logics on the white male counter-terrorist, arguing that the figure often held as the 'saviour' (Mutua 2001) is actually the violent one who harms; in other words, the white man is queered, transforming from a *counter*-terrorist into a counter-terrorist/terrorist figuration.

Valourising the West and the security of those within it has led to another problem. Women's precarity is often dichotomised: women in the West are reaping the benefits of liberal equality and face few problems (for a critique of this perspective, see Gentry 2017) while women outside of the West have to contend with numerous inequalities, ranging from a lack of education to prevalent domestic violence. This dichotomy exists for a reason, playing into the hierarchies of international politics. It upholds the West as a paragon of liberal virtue, a place where people flourish and where rationality and justice exist, and it demotes the non-West.

Yet, this is a myth. Not all people flourish in the West – the racial and misogynist structures make sure of that. While the last chapter touched all too briefly on the violence and harm that people of colour face, this chapter looks at the harm women face. The homicide rate for women of colour is nearly double the national average: according to a 2017 Centre for Disease Control report:

Black women are killed at a rate of 4.4 per 100,000 people, and indigenous women at a rate of 4.3 per 100,000; every other race has a homicide rate of between 1 and 2 per 100,000. (Domonoske 2017)

Women are the largest victims of mass shootings[3] in the United States.[4] The shooters are mainly white men (there has been one female shooter)

(Follman et al. 2018). While a substantial number of the attackers showed signs of untreated mental illness (Follman et al. 2018), bringing up the tension that exists in lone wolf terrorism as highlighted in Chapter 3, a significant number have also relied upon a misogynistic and white supremacist belief system in attacks beyond the US, including Canada, the UK and Norway. For instance, while it was immediately recognised after the 2018 Toronto van attack that the perpetrator believed he was engaged in the 'incel rebellion' (Crilly et al. 2018), it is less known that Breivik was also inspired by misogyny that worked in tandem with his white supremacy (Jones 2011). This intersection of misogyny and racism is not surprising, yet it needs further exploration, particularly in the light of the theme of this chapter: misogynistic terrorism. This risks doing what many resist: seeing white men as the terrorist – as the perpetrators of political violence in a Western state, independent of war or high-intensity conflict.

Three prominent attacks help to illustrate this connection. On 23 May 2014, Elliot Rodger first stabbed his two Chinese roommates and their friend, also Chinese, before driving to the area surrounding the University of California, Santa Barbara known as Isla Vista, intending to kill the women of the 'hottest' sorority on campus. When his loud knocking at the sorority house was not answered, he shot three women outside of the house, then drove around Isla Vista, shooting and running over fourteen other individuals. He killed two women and four men in total. On 17 June 2015, Dylann Storm Roof entered a black Methodist church in Charleston, South Carolina, killing six black women and three black men gathered for a bible study. Even though his motivation is described as white supremacist, as he stated that his hope was to start a race war, during the attack Roof articulated his fear of black men's sexual relationships with white women (Roof 2014; Bell 2017). Additionally, Breivik's manifesto expresses a clear misogyny, one that links explicitly to his political goals: where 'feminist ideology' aims at 'transforming a patriarchy into a matriarchy and intends to deny the intrinsic worth of native Christian European heterosexual males' (as cited in Jones 2011).

While Rodgers is often listed within the many shooting attacks on women in the United States, Roof is only listed as a white supremacist. Yet, these shootings are not just one or the other. I made a point of including Rodgers' stabbing of his roommates and their friend – an intimate and aggressive killing – because of the strong relationship between misogyny and racism. Additionally, two-thirds of Roof's victims were women: a factor that may be explained because women make up the majority of church-goers (Fahmy 2018); yet something that should not be chalked up as merely coincidental either. Finally, Breivik was not just concerned with feminism, but with Islam and his perception of its growing power within Europe (Jones 2011). Intersecting the identity of victims of mass shootings is key to understanding these attacks, and to seeing them as terrorist violence.

This chapter will begin by tracing out the intellectual history of 'patriarchal terrorism', a concept that has grown out of sociology and psychology. It has evolved over the years from 'patriarchal' (Johnson 1995) to 'intimate' (Anderson 2008; Gradinariu 2007; Dobash and Dobash 2004) to 'everyday' terrorism (Pain 2014 and 2012). While the literature discusses race and patriarchy as structures, it does not fully connect the structures of misogyny with the structures of racism. When asking the other question, these cannot be divorced. Thus, the next section will look at how this violence fits into an orthodox definition of terrorism, drawing upon the key areas as outlined in Chapter 1. In particular it will focus on the ideology of the alt-right, a new form of white supremacist misogyny that takes inspiration from and for multiple attacks that target women.

Patriarchal/Intimate/Everyday Terrorism

R. Emerson Dobash and Russell P. Dobash began their work on the form of domestic violence that became known as 'patriarchal terrorism' by making the argument that domestic violence against women was a long-standing Western norm – from the Romans and Anglo-Saxons through to present-day America – that formed male domination 'through socially approved marital hierarchy' (1979, back cover). Dobash and Dobash's (1984: 269) early research was to locate domestic abuse against women within the same realm of study as 'interpersonal violence, homicides, and assaults' while also differentiating it from these other violences. For instance, other forms of violence were then seen as discrete and episodic, where men (as the primary perpetrators) 'sought out violent encounters and interactional settings with the intention of using violence' in the short term (Dobash and Dobash 1984: 271–2, 286).

In contrast, domestic violence was part of the structure of some marital relationships and therefore a constant and always present threat (Dobash and Dobash 1984: 271–2). It is intentional and purposeful violence:

[T]he majority of men who use violence against their wives usually enter verbal confrontations with the intentions of punishing, regulating, and controlling their wives through . . . the use of physical force. (Dobash and Dobash 1984: 286)

When men were abusive, the violence was paradigmatic of patriarchy; these men 'are deeply embedded in the existing intentions of male aggressors and these in turn are shaped and legitimated by a wider, socio-cultural context of patriarchal domination' (Dobash and Dobash 1984: 286–7). Therefore, Dobash and Dobash's (1998) additional research continues to draw connections between what occurs domestically in the home and what public – political, sociological, cultural – structures exist. Thus, domestic abuse is not simply about the control of that *one* woman, but about all women. Domestic abuse is one means amongst many of upholding the patriarchy. Domestic abuse is intimately tied to sexual violence, female genital mutilation and higher violence against women in conflict zones (see Dobash and Dobash 1998).

Building upon the work of Dobash and Dobash, Michael Johnson (1995) was one of the first to articulate and define a specific form of domestic abuse as 'patriarchal terrorism'. By emphasising the 'historical traditions of patriarchal family, contemporary constructions of masculinity and femininity, and structural constraints that make escape difficult for women who are systematically beaten', he specifies that 'patriarchal terrorism' is an escalating form of physical, emotional and economic abuse via 'subordination, threats, isolation, and other control tactics' borne of the patriarchal attitudes of the male abusers' ownership of 'their' women (Johnson 1995: 284). Furthermore, the use of 'terrorism' maintains the focus upon the 'systematic, intentional nature' of the violence, whereas the use of 'patriarchal' draws attention to the male perpetrator and the historical and cultural roots of this form of violence (Johnson 1995: 284).

There are some evident limitations of this earlier research. One, there is a typical understanding of men as the primary perpetrators, even if a patriarchal system demands conformity and complicity of all actors. Women may also learn to use violence in order to enforce gender norms. Therefore, in the early 2000s, the scholarship on patriarchal terrorism began to morph based upon the need to incorporate the statistics that demonstrated violence against men was a growing phenomenon (Dobash and Dobash 2004; see also Anderson 2008; Gradinariu 2007). Thus, Nicola Graham Kevan and John Archer (2004) coined 'intimate terrorism' as a 'gender-neutral' term. Unlike Johnson (1995), Kevan and Archer (2004) found that both men and women engage in the controlling, spiralling aggression that forms this style of terroristic violence. Yet, this argument also fails to capture the complexity of patriarchal/intimate terrorism. Therefore, second, these earlier conceptions, while relating the violence back to the larger ideology of patriarchy, remain focused upon domestic violence, instead of the larger incorporation of all violences that may come under patriarchal terrorism, or my preference, misogynistic terrorism.

There are two key pieces of scholarship that demonstrate the connections between domestic abuse and other forms of patriarchal violences. First, Candice Ortbals and Lori Poloni-Staudinger (2014) provide evidence for the relationship between three levels of political violence in Spain. They first identify intimate terrorism, highlighting the discursive and social connections it has with the second type, the ethno-nationalist violence of the Basque group ETA. The third form is the Spanish government response to the ETA, specifically identifying this as state terrorism. *Terrorismo machista*, 'the violence associated with extreme masculinity', links all three forms of terrorism (Ortbals and Poloni-Staudinger 2014: 348). To them, the connection between all three forms of terrorism is evident in the fact that

> [s]tate and societal responses to said [ETA] terrorism overlap with responses to other terrorisms; among them, the use of protest through women in movements and state resources harnessed to stop terrorist violence (Ortbals and Poloni-Staudinger 2014: 351)

Importantly, recognising these 'intersections between terrorism types problematises mainstream definitions' and allows them (and others) to 'rais[e] future inquiries about how gender structures each terrorism type' (Ortbals and Poloni-Stuadinger 2014: 351). In other words, the 'personal' terrorism of domestic violence is not separate from the sociopolitical terrorism of ETA and the Spanish response because patriarchal values – *machista* – organise all three of them. If a society prioritises a masculinised ideal of violence, then such a prioritisation is going to structure that society.

The second piece of scholarship is by human geographer Rachel Pain (2014: 531–2), who connects intimate terrorism – or everyday terrorism – with global terrorism. She argues that global terrorism – the terrorism specifically articulated during the War on Terror – was framed as both global and intimate (Pain 2014: 531–2). The global is obvious to those who know the rationale behind the War on Terror – that al Qaeda operatives are likely to be hidden within Western societies, ready to be randomly activated at any moment; and that al Qaeda had infiltrated multiple regional conflicts, such as Chechnya, Pakistan and Palestine. Equally, it was *intimate* in that US discourse made women's insecurity in Afghanistan part of the intervention justification. In one of First Lady Laura Bush's only national addresses, she used women's vulnerability to domestic violence and micro-level social coercion by the Taliban in Afghanistan to find support for the US intervention there.

Because of this connection, Pain (2014: 535) begins to explicitly connect everyday terrorism with racialised violence, reversing the American exceptionalised justifications of the War on Terror by instead focusing on domestic violence '*in the West* [where] women of colour are *also* at high risk of racist violence, particularly when leaving violent domestic relationships' (emphasis added). Unlike Ortbals and Poloni-Staudinger (2014), fear is Pain's (2012) central organising feature. By looking at 'fear' as the central element of terrorism, Pain is able to

> highlight the frequency and severity of domestic abuse, the serious effects of the fear that it invokes, and the control that this fear makes possible . . . Drawing this parallel also muddies the boundaries between forms of violence that are usually framed as public, political, and spectacular, and forms of violence that are usually framed as private, apolitical, and mundane. (Pain 2012: 8)

While this is crucially important and helps to establish this form of violence as terrorism, it minimises the importance of patriarchy as a socio-political organising hierarchy. Pain's (2012) focus on 'fear' as the central connecting point to terrorism fails to go far enough. Instead the connections to terrorism are evident if one follows those central themes outlined in Chapter 1. Therefore, the next section looks at misogyny and violence against women before working through how these are violences that fit into the definitional elements of terrorism, including extranormativity, perpetrators, coercion and fear, victim–target differentiation, and, most importantly, the guiding political purpose of ideology.

Misogyny and Terrorism

Some may ask – indeed, some have asked – is it not awkward, a bit weird, even hypocritical in light of Chapter 1, to say, write or think 'misogynistic terrorism'? This awkwardness is something we should pay attention to; it *tells* me something. First, as Ortbals and Poloni-Staudinger (2014) and Pain (2014 and 2012) point out: it destabilises the notion of terrorism when the standard counter-terrorist – Western, white man – is suddenly more aligned with the terrorist. While I might resist the proliferation of the term, I think it is deeply instrumental to look at a rejected form of terrorism (i.e., mainstream Terrorism Studies' rejection of patriarchal terrorism) and tease out why it was rejected, especially when it fits the definition.

Second, this awkwardness is what misogyny wants. For instance, when feminist philosopher Kate Manne (2018a: xx) reflects on the Isla Vista killings from 'the perspective of the women who were targeted and killed': 'I felt morally embarrassed' and 'embarrassed . . . to dwell on them at all – as if I should be detached and cool'. Patriarchy and misogyny demanded that Manne realign herself with them again – to be masculinist: rational, logical, cool and detached. Misogyny operates to bring our focus back to supporting the dominant system; as Manne (2018a: xxi) clarifies:

> [W]e channel and enact social forces far beyond our threshold of conscious awareness or even ability to recover – and sometimes, markedly contrary to our explicit moral beliefs and political commitments.

In fact, Manne discusses how misogyny demands that we be sympathetic to those who uphold a misogynist order. This becomes shockingly clear when we consider the murder of Anne Searle by her husband, Stephen Searle. Searle, a former UKIP (far-right UK party) politician, when arrested, said, 'I've been a very naughty boy' (Enright 2018). News outlets 'including the BBC, publishing sympathetic comments' about Searle, reinforced an attitude that men must be sympathised with when they do wrong, abnegating any sense of responsibility towards or sympathy for their victims, like Anne (Enright 2018).

More importantly, the problem here is not the definition of terrorism – it is about who the signified is when we say it. In the interpellation of terrorism, particular elements of a society are signified – sub-state elements. One *raison d'être* of Critical Terrorism Studies' focus upon *state* terrorism was to destabilise the conventional wisdom of terrorism. The interpellation differentiated terrorist violence from state violence, allowing terrorist violence to be delegitimised, while state violence remained legitimate. Therefore, when Pain (2014: 535) argues that everyday terrorism is not like colonial violence, I disagree. It is just like it. Even if what we know of as terrorism is not the encompassing weight of the panopticon, patriarchal/everyday/misogynistic terrorism is just that, embedded in the everyday activities that are enforced, just as colonial governance was enforced. Thus, we have to look at all of the ways, large and small, that patriarchy uses misogyny – as the hatred of women – to govern.

Patriarchy and misogyny contribute to an epistemic bias against women, one in which women have a credibility deficit. Women's truths are not believed, nor taken as seriously as men's. This is clearly illustrated in the confirmation hearings for Judge Brett Kavanaugh to the US Supreme Court. Dr Christine Blasey Ford, along with two other women, accused him of attempted rape and sexual violence. While Dr Blasey Ford's testimony was largely seen as credible, Judge Kavanaugh's angry and tear-filled testimony was seen as deeply partisan and driven by his threatened misogyny. The Republican-controlled Senate Judiciary Committee supported the nomination, but it was slowed by the demand from Republican Senator Flake for an FBI investigation after he was confronted by two women in an elevator in the Capitol Building. The support given by the Republican party and President Trump to Judge Kavanaugh is what Manne (2018b) describes as 'himpathy' – or

> the inappropriate and disproportionate sympathy powerful men often enjoy in cases of sexual assault, intimate partner violence, homicide and other misogynistic behaviour.

Attitudes like these support the patriarchy and are formed through misogyny.

In her book on misogyny and the patriarchy as it functions currently, Manne (2018a: 20) makes these key points:

1. 'sexism [is] the branch of patriarchal ideology that *justifies* and *rationalises* a patriarchal social order';
2. 'misogyny [is] the system that *polices* and *enforces* its governing, norms, and expectations'.

In order to better understand this,

> we should think of misogyny as serving to uphold patriarchal order, understood as one strand among various similar systems of domination (including racisms, xenophobia, classism, ageism, ableism, homophobia, transphobia, and so on). Misogyny does this by visiting hostile or adverse social consequences on a certain (more or less circumscribed) class of girls or women to enforce and police social norms that are gendered either in theory (i.e., content) or in practice (i.e., norm enforcement mechanisms). (Manne 2018a: 13)

Indeed, misogyny works like a colonial system of governance, by classifying people and by punishing them for operating outside of them. For instance,

> Misogyny takes a girl or a woman belonging to a specific social class (of a more or less fully specified kind, based on race, class, age, body type, disability, sexuality, being cis/trans, etc.). It then threatens hostile consequences if she violates or challenges the relevant norms or expectations as a member of this gendered class of persons. (Manne 2018a: 20)

Furthermore, misogyny is 'psychological, structural, and institutional . . .'; it is 'a system of hostile forces that by and large *makes sense* from the perspective of patriarchal ideology, inasmuch as it works to police and enforce patriarchal order' (Manne 2018a: 27). It is *political* and upholds a *political* system. Misogyny operates in the everyday as a form of governance: it demands complete compliance and obedience by subordinating women. It is a form of coercive control – just as terrorism aims to be – and it uses violence or the threat of violence to gain this control.

Domestic violence works with other violences against women, and by recognising this we can finally begin to recognise the operational hierarchy of patriarchy and how it governs all of our lives. It does not just govern through normative restrictions that result in the unequal pay of women, in the control of women's reproductive health and in the structural limitations that lead to fewer women in science, technology, engineering and math (STEM), but in the threatened and actual violence when women dare to object to men's perspectives and hegemony.

Misogyny is seen in the online abuse directed at women. Whether it is the doxing of a specific woman's details or death and rape threats, like those levelled against Caroline Criado-Perez, the person who suggested placing Jane Austen on the £10 note (Philipson 2013) or at UK politicians (Marsh 2018; Dhrodia 2017), online abuse against women is significant. A 2018 Amnesty International poll found

> that nearly a quarter (23%) of the women surveyed across the . . . countries said they had experienced online abuse or harassment at least once, including 21% of women polled in the UK and 1/3 (33%) of women polled in the US. In both countries, 59% of women who experienced abuse or harassment said the perpetrators were complete strangers. (Amnesty 2018)

Additionally, Amnesty International (2018) connected this with domestic abuse:

> 97 per cent of domestic violence programs reported that abusers use technology to stalk, harass, and control victims. It also found that 86 per cent of domestic violence programs reported that victims are harassed through social media. In the UK, research on domestic online abuse by domestic violence organisation Women's Aid found that 85% of respondents said the abuse they received online from a partner or ex-partner was part of a pattern of abuse they also experienced offline. Additionally, 50% of respondents stated that the online abuse they experienced also involved direct threats to them or someone they knew.

Misogyny is seen in the response to women who report sexual violence. Out of 1,000 rapes in the US, only 310 will be reported to the police; only fifty-seven reports will lead to an arrest; from there only eleven cases will go to the prosecutor's office; seven of these cases will be convicted; and only six of the accused will serve prison time (RAINN 2018).

Misogyny is seen in the physical violence directed towards women. For example, in 2008, Katie Piper was a UK model early in her career. She dated a man for *two weeks*, one who had followed her career via social media and then asked her out, before he raped and stabbed her in a hotel room. When she refused to see him again, he stalked her and, with an accomplice, threw acid in her face, leading to significant scarring and the loss of sight in one eye.

Misogynoir is seen in the fact that the homicide rate for women of colour is nearly double that of white women. A 2017 CDC report found that 3,519 women and girls were killed by homicide in 2015, and half of these were by a 'current or former male intimate partner' (Petrosky et al. 2017). While 'non-Hispanic white women' were killed at a rate of 1.5 out of 100,000, non-Hispanic black women were killed at a rate of 4.4, American Indian/Alaskan Native women at 4.3, and Hispanic women at 1.8. The lowest rate was among Asian/Pacific Islanders, at 1.2 women per 100,000 (Petrosky et al. 2017).

Misogynoir is seen in the incredible levels of hostility black women face in public life. Politicians, like Diane Abbott, the Labour Shadow Home Secretary in the UK, are particularly targeted. In the UK general election in June 2017,

> Amnesty researchers found Abbott received 45 per cent of all abusive tweets sent to female MPs in the six weeks before election day. In the previous six months, she received just under a third of all abuse sent to the same group. (Elgot 2017)

Maxine Waters, a Californian member of the US House of Representatives, has faced increasingly targeted threats and violence, including a fake anthrax scare and death threats, and has been the target of a significant number of Trump's Twitter tirades (Castillo 2018). Other prominent black women also face abuse. Even before the summer of 2018, Serena Williams has had serious run-ins with tennis umpires making egregiously biased calls against her. This has led to a righteous anger on her part, which came acutely to the surface at the US Open final in 2018. Instead of seeing her anger as relatable, or at the very least in line with the anger of male tennis stars, Williams was blasted for hers, including through some racist cartoons (Sharma 2018; see also Rankine [2015: 27–32] for a detailed discussion of Williams's treatment over the years and how this relates to racial politics).

Transmisogyny is seen in the abuse and violence against transwomen. Linking the devalorisation of femininity, 'transmisogyny' is the hatred not just of (cis) women, but of those who identify and perform femininity. It is an intersectional problem:

> Trans women experience a particular kind of sexist marginalization based in their unique position of *overlapping oppressions* – they are both trans and feminine. They are devalued by society on both accounts. (Battered Women's Support Services 2018)

It is in the fear of transwomen using 'female' bathrooms in the United States, but it is most evident in the growing rate of homicide against transwomen (Human Rights Campaign 2018).

All of these together connect the notion that patriarchy is neither benign nor without harm. Coupled with the hatred of misogyny, women are not safe, particularly when their right to an equal existence is seen at odds with the survival of men.

Misogynistic Terrorism as Political Violence

Domestic violence, joined by other forms of violence against women, such as rape and sexual assault, harassment and mass violence, controls women's lives. If we then think about the steps that women and other targeted groups take every day to make themselves safe: taking the long way around a dark park; lacing their keys between their fingers; carrying a rape alarm or pepper spray; letting people know where they are going on a first date, etc. – it is clear that all of these actions constitute an awareness of behaviour and a changing of behaviour because of fear, yes, but also because of who they are and how their status marks them as targets. Terrorism, as the actual or perceived threat of violence for strategic ends, encapsulates this level of coercion. And the patriarchal/intimate/everyday terrorism must now go further: domestic violence and mass shootings are intrinsically connected. Every Town for Gun Safety, a non-profit campaign organisation, 'found that in 54% of the shootings, the perpetrator shot a current or former intimate partner, or other family members' (Casciani 2017).

The perpetrators of terrorism are generally said to be sub-state groups, but many scholars also include states and individuals (Hoffman 2006: 19); while in typical responses to domestic violence, the focus is upon the individual perpetrator, without recognising the structure within which the perpetrator operates – creating perhaps more of a group dynamic than it is comfortable to admit. The complicity wrought by patriarchy means that all agents/individuals are active in it – not necessarily just the perpetrators of violence. However, this should not minimise or detract from the primary perpetrators of domestic violence, sexual violence and mass shootings: individual men. Misogynistic terrorism is perpetrated by individuals who are invested in a larger patriarchal system, which is complicit in as well as *dependent* upon the violence to maintain power structures. This is why addressing these concerns is slow.

While terrorist violence is also discussed as extranormative (Schmid and Jongman 2005: 4–6) – or outside the bounds of legality and normative social practices – domestic violence, rape and mass shootings are also illegal. *Yet*, they are also allowed to continue. Therefore, while domestic violence, rape, homicide and gun violence are condemned in principle, all are allowed and condoned in reality: just refer back to how few rape cases actually lead to an arrest, trial and conviction. This has everything to do with who the perpetrators of this form of violence are. Those who benefit from a patriarchal system are also the people who have been most identified as the rational, logical counter-terrorist who is legitimate and credible. Thus, this creates a level of complicity of the 'normal' counter-terrorist with the terrorist violence.

The victims of terrorism are often agreed to be non-combatants (Bellamy 2008; Schmid 2004; Ganor 2002). The victims of misogynistic terrorism are clearly non-combatants but, most importantly, they do not have as much access to power as men do. Misogynistic terrorism is systematic and strategic – the escalating nature of it is an intentional means of controlling the subordinates. While there is normally a victim–target differentiation in terrorism, in misogynistic terrorism, like imperial violence, there is an overlap between the victim and the target audience.

In other forms of terrorism, the target audience of terrorism is the one whose behaviour the terrorist wishes to control through its actions. It is not necessarily the same as the victim. Schmid (2004: 206–7) makes this argument about victim-target differentiation:

> Violence aims at behaviour modification by coercion. Propaganda drives at the same by persuasion. . . . Terrorism, by using violence against one victim, seeks to coerce and persuade others. The immediate victim is merely instrumental . . .

Victims and targets in misogynistic terrorism, however, significantly overlap, given that patriarchy and misogyny demand complicity of all subjects. While that one person abusing a feminised subject may only intend to harm a single individual, the above-mentioned futility in reporting rape is similar to domestic violence. This is indicative of a system of complicity and insidious acceptance of it. Of the limited cases of abuse reported to the police, the number that go forward to criminal prosecution is shockingly low.

Accordingly, the goal of terrorism is to coerce a target to align with one's ideology and to give in to the related demands. Ideology may range from religious to secular, right- to left-wing, anarchist to fascist, but all of these ideologies articulate political goals and demands. In a key Terrorism Studies text, C. J. M. Drake (1998: 56) argues that ideology is central to understanding why a group uses violence and 'who or what' will be targeted. Drake (1995: 56) finds

> A group's ideology is extremely important in determining target selection because it defines how the group's members see the world around them. The ideology of a terrorist group identifies the 'enemies' of the group by providing a measure against which to assess the 'innocence' or 'guilt' of people and institutions. This gives rise to the idea that certain people or things are somehow 'legitimate targets'.

The goal of misogynistic terrorism is also to coerce the target to behave in a certain way that seeks compliance with patriarchy. The perpetrator resorts to violence to control the immediate situation or to seek revenge for a slight (as explored in the next section). The repeated nature of these assaults and the fact that they happen to many, many different women has the outcome of provoking fear in a larger population. It is not necessarily about the women hurt, but that all women live with the threat of being hurt. While the perpetrators may not necessarily explicitly articulate patriarchal goals like a terrorist communiqué might (although the perpetrators explored next do), their actions and attitudes towards feminised subjects are physical representations of an ontology and epistemology that power belongs to the dominant.

'Everyday terrorism', like other descriptions of this type of terrorism, simply does not go far enough, and indeed, skitters away from describing the heart of the matter: the ideology of misogyny. Pain's (2014) focus on fear is certainly apt – women's fear results in constrained behaviours – but it also detracts from what this control ultimately does: ensuring compliance with patriarchy. If terrorism is political, and if terrorism strikes at symbolic targets, it needs ideology to articulate political aims. Patriarchy continues to be the dominant structuring order and it works hand in hand with misogyny, which justifies violence against women. Violence against women has always been hidden or dismissed within patriarchal societies in order to protect men and men's superiority, and to preserve women's inferiority. Furthermore, it is deeply *entrenched* with racism. Therefore, the next section looks at the relationship between 'toxic masculinity' and mass shootings, finding that these need to be central to any conversation about misogynistic terrorism moving forward.

Toxic Masculinity: The Ideology behind Misogynistic Terrorism

Mass shootings and misogyny are particularly linked in the US because of the 'persistent pressure to constantly be proving manhood and warding off anything considered feminine or emasculating' (Hamblin 2016). Online culture has enabled the rise – or at least the emergence from the shadows – of toxic masculinity, a culture that believes women's utility lies in their attractiveness and ability to give birth, and that men are fulfilled only when they are 'alphas', men who display power, domination and sexual attractiveness. From the École Polytechnique shooting in Montreal in 1989, to Isla Vista in 2014, to Toronto in 2018, these attacks have targeted women and have been justified by an ideology of misogynistic, toxic masculinity.

Toxic masculinity[5] is co-constituted by the opposing forces of feminist voices and the men who use social media to articulate their virulent form of misogyny. According to feminist journalists, toxic masculinity is

> a specific model of manhood geared towards dominance and control. It's a manhood that views women and LGBT people as inferior, sees sex as an act not of affection but domination, and which valorises violence as the way to prove one's self to the world. (Marcotte 2016)

Furthermore, it drives violence in a very specific way. As Penny (2014) observes:

> Women owe men. Women, as a class, as a sex, owe men sex, love, attention, 'adoration', in [Elliott] Rodger's words. We owe them respect and obedience, and our refusal to give it to them is to blame for their anger, their violence – stupid sluts get what they deserve. Most of all, there is an overpowering sense of rage and entitlement: the conviction that men have been denied a birthright of easy power.

Thus, it is all too easy to see toxic masculinity in domestic abuse, but also the abuses mentioned above including rape, (online) harassment and mass shootings, especially when women's gains in the workplace, in government and in equal rights threaten men's status. Additionally, several feminists, beyond Solnit (CBC 2018), have called for the use of 'misogynistic terrorism' (Matthews 2018; Valenti 2018).

The men involved are often conceived as independent actors, something akin to lone wolf actors. Yet, misogynistic terrorists' violent agencies are often minimised because of their whiteness and suspected mental ill health. Furthermore, misogynistic terrorists are not isolated individuals – in misogynistic terrorism the offenders are often inspired by and immersed in online and community politicisation processes (Valenti 2018). In these online forums they find support and encouragement from like-minded individuals, who often view men like Rodgers and Breivik as heroes. There are multiple groups of men who contribute to toxic masculinity, including men's rights activists,[6] pick-up artists[7] and incels[8] (Anti-Defamation League 2018: 5; Valenti 2018). Additionally, they share characteristics with white supremacists, to the point that the Southern Poverty Law Centre (SPLC) added misogynist hate groups to their watch lists in 2018 (Collins and Zadronzy 2018). Heidi Beirich, the director of the SPLC's Intelligence Project, said

> They're young, frustrated white males in their late teens into their early twenties who are having a hard time adjusting to adulthood. They're the same kinds of people you find in white supremacy writ large. . . . They have grievances about the world they've placed onto women and black people. (Collins and Zadronzy 2018)

These grievances become clear when one delves into the social media postings.

Toxic masculinity maintains strict gender roles. The 'alpha male' claim is central to the Red Pill, an extremist men's rights forum located primarily on Reddit. Alpha males are conceptualised as the only men who hold women's interest because they are physically fit and domineering in attitude. The Red Pill defines 'alpha' as:

> Socially dominant. Somebody who displays high value, or traits that are sexually attractive to women. Alpha can refer to a man who exhibits alpha behaviours (more alpha tendencies than beta), but [is] usually used to describe individual behaviours themselves. (Red Pill 2015a)

Alpha males have 'game', which is a 'sexual strategy' men need to adopt because women, in a biologically essentialist move, select mates 'to locate the best dna [sic] possible, and to garner the most resources' (Red Pill 2011). In juxtaposition, 'betas' are 'low value to women' because they do not dominate women, something that women inherently (biologically) desire (Red Pill 2015b). This leads beta males into a life of involuntary celibacy, or 'incel', a 'man who wants to get laid, but can't' (Red Pill 2015b). The Red Pill uses a misunderstanding of evolutionary biology to argue that women's and men's reproductive needs are mismatched. Women instinctively 'filter' men for economic 'security' (Red Pill 2011), meaning they often chose betas because these men are good providers. Yet, rather contradictorily, sexual attraction will also instinctively prevail, leading women to eventually cheat on betas or leave betas for alphas. On the other hand, alphas, in particular, must have sex because of their testosterone level and choose women because they are 'hot' or desperate ('no one's ugly after 2am') (Red Pill 2011). Once a man understands this dilemma, he can use the game to become an alpha (Red Pill 2015b).

The ideology of toxic masculinity sets out a vision of the world in which women are compliant, submissive and sexually attractive. It blames feminism for most, if not all, social ills. As Christopher Cantwell, a white supremacist, posted on his blog,

> The vagina is the perfect representation of the nature of females. An empty vessel, a hole, a void with no identity of its own. Without a man to fill her with his essence, she is as useless as a crabapple [sic] rotting on the sidewalk. (Anti-Defamation League 2018: 6)

Women are referred to as 'thots' – That Ho Over There – or 'tradhots' – alt-right women who perform traditional gender roles (Anti-Defamation

League 2018: 7). Women are seen to have 'too much freedom to choose their partners,' which leaves some men cheated out of their sexual birth-right' (Anti-Defamation League 2018: 12). By being able to say no to sex, incels argue that 'women are committing "reverse rape" – which they argue is just as damaging and harmful as actual rape' (Anti-Defamation League 2018: 12). This argument is related to race. F. Roger Devlin, described as 'a longtime white nationalist academic', claims that 'wom-en's liberation has actively hurt (white) men's ability to procreate because when white women have choices, they are less likely to get married, have children, and perpetuate the white race' (Anti-Defamation League 2018: 7).

As women are simply seen as submissive pawns, violence is not a surprising outcome. Well-known neo-Nazi Andrew Anglin believes: 'Women crave men who call them stupid and claim they shouldn't have any rights. They also crave being tied up, beaten, and raped' (Anti-Defamation League 2018: 7). This is echoed by white supremacist Richard Spencer who, in a *Newsweek* interview, articulated the necessity of total control:

> As men, it is our responsibility to bring girls back to their proper place. To lead them into their natural roles as wives and mothers. We men do not choose or reward girls for their clown college degrees, their meaningless cubicle jobs, or their supposed 'intelligence'. We reward them for their will-ingness to please us and make us happy, and in doing so make themselves happy. No amount of phony education or career 'success' will scratch that deep itch in a girl's soul: the desire to serve a man. (Anti-Defamation League 2018: 9)

Needless to say, Spencer also believes women should not have the right to vote.

Feminists have long argued that gender relations speak to politi-cal order (Elshtain 1981; Pateman 1980). Socio-political ordering becomes clearer when looking at the statements left by the various shooters – statements that have become memorialised and lauded within these communities. To control women is to control society and preserve an order that serves white men. Misogyny and racism is evi-dent in the shooters' manifestos and in the websites that memorialise them, effectively presenting them men as martyrs to a cause who serve to inspire others.

Even though there is a 'newness' to online toxic masculinity, the web-sites also demonstrate that this violence is in part historic. One central figure is Marc Lépine, a Canadian mass shooter, who entered the École Polytechnique in Montreal on 6 December 1989, murdering fourteen women, wounding ten women and four men. He was driven by his hatred of feminism. An extract from his very brief suicide note reads:

> . . . the feminists have always enraged me. They want to keep the advantages of women (e.g. cheaper insurance, extended maternity leave preceded by a preventative leave, etc.) while seizing for themselves those of men . . .
> They [feminists] are so opportunistic they [do not] neglect to profit from the knowledge accumulated by men through the ages (Langman 2014).

On a website dedicated to his actions and memory, Lépine is hailed as 'liberating' women from feminism, which is often conflated with abortion:

> He liberates women from the unhealthy thoughts of genocide and gender-cide that were prevalent in the feminist discourse since the days of Valerie Solanas and Mary Daly, and helps them STOP their planned monstrosities. The message is here: stop hurting men and be good to them, and they will stop hating you. They could even start to like you again some day [sic]. (mar-clepine.blogspot.com 2009)

The graphics for this page are telling: two illustrations sit side by side at the top of the page. One is of an overweight woman throwing a small, bloody baby into a waste bin next to an image of Lépine's face on the body of a woman throwing away a 'femi-nazi' symbol (a swastika inside the loop of the Venus symbol, ♀). Below it, the text declares:

> Marc Lepine tells women and feminists YOU DON'T HAVE TO BE MONT-ERS [sic] ANYMORE. He tells these thousands of women and feminists who have stolen their partner's house, their car, their money, he tells those who have stolen their ex-husband's children, their jobs and drove them to sui-cide: STOP TO BE [sic] MONSTERS, stop to [sic] secretly dream of killing men and planning gendercide, and we will perhaps begin again to love you some day. This is a powerful message, A MESSAGE OF LOVE, worthy of a new Christ. (marclepine.blogspot.com 2009)

Building up Lépine as a martyr aims to politicise more men to the point of violence.

Similar anger and entitlement shows up in Elliot Rodger's (2014) 141-page manifesto. It is an arrogant reflection on what he describes as a fairly normal childhood. During his early adulthood and university, he moved to 'Isla Vista with the goal of losing his virginity and attaining the life I desire' (Rodger 2014: 125). He saw himself as an incel, unable to fit into university life: 'I often call USC [University of Southern California] the "University of Spoiled Cunts", just like I call UCSB the "University of California's Spoiled Brats"' (Rodger 2014: 125). In describing a blonde-haired woman on Facebook and her friends, his incel status, entitlement and misogyny comes through:

> They were the kind of beautiful, popular people who lived pleasurable lives and would look down on me as inferior scum, never accepting me as one of them. They were my *enemies*. They represented everything that was wrong with this world. . . . I would take great delight in torturing and flaying her and every single one of her spoiled, obnoxious evil friends. (Rodger 2014: 125–6)

After being in a fight – a rather violent one – in Isla Vista, Rodger began to plan his attack during his recuperation. He mused,

> I was bullied by thugs, and the girls adored the bullies instead of me. . . .
>
> Only now, I was ready and capable of fighting back against the cruelty of women. . . . All of the suffering, loneliness, rejection, and humiliation I had to experience since then had strengthened me. The hatred that festered inside of me in all of those years leading up to this point had empowered me in a dark, twisted way. I was now armed with weapons, possessed great intelligence and philosophical insight, with the willpower to exact the most catastrophic act of vengeance the world will ever see.
>
> I spent the next week . . . brooding the injustices of life and my place in the world. It fully dawned on me that I would now have to bring about the Day of Retribution. There was no other hope. I mused that once I descend upon Isla Vista, armed with my weapons and my burning hatred, I would definitely make sure to target the people who lived in that house I was attacked in. The plan was to destroy the entirety of Isla Vista, and kill every single person in it, or at least kill as many popular young people I could before the police arrive and I'd have to kill myself. (Rodger 2014: 124)

Race is also threaded throughout. He describes his Chinese roommates as a contrast to his previous roommates:

> They were two foreign Asian students. . . . These were the biggest nerds I had ever seen, and they were both very ugly with annoying voices. . . . These two new ones were utterly repulsive. (Rodger 2014: 128)

His younger sister's 'half White, half Mexican' boyfriend is an 'obnox-
ious', 'freeloading', 'slob' and Rodger was livid that this guy's former
girlfriend was 'a pretty brunette white girl. My hatred towards him only
intensified after that' (Rodger 2014: 128–9).

Rodger's (2014: 131) 'Day of Retribution' was all about revenge and
control.

> I had been rejected, insulted, humiliated, cast out, bullied, starved, tortured,
> and ridiculed for far too long. Humanity is a cruel and brutal species, and
> the only thing I could do to even the score was to return that cruelty one-
> thousand fold. Women's rejection of me is a declaration of war, and if it's
> war they want, then war they shall have. It will be a war that will result in
> their complete and utter annihilation. I will deliver a blow to my enemies
> that will be so catastrophic. It will redefine the very essence of human nature.

In fact, the second phase of his Day of Retribution was his 'War on
Women', which Rodger (2014: 132) justifies as follows:

> Punish[ing] all females for the crime of depriving me of sex. They have starved
> me of sex for my entire youth, and gave that pleasure to other men. . . . I
> cannot kill every single female on earth, but I can deliver a devastating blow
> that will shake all of them to the core of the wicked hearts.

His thinking and intention are both clear: only a few women may be
his future victims, but he aims to 'shake' all women 'to the core' – thus
cohering with the idea that terrorism has fewer direct victims, but a
larger targeted population.

Dylann Roof's two manifestos convey a similar sense of superiority and
entitlement to Rodger's – the first he wrote before his Charleston shooting, and the second he wrote from jail. Roof's racism is most evident. He
mentions Jews, Hispanics and Asians. All black people are violent and
have 'lower iqs [sic], lower impulse control, and higher testosterone levels'
(Roof 2014: 3) and black-on-white crime is an unreported epidemic. He
wishes that slavery still existed, and that white people still controlled black
people. He paints himself as helpless in the face of this 'knowledge':

> I have no choice. I am not in a position to, alone, go into the ghetto and
> fight. I choose Charleston because it is the most historic city in my state,
> and at one time had the highest ratio of blacks to Whites in the country. We
> have no skinheads, no real KKK, no one doing anything but talking on the
> internet. Well someone has to have the bravery to take it to the real world,
> and I guess that has to be me. (Roof 2014: 5)

His discussion of women is limited, but coheres with the previous discourse. Women are victims and seen in light of what they are (or should be) for white men. For instance, women in interracial relationships are victims in need of saving (Roof 2014: 5). During the shooting, when asked by one of the male victims why he was doing this, he responded, 'I have to do this, because y'all are raping our women . . .' Later he cited '1488', which is a supremacist code where '14 refers to a micro-creed, fourteen words long – "We must secure the existence of our people and a future for white children"' and 88 is code for 'Heil Hitler', as 'H' is the eighth letter (Ball 2017).

Breivik's loathing of women follows similar lines. Breivik believes that the PC project 'intends to deny the intrinsic worth of native Christian European heterosexual males' (Jones 2011). Breivik is haunted by a 'terror of feminisation', believing that men are forced to be metrosexual emotional beings, and says that only the restoration of patriarchy can save European culture (Goldberg 2011). It is feminism's attack on the nuclear family that has led to a 'demographic collapse' 'open[ing] Europe to Muslim colonisation' (Jones 2011). In Section 2.89 of his manifesto, Breivik compares Europe to a woman who has submitted to rape (Jones 2011).

Therefore, even though neither Roof nor Breivik's overriding ideological bent may be misogynistic, it is becoming clear to the SPLC as well as the Anti-Defamation League that

[t]here is a robust symbiosis between misogyny and white supremacy, the two ideologies are powerfully intertwined . . . a deep-seated loathing of women acts as a connective tissue between many white supremacists, especially those in the alt-right. (Anti-Defamation League 2018: 5)

Together, all of these men serve as inspiration to those who read and contribute to the toxic masculinity online.

The martyrdom angle was especially salient in the reactions to Alek Minassian's van attack in Toronto on 23 April 2018, which killed ten people and hospitalised fifteen. He was inspired by social media misogyny, self-identified as an incel and praised Rodger (Crilly et al. 2018). In a Facebook post, Minassian wrote:

Private (Recruit) Minassian Infantry 00010, wishing to speak to Sgt 4chan[9] please. C23249161. The Incel Rebellion has already begun! We will overthrow all the Chads and Stacys![10] All hail the Supreme Gentlemen [sic] Elliot Rodger! (Collins and Zadronzy 2018)

Responses to Minassian's attack on incel.me, 'a forum where incels congregate', 'hailed him as a hero of the movement' (Collins and Zadronzy 2018). Specific responses on incel.me included:

'I hope this guy wrote a manifesto because he could be our next new saint'
    'Spread that name, speak of his sacrifice for our cause, worship him for he gave his life for our future'
    'I want to see some mass food poisoning deaths, maybe a pipe bomb or two, or hopefully somebody finally uses a fucking truck to just ram down [women] during a school parade or something, mix it up a little' (Collins and Zadronzy 2018)

As to be expected, the violence continues. In November 2018, three mass shootings occurred: at a synagogue, a yoga studio and a country-and-western bar. At all three shootings, people were present who had survived the Holocaust and other mass shootings in the US.

Conclusion

If we argue that misogynistic terrorism exists in the US, then we are arguing that terrorist perpetrators exist in the US. And if there are so many *reported* cases of domestic abuse in the US, this means that male citizens of the US are implicated as *terrorists*. And if there are so many cases between white couples a year, this means *white men* are implicated as terrorists. This is a designation that the US has gone to great pains to avoid, as noted in the previous chapter. Moreover, we need to start caring and recognise the precarity of black women and transwomen, where the intersecting identity politics collude to make violences against them more targeted and more lethal.

Where the ending of Chapter 4 focused on the fallacy of Black Identity Extremism, this chapter has focused on the intersecting violences of white men who feel their privilege, entitlement and masculinity are under threat. The violence continues because of what we have – and have not – considered terrorism. White men, given the effects of coloniality and Western privilege, have not historically been considered terrorists. Yet, this is only recently: in the 1980s in the US, the US law enforcement effectively and efficiently removed the threat of the Order and (mostly) of the Aryan Nations, two white supremacist right-wing groups. These left the public psyche and evidently the psyche of law enforcement as the new terrorism thesis reinforced a colonial imaginary, re-establishing brown men as violent deviants and reaffirming white men as counter-terrorists. This needs to change. Violence is violence, no matter who commits it. But when white male domestic abusers, who are prohibited in a significant number of states from buying guns, manage to buy guns and then commit mass shootings, where women are the largest number of victims – when a country would rather bury children than make substantial changes – then the priorities of this country are with the violent perpetrators, not the victims.

Notes

1. Kim Wall was a journalist murdered while interviewing Danish entrepreneur Peter Madsen on board his mini-sub. He dismembered her body and scattered it at sea.
2. Cosby has since been sentenced to three to ten years in prison (Levenson and Cooper 2018).
3. The Mother Jones database on mass shootings between 1982 and the present defines them as 'indiscriminate rampages in public places resulting in four or more victims by one perpetrator' (except in the cases of the Columbine High School and Westside Middle School shootings).
4. Thinking intersectionally, one also has to recognise that this does not just apply to those who identify as 'women' but to any person who has been feminised, or seen as less than, and is therefore more precarious.
5. Scholarship (Kimmel and Wade 2018; Duriesmith 2017) on toxic masculinity discusses it in terms of where it has arisen in particular culture, and even how men respond to and feel conflict with the term. I am less interested in this approach, as I am concerned with how this position plays out on women and contributes to particular social forces.
6. Men who believe that feminism and laws that support women in divorce settlement adversely affect men.
7. A movement of men whose goal is to seduce women. It is related to 'The Game', or a specific sequence of events to seduce women, seeing them as passive in the game and as pawns in men's sexual fulfilment (Conger 2018).
8. 'Involuntary celibates', or beta males.
9. 4chan is another online forum associated with toxic masculinity and white supremacy.
10. 'Chads' are hyper-manly alpha males. 'Stacys' are women who sleep around.

References

Amnesty International (2018), *Toxic Twitter – Women's Experiences of Violence and Abuse on Twitter*, <https://amnesty.org/en/latest/research/2018/03/online-violence-against-women-chapter-3/> (last accessed 25 November 2018).

Anderson, Kristin L. (2008), 'Is Partner Violence Worse in the Context of Control?', *Journal of Marriage and Family*, 70(5): 1157–68.

Anti-Defamation League (2018), *When Women Are the Enemy: The Intersection of Misogyny and White Supremacy*, <https://www.adl.org/resources/reports/when-women-are-the-enemy-the-intersection-of-misogyny-and-white-supremacy> (last accessed 25 November 2018).

Bailey, Moya, and Trudy (2018), 'On Misogynoir: Citation, Erasure, and Plagiarism', *Feminist Media Studies*, 18(4): 1–7.

Ball, Edward (2017), 'United States v. Dylann Roof', *The New York Review of Books*, 9 March, <https://www.nybooks.com/articles/2017/03/09/united-states-versus-dylann-roof/> (last accessed 25 November 2018).

Bell, Harriet (2017), 'Dylann Roof Sentenced to Death for Charleston Church Shooting', *The Telegraph*, 10 January, <https://www.telegraph.co.uk/news/2017/01/10/dylann-roof-sentenced-death-charleston-church-shooting/> (last accessed 25 November 2018).

Bellamy, Alex (2008), *Fighting Terror: Ethical Dilemmas* (London: Zed Books).

Caciani, Dominic (2017), 'Texas: Is Domestic Violence a Common Theme in Mass Shootings', *BBC News*, 8 November, <https://www.bbc.co.uk/news/world-us-canada-41906203> (last accessed 25 November 2018).

Castillo, Monica (2018), 'Misogynoir', 25 July, *The Lily*, <https://www.thelily.com/the-violence-and-threats-against-maxine-waters-are-rooted-in-misogynoir/> (last accessed 25 November 2018).

CBC (2018), 'The Current Transcript for April 26, 2018', <https://www.cbc.ca/radio/thecurrent/the-current-for-april-26-2018-1.4636157/thursday-april-26-2018-full-episode-transcript-1.4637420> (last accessed 25 November 2018).

Collins, Ben, and Brandy Zadrozny (2018), 'After Toronto Attack, Online Misogynists Praise Suspect as "New Saint"', *ABC News*, 24 April, <https://www.nbcnews.com/news/us-news/after-toronto-attack-online-misogynists-praise-suspect-new-saint-n868821> (last accessed 25 November 2018).

Conger, Christen (2018), 'How Pickup Artists Work', *How Stuff Works*, <https://people.howstuffworks.com/pickup-artist.htm> (last accessed 25 November 2018).

Crilly, Rob, Christopher Guly and Mark Molloy (2018), 'What Do We Know About Alek Minassian, Arrested after Toronto Van Attack?', *The Telegraph*, 24 April, <https://www.telegraph.co.uk/news/2018/04/24/do-know-alek-minassian-arrested-toronto-van-attack/> (last accessed 25 November 2018).

Dhrodia, Azmin (2017), 'We Tracked 25,688 Abusive Tweets Sent to Women MPs – Half Were Directed at Diane Abbott', *The New Statesman*, 5 September, <https://www.newstatesman.com/2017/09/we-tracked-25688-abusive-tweets-sent-women-mps-half-were-directed-diane-abbott> (last accessed 25 November 2018).

Dobash, R. Emerson, and Russell Dobash (1979), *Violence Against Wives: A Case Against The Patriarchy* (New York: Free Press).

Dobash, R. Emerson, and Russell P. Dobash (1984), 'The Nature and Antecedents of Violent Events', *The British Journal of Criminology*, 24(3): 269–88.

Dobash, Russell P., and R. Emerson Dobash (eds) (1993), *Women, Violence, and Social Change* (Abingdon: Routledge).

Dobash, Russell P., and R. Emerson Dobash (2004), 'Women's Violence to Men in Intimate Relationships: Working on a Puzzle', *British Journal of Criminology*, 44(3): 324–49.

Domonoske, Camila (2017), 'CDC: Half of All Female Homicide Victims Are Killed by Intimate Partners', *NPR*, 21 July, <https://www.npr.org/sections/thetwo-way/2017/07/21/538518569/cdc-half-of-all-female-murder-victims-are-killed-by-intimate-partners> (last accessed 25 November 2018).

Drake, Charles J. M. (1998), 'The Role of Ideology in Terrorists' Target Selection', *Terrorism and Political Violence*, 10(2): 53–85.

Elgot, Jessica (2017), 'Diane Abbott More Abused Than Any Other Female MP During Election', *The Guardian*, 5 September, <https://www.theguardian.com/politics/2017/sep/05/diane-abbott-more-abused-than-any-other-mps-during-election> (last accessed 25 November 2018).

Elshtain, Jean Bethke (1981), *Public Man, Private Woman: Women in Social and Political Thought* (Princeton, NJ: Princeton University Press).

Enright, Lynn (2018), 'We Cannot Afford to be Flippant about the Murder of Women', *The Pool*, 20 July, <https://www.the-pool.com/news-views/opinion/2018/29/Lynn-Enright-on-Anne-Searle-death-domestic-violence> (last accessed 25 November 2018).

Fahmy, Dalia (2018), 'Christian Women in the US Are More Religious than Their Male Counterparts', *Pew Research Centre*, 4 June, <http://www.pewresearch.org/fact-tank/2018/04/06/christian-women-in-the-u-s-are-more-religious-than-their-male-counterparts/> (last accessed 25 November 2018).

Follman, Mark, Gavin Aronsen and Deanna Pan (2018), 'A Guide to Mass Shootings in America', *Mother Jones*, 19 November, <https://www.motherjones.com/politics/2012/07/mass-shootings-map/> (last accessed 25 November 2018).

Ganor, Boaz (2002), 'Defining Terrorism: Is One Man's Terrorist Another Man's Freedom Fighter?', *Police Practice and Research*, 3(4): 287–304.

Gentry, Caron E. (2017), 'The "Duel" Meaning of Feminisation in International Relations: The Rise of Women and the Interior Logics of Declinist Literature', *Global Responsibility to Protect*, 9(1): 101–24.

Goldberg, Michelle (2011), 'Norway Massacre: Anders Breivik's Deadly Attack Fueled by Hatred of Women', *The Daily Beast*, 24 July, <https://www.thedaily-beast.com/norway-massacre-anders-breiviks-deadly-attack-fueled-by-hatred-of-women> (last accessed 26 November 2018).

Goldstein, Joshua S. (2012), *Winning the War on War: The Decline of Armed Conflict Worldwide* (New York: Plume Books).

Gradinariu, Laura (2007), 'Domestic Violence – A Micro-Level Terrorism? Empirical Findings of Significant Similarities between Two Human Rights Violations', <https://ssrn.com/abstract=993278 or http://dx.doi.org/10.2139/ssrn.993278> (last accessed 25 November 2018).

Hamblin, Drake (2016), 'Toxic Masculinity and Murder: Can We Talk About Men?', *The Atlantic*, 16 June, <https://www.theatlantic.com/health/archive/2016/06/toxic-masculinity-and-mass-murder/486983/> (last accessed 25 November 2018).

Hoffman, Bruce (2006), *Inside Terrorism* (New York: Columbia University Press).

Human Rights Campaign (2018), 'Violence Against the Transgender Community in 2018', <https://www.hrc.org/resources/violence-against-the-transgender-community-in-2018> (last accessed 25 November 2018).

Jackson, Laur (2014), 'Memes and Misogynoir', *The Awl*, 28 August, <https://www.theawl.com/2014/08/memes-and-misogynoir/> (last accessed 25 November 2018).

Johnson, Michael P. (1995), 'Patriarchal Terrorism and Common Couple Violence: Two Forms of Violence against Women', *Journal of Marriage and the Family*, 57(2): 283–94.

Jones, Jane Clare (2011), 'Anders Breivik's Chilling Anti-Feminism', *The Guardian*, 27 July, <https://www.theguardian.com/commentisfree/2011/jul/27/breivik-anti-feminism> (last accessed 25 November 2018).

Kevan, Nicola Graham, and John Archer (2004), 'Using Johnson's Domestic Violence Typology to Classify Men and Women in a Non-Selected Sample', *International Family Violence Research Conference*, <http://www.mendeley.com/catalog/using-johnson-s-domestic-violence-typology-classify-men-women-non-selected-sample/> (last accessed 11 February 2013): 1–45.

Langman, Peter (2014), 'Lepine Suicide Note', <https://schoolshooters.info/sites/default/files/lepine_note_1.1.pdf> (last accessed 25 November 2018).

Levenson, Eric, and Aaron Cooper (2018), 'Bill Cosby Sentence to 3 to 10 Years in Prison for Sexual Assault', *CNN*, 26 September, <https://edition.cnn.com/2018/09/25/us/bill-cosby-sentence-assault/index.html> (last accessed 25 November 2018).

Manne, Kate (2018a), *Down Girl: The Logic of Misogyny* (Oxford: Oxford University Press).

Manne, Kate (2018b), 'Brett Kavanaugh and America's "Himpathy" Reckoning', *The New York Times*, 26 September, <https://www.nytimes.com/2018/09/26/opinion/brett-kavanaugh-hearing-himpathy.html> (last accessed 25 November 2018).

Marcotte, Amanda (2016), 'Overcompensation Nation: It's Time to Admit that Toxic Masculinity Drives Gun Violence', *Salon*, 13 June, <http://www.salon.com/2016/06/13/overcompensation_nation_its_time_to_admit_that_toxic_masculinity_drives_gun_violence/> (last accessed 25 November 2018).

Marsh, Sarah (2018), 'Surge in Crimes against MPs Sparks Fears Over Intimidation and Abuse', *The Guardian*, 23 October, <https://www.theguardian.com/politics/2018/oct/23/crimes-mps-uk-online-intimidation-abuse> (last accessed 25 November 2018).

Matthews, Heidi (2018), 'If Misogyny Was a Factor, Is Toronto Rampage a Terrorist Act Against Women?', *The Conversation*, 27 April, <https://theconversation.com/if-misogyny-was-a-factor-is-toronto-rampage-a-terrorist-act-against-women-95633> (last accessed 25 November 2018).

Mutua, Makau (2001), 'Savages, Victims, and Saviours: The Metaphor of Human Rights', *Harvard International Law Review*, 42(1): 201–45.

Ortbals, Candice D., and Lori Poloni-Staudinger (2014), 'Women Defining Terrorism: Ethnonationalist, State, and *Machista* Terrorism', *Critical Studies on Terrorism*, 7(3): 336–56.

Pain, Rachel (2012), *Everyday Terrorism: How Fear Works in Domestic Abuse* (Durham: Centre for Social Justice and Community Action).

Pain, Rachel (2014), 'Everyday Terrorism: Connecting Domestic Violence and Global Terrorism', *Progress in Human Geography*, 38(4): 531–50.

Pateman, Carole (1980), '"The Disorder of Women:" Women, Love, and the Sense of Justice', *Ethics*, 91(1): 20–34.

Penny, Laurie (2014), 'Let's Call the Isla Vista Killings What They Were', *New Statesman*, 25 May, <http://www.newstatesman.com/lifestyle/2014/05/lets-call-isla-vista-killings-what-they-were-misogynist-extremism> (last accessed 25 November 2018).

Petrosky, Emiko, Janet M. Blair, Carter J. Betz, Katherine A. Fowler, Shane P. D. Jack and Bridget H. Lyons (2017), 'Racial and Ethnic Differences in Homicides of Adult Women and the Role of Intimate Partner Violence – United States, 2003–2014', Centres for Disease Control and Prevention, 21 July, <https://www.cdc.gov/mmwr/volumes/66/wr/mm6628a1.htm> (last accessed 26 November 2018).

Philipson, Alice (2013), 'Woman Who Campaigned for Jane Austen Bank Note Receives Twitter Death Threats', *The Telegraph*, 28 July, <https://www.telegraph.co.uk/technology/10207231/Woman-who-campaigned-for-Jane-Austen-bank-note-receives-Twitter-death-threats.html> (last accessed 25 November 2018).

Pinker, Stephen (2011), *The Better Angels of Our Nature: A History of Violence and Humanity* (New York: Penguin).

RAINN (2018), 'The Criminal Justice System: Statistics', <https://www.rainn.org/statistics/criminal-justice-system> (last accessed 25 November 2018).

Rankine, Claudia (2015), *Citizen: An American Lyric* (New York: Penguin).

Red Pill (2011), 'Schedules of Mating', <https://therationalmale.com/2011/08/23/schedules-of-mating/> (last accessed 26 November 2018).

Red Pill (2015a), 'Introduction', <http://archive.is/20150610190226/www.reddit.com/r/TheRedPill/comments/12v1hf/almost_a_hundred_subscribers_welcome_newcomers/> (last accessed 26 November 2018).

Red Pill (2015b), 'Updated Glossary of Terms and Acronyms', <https://www.reddit.com/r/TheRedPill/comments/2zckqu/updated_glossary_of_terms_and_acronyms/> (last accessed 26 November 2018).

Rodger, Elliot (2014), 'Manifesto', <https://www.documentcloud.org/documents/1173808-elliot-rodger-manifesto.html> (last accessed 25 November 2018).

Roof, Dylann Storm (2014), 'Manifesto', <https://assets.documentcloud.org/documents/3237779/Dylann-Roof-manifesto.pdf> (last accessed 25 November 2018).

Schmid, Alex P. (2004), 'Frameworks for Conceptualising Terrorism', *Terrorism and Political Violence*, 16(2): 197–221.

Schmid, Alex P., and Albert J. Jongman (2005), *Political Terrorism* (London: Transaction).

Sharma, Ruchira (2018), 'Serena Williams: Why People Are Saying Her US Open Final Treatment Is an Example of "Misogynoir"', 10 September, <https://inews.co.uk/inews-lifestyle/women/serena-williams-outburst-us-open-final-2018-naomi-osaka/> (last accessed 25 November 2018).

True, Jacqui (2015), 'Winning the Battle but Losing the War on Violence: A Feminist Perspective on the Declining Global Violence Thesis', *International Feminist Journal of Politics*, 17(4): 554–72.

Valenti, Jessica (2018), 'When Misogynists Become Terrorists', *The New York Times*, 26 April, <https://www.nytimes.com/2018/04/26/opinion/when-misogynists-become-terrorists.html> (last accessed 25 November 2018).

Conclusion: Disordered Violence

Place yourself in a city with palm trees and freeways, beaches and deserts, mansions and ghettos. Imagine that this city experiences regular police patrols, both by helicopter and by car. Imagine that there are shootings every day. Imagine that there is little chance for black boys to become men without a violent police encounter, or spending time in police detention or prison. Imagine that the police have been sued for torturing those under arrest – raping men with police batons, withholding food, water and necessary medicine.

What would you do to stop this violence? Imagine living in a small artistic community where part of the purpose is to provide a different vision for the future, one different from guns and gangs and drugs and violence. Where the intention of the movement you are creating is to be non-violent, but to also be a confrontation. Is it surprising then that the police raid your small bungalow twice, both times with over a dozen officers in full protective gear and guns pointed at you? Is it surprising that some of the media call you a terrorist? This sounds like Chile, Argentina, Uruguay or Paraguay under the *juntas*. It sounds like something opposite to the liberal ideal.

This is the experience of Patrisse Khan-Cullors (2018), one of the co-founders of Black Lives Matter. The city is Los Angeles. After watching her father die young as a result of addiction, which is criminalised in an over-eager prison industry, witnessing the effects of police brutality against her mentally ill brother, and growing up in poverty in Los Angeles, she became a community organiser and activist, one committed to non-violence. After the killing of Trayvon Martin, she created, with Opal Tometi and Alicia Garza, the #blacklivesmatter hashtag and organised marches to raise awareness about police brutality, amongst other causes. Only in a system of white supremacy, something in which the police are complicit, can a peace activist be called a terrorist by Bill O'Reilly of Fox News, who compared Black Lives Matter to the Ku Klux Klan (Launder 2018). When faced with these labels, Khan-Cullors (Launder 2018) responded:

> It was important to question: What is terror? Who is committing terrorism? Is it really black activists or is it really the police who have plagued our communities for decades?

It is not surprising, even though it is regrettable, that Khan-Cullors has faced this label and faced the violent consequences of it. There is coherence in the label: like members of the Tupamaros, Weather Underground or the Red Army Faction, Khan-Cullors is a community activist and highly critical of the police, the prison-industrial complex and US politics. Yet, the threat that Black Lives Matter and Khan-Cullors represent is *fundamentally different*, and this is what the label of terrorist glosses over: the movement and Khan-Cullors are non-violent, but they are *perceived as violent* because they represent a threat to the dominant system. And this is the crux of the terrorism label: violence so *disordered* that it threatens the dominant system *must be seen* as irrational, illegitimate and immoral, or the system cannot be preserved.

If the example of Khan-Cullors and Black Lives Matter seems flagrant, then think back to the examples given in the introduction: the takeover of the Malheur National Wildlife Refuge in Oregon and the Austin bomber. The occupation of the Refuge was carried out by white men, white men who were never charged with terrorism and were acquitted of all crimes. In Austin, there was an immediate assumption that the bomber was a young black man (indeed, one of the first victims) – and when it was clear it was a young white man, Mark Conditt, the response was to treat his actions with understanding and compassion.

Because of the disordering of terrorism, the label of terrorism does not seem to stick to Conditt or the men involved in the occupation of Malheur. As Terrorism Studies experts have known for a very long time, the label of terrorism is simply a construction. Other than to state that it is a pejorative, orthodox Terrorism Studies scholars have never fully investigated why this is. Even Critical Terrorism Studies scholars will point to larger discursive structures, particularly between Western states and non-Western bodies, yet even these investigations do not go far enough. Terrorism as a label works because it makes sense given the historical legacies of whose violence is legitimated, whose lives matter more and whose bodies are seen as expendable. This is the ordering of violence, in which state violence is legitimated and terrorism is always seen in opposition.

When I first began this book, I proposed to look in more depth at gendered neo-Orientalism, thinking this was the way forward within Critical Terrorism Studies. Yet, when I wrote the first few chapters, I felt that something was missing. With this nagging doubt in mind, I turned my attention to the profiles in Chapter 3. I was already cognisant of some of the 'strange bedfellows' that would emerge, but I realised as I wrote that racialised identities persisted before and after the specific focus of neo-Orientalism during the War on Terror (not that it is over). This was a pivotal moment, and one that captured why I felt Critical Terrorism Studies' critique was flagging: it not only needed to deal in a more intensive and instrumental way with gender and heteronormativity, but it needed to deal with the racial legacies of imperialism in more depth.

Intersectional feminism helps us do this. By asking the other question, it interrogates the various structures that harm individual lives and dictate the operation of international politics: race, gender and heteronormativity, amongst others. These determine who we see as a terrorist because these order how we understand legitimacy, rationality and morality, particularly when it comes to political violence. These work to uphold a Westphalian order that assumes the lessons of Enlightenment and imperialism: that women and people of colour are lesser beings, incapable of acting as good citizens because they cannot access higher-ordered thinking that leads to rational and capable citizenship. More so, intersectional feminism cannot privilege one identifier over another: gender does not always create the most harm; racism is persistent and ever-present; heteronormativity is still so naturalised for many that it is sometimes impossible to recognise. Above all, intersectionality compels its followers to look at the individuals, and to pay attention to them.

In Chapter 2, I retold Toni Morrison's parable of the children with the bird who antagonise the blind woman. The blind woman calls the children on their power and their abuse of the bird that they hold in their hands. I asked that the academics within Terrorism Studies see themselves not as the blind woman (as we might want to), but as the children –because we hold the power in this dynamic. Terrorism Studies and Critical Terrorism Studies are power-filled disciplines, making epistemic judgements about violence and politics, helping to determine and shape counter-terrorism policy. We hold the power – and our subject, and the individuals that make up our subject, are the bird. We determine whether that bird stays safe.

This bird may be violent and it may struggle in our hands, but there are sometimes peaceful birds we hold in our hands. Patrisse Khan-Cullors is one such bird. So was Nelson Mandela. When the LTTE were forced to the edge of the Sri Lankan island, was there a peaceful individual in there that we lost because of genocide? It is hard, sometimes, in this violently, virulently discursive moment of terrorism, to see those individuals. It is hard to admit that even violent actors deserve human rights. There is no doubt that those who use violence do harm. This book does not seek to excuse violence, but it does seek to understand how we see the political violence of certain actors as more violent, more harmful and more problematic, and thereby as individuals who are easily expendable, easily eradicated.

Therefore, I also ask us to see the holding of that bird as a moment of antagonism. A moment where we interrogate what is happening when some violence gets described as terrorist and some violence does not. These determinations are made, I argue, due to the wilful 'forgettings' of race, gender and heteronormativity. The forgettings are not necessarily conscious decisions, as they are embedded in the literature of IR and Terrorism Studies and, indeed, Western society at large. The forgettings get written into our textbooks, our course listings, in what we assign, and in the anecdotes or stories we tell. Thus, our students learn to never question the absence of this information and to treat with suspicion the subjects that bring these forgettings to the surface.

The forgettings have ordered how violence is conceived. State violence, with its ties to Westphalia, Enlightenment principles and imperialist socio-cultural politics of ordering people, knowledge and power, is often tacitly accepted. Even if scholars claim that state violence is not terrorist violence because it falls within the remit of war crimes, this is a semantic difference that is allowed because of forgettings. Non-state violence challenges the normative status quo of Westphalian and imperialism – it is therefore illegitimate and immoral. It is terrorist violence. Even if this sentiment seems counter-intuitive to the arguments made in earlier chapters, it is not. Calling out violence not normally seen as terrorism forces the writer, her audience and her readers to stand in a moment of antagonism. By querying how violence is determined to be terrorism, it forces these multiple audiences to constantly and consistently engage in the moment of antagonism, never forgetting the power dynamics of the label of terrorism.

In using Morrison's parable and Piki Ish-Shalom's (2009) ethical interrogation of theory, I ask that all of us take responsibility for how we theorise terrorism. We have an ethical responsibility for how our words, publications, consulting and teaching on terrorism are used outside of our academic ivory towers. I have purposefully turned the tables back on 'the counter-terrorist' and how the counter-terrorist is automatically assumed to reside in a place of legitimacy and credibility. I do this in part by turning the tables back on the West and the United States in order to dispel the myth of a teleological liberal progressive vision that presumes Western superiority. Violence and harm exists in the West. All people may experience this harm, but the system is built in a way that means people of colour and women feel this harm more and have a harder time finding their way out of the harm.

Therefore, when I turn the attention back to the West, it is not a way of re-centring the conversation on whiteness or masculinity to lament the risk of terrorism that exists in the West. Instead, it is to examine how insecurity is constructed within the West and to interrogate the conflation of white masculinity with counter-terrorism. In doing so, it mourns how some violences are simply unseen because the perpetrators benefit the most from a white supremacist patriarchal order, as they do in looking at the full spectrum of misogynistic terrorism. Additionally, it laments how privileged people have constructed a risk to their privilege that is intimately connected with race and the gendering of non-white masculinity as violent and threatening. In turn, it problematises the easy use of women, conceiving of them in gender-essentialised ways, in programmes like Prevent Tragedies.

One book, however, cannot and does not do all of the necessary work. While this book is entirely dependent upon the work that preceded it – in Critical Military Studies, Critical Terrorism Studies, Feminist Security Studies, Critical Race scholarship and queer theory – there are still some subjects it cannot fully tackle. This is particularly true when it comes to queer theory. I find queer theory to be a necessary development within feminist and gender theorising. Feminism has done an excellent job of pointing out the binaries that have trapped humanity, but it has not necessarily fully articulated a way past those binaries. Queer theory does this, particularly in the use of queer logics and in the interrogation of pluralities in figurations and constructions. Yet what does it mean for me, a cis-gender heterosexual woman, to use queer theory?

When Laura Sjoberg and I co-edited a special issue on everyday terrorism for *Studies in Critical Terrorism* in 2015, our articles sat in tension with one another. Where I argued for the recognition of domestic abuse as a form of terrorism (as I do here in Chapter 5), Sjoberg (2015) argued convincingly against this, stating that there was no need to further invite the state, the counter-terrorist, into the bedroom. For instance, it is only a recent development that laws in the US that made sodomy or gay sex illegal were repealed. Why would we invite the police back into the bedroom, allowing for further abuses and violences? While she believes that domestic violence is a problem that needs legal recourse, to name something as terrorism summons a securitised response.

Queer theorists have argued something similar, asking those of us who would use queer theory to think about the impact of queer theorising on the lives of queer people. What does it do when I 'queer' the counter-terrorist, as I have in both Chapters 4 and 5, highlighting how the counter-terrorist, or the figure most closely aligned with the state, is the one creating more insecurity for some individuals? What impact might this have on queer individuals, particularly to queer the roles of the very people who might threaten them, especially when we consider the violence and bigotry transwomen face? This is one reason I have tried to think parsimoniously about the use of queer theory. While I fundamentally believe that heteronormative structures have established how we think of belonging and identity, there are other scholars, such as Cynthia Weber (2016), Jasbir Puar (2017) and Melanie Richter-Montpetit (2014), who queer the dynamics of terrorism in ways far superior to my own.

I recognise that, on some level, to even critically interrogate the notion that a woman like Patrisse Khan-Cullors is a terrorist re-inscribes her as a terrorist: simply by recording it again, this feeds the biased, problematic narrative on some level. This book, like any academic project, carries with it epistemic power – a power to name, claim and describe (Brunner 2015). As an academic in a field that has had direct impact on conflict and people affected by conflict, neither I nor any other student of terrorism can ever escape multiple, criss-crossing layers of power. This to me is why the definition question is both so important and so impossible. The definition quest continues precisely because it seeks to hide the legacies of racialised imperial structures. The need for a definition of terrorism to be objective is built on the notion that terrorism itself can be approached objectively. However, there is nothing (or at least very little that is) objective in Terrorism Studies. Thus, to be responsible for our own theorising would mean we have to be responsible for, or at least deeply attenuated towards, the erasures and exclusions upon which Terrorism Studies is founded. Indeed, the ethical approach would demand that Terrorism Studies as a field of study be willing to have difficult conversations about how best to continue to navigate the power/knowledge nexus. Terrorism will never stop. Yet it would help to recognize how terrorism is constructed as the worst, the most evil, the most reprehensible – and to realize that this is formed by an epistemic bias that upholds the dominant global system.

References

Brunner, Claudia (2015), 'Knowing Suicide Terrorism? Tracing Epistemic Violence Across Scholarly Expertise', Centre for Peace Research and Peace Education, <http://www.uni-klu.ac.at/frieden/downloads/knowing_suicide_terrorism_brunner_2015(1).pdf> (last accessed 22 November 2018).

Ish-Shalom, Piki (2009), 'Theorising Politics, Politicizing Theory, and the Responsibility That Runs Between', *Perspectives on Politics*, 7(2): 303–16.

Khan-Cullors, Patrisse (2018), *When They Call You a Terrorist: A Black Lives Matter Memoir* (Edinburgh: Canongate).

Launder, Mimi (2018), 'The Founder of Black Lives Matter Has a Message for Anyone Calling Her a Terrorist', *The Independent*, <https://www.indy100.com/article/patrisse-cullors-black-lives-matter-racism-usa-when-they-call-you-a-terrorist-book-8244506> (last accessed 26 November 2018).

Puar, Jasbir K. (2017), *Terrorist Assemblages: Homonationalism in Queer Times* (Durham, NC: Duke University Press).

Richter-Montpetit, Melanie (2014), 'Beyond the Erotics of Orientalism: Lawfare, Torture and the Racial–Sexual Grammars of Legitimate Suffering', *Security Dialogue*, 45(1): 43–62.

Sjoberg, Laura (2015), 'The Terror of Everyday Counterterrorism', *Critical Studies on Terrorism*, 8(3): 383–400.

Weber, Cynthia (2016), *Queer International Relations: Sovereignty, Sexuality, and the Will to Knowledge* (New York: Oxford University Press).

INDEX

EU representative:
Easy Access System Europe
Mustamäe tee 50, 10621 Tallinn, Estonia
Gpsr.requests@easproject.com

www.ingramcontent.com/pod-product-compliance
Lightning Source LLC
Chambersburg PA
CBHW070844300326
41935CB00039B/1443